LIBRARIES AMID PROTEST

A VOLUME IN THE SERIES
Studies in Print Culture and the History of the Book

EDITED BY

Greg Barnhisel, Robert A. Gross,
Joan Shelley Rubin, and Michael Winship

LIBRARIES AMID PROTEST

BOOKS, ORGANIZING, AND GLOBAL ACTIVISM

Sherrin Frances

University of Massachusetts Press
Amherst and Boston

Copyright © 2020 by University of Massachusetts Press
All rights reserved
Printed in the United States of America

ISBN 978-1-62534-491-5 (paper); 490-8 (hardcover)

Designed by Sally Nichols
Set in Minion Pro

Cover design by Rebecca Lown
Cover photo by David Shankbone, "The People's Library at Occupy Wall Street," 2011
(CCBY2.0)

Library of Congress Cataloging-in-Publication Data

Names: Frances, Sherrin, author.
Title: Libraries amid protest : books, organizing, and global activism / Sherrin Frances.
Description: Amherst : University of Massachusetts Press, [2020] | Series: Studies in print culture and the history of the book | Includes bibliographical references and index.
Identifiers: LCCN 2019042780 | ISBN 9781625344908 (hardcover) | ISBN 9781625344915 (paperback) | ISBN 9781613767368 (ebook) | ISBN 9781613767375 (ebook)
Subjects: LCSH: Libraries and society. | Libraries and society—Case studies. | Libraries and community. | Libraries and community—Case studies. | Libraries—Political aspects. | Libraries—Political aspects—Case studies. | Protest camps.
Classification: LCC Z716.4 .F73 2020 | DDC 021.2—dc23
LC record available at https://lccn.loc.gov/2019042780

British Library Cataloguing-in-Publication Data
A catalog record for this book is available from the British Library

Portions of chapters 3 and 4 first appeared in "OWS People's Library and Jorge Luis Borges: Radical Politics, Heterotopic Spaces, and the Practice of Hope," in *CTheory* (July 20, 2014). Portions of chapters 6 and 7 first appeared in "In Carnegie's Shadow: The Biblioteca Popular as a Biopolitical Exception," in New Urban Languages conference proceedings, 2016. Licensed for use under CC BY 4.0 (https://creativecommons.org/licenses/by/4.0/). Portions of chapters 9 and 10 first appeared in "Maidan Library: The Emergence of a Protest Library within Ukraine's Revolution of Dignity," in *Pacific Coast Philology* 52, no. 2 (2017): 314–23. Copyright © 2017 The Pennsylvania State University. This article is used by permission of The Pennsylvania State University Press.

CONTENTS

PREFACE AND ACKNOWLEDGMENTS
ix

INTRODUCTION
1

PART ONE
Definition of a Protest Library
13

CHAPTER 1
ORIGINS
BiblioSol, Madrid
15

CHAPTER 2
MATERIALITY AND VIRTUALITY
BiblioSol, Madrid
27

CHAPTER 3
BEHAVIOR IN SPACE
Occupy Wall Street People's Library, New York
40

CHAPTER 4
VISUAL SPECTACLE
Occupy Wall Street People's Library, New York
54

CHAPTER 5
LIBRARY AS A DEMOCRATIC INSTITUTION
NYPL Main Branch, New York
65

PART TWO
Libraries and Undercurrents
77

CHAPTER 6
CARNEGIE'S INFLUENCE
Biblioteca Popular Victor Martinez, Oakland
79

CHAPTER 7
LIBRARY AS SOCIAL SPACE
Biblioteca Popular Victor Martinez, Oakland
92

CHAPTER 8
BORDERS AND BARRICADES
Gezi Park Library, Istanbul
104

CHAPTER 9
ENGAGING IN NATION-BUILDING
Maidan Library, Kiev
118

CHAPTER 10
A LIBRARY WITHOUT BOOKS
Library of Ukrainian Literature, Moscow
132

PART THREE
Reinvention
145

CHAPTER 11
THE NEW SHAPE OF SPACE
BiblioDebout, Paris
147

CHAPTER 12
PHASES OF THE PROTEST LIBRARY
BiblioDebout, Paris and Lyon
161

CHAPTER 13
REINVENTION AS COLLECTIVE
Freedom Square Library, Chicago
172

CHAPTER 14
CIRCLING BACK
BiblioSol Reinvented as Tres Peces Tres, Madrid
186

NOTES
199

INDEX
225

PREFACE AND ACKNOWLEDGMENTS

I love libraries. I love the books, the information, and being in that kind of space. But I also really love the different types of categorization that relegate the same book to different places. The materiality of the card catalogs. The dramatic and important history of the index card.[1] And the stacks that (back in the day) were so close together that they had to be hand-cranked along tracks to make enough space to reach the books. I love the math and systems and organization undergirding all of this. If you're reading this preface, then my guess is that you know exactly what I mean.

In 2011, a story about the raucous protests in New York called Occupy Wall Street popped up on my Facebook newsfeed. A friend had tagged me in the comments because the article mentioned the People's Library that had been built as part of the occupation of Zuccotti Park. A library, in the plaza, built with crates and boxes and protected by tarps, that had thousands of books. Two years later a blog post made its way onto my screen, this time about a library in the middle of the Gezi Park protests in Istanbul. It had a picture of books lined up on cinderblock shelves and a handmade spray-painted sign that read "Gezi Park Kütüphane" (Gezi Park Library). Then I learned about a *third* "library of protest," the Biblioteca Popular Victor Martinez, which happened to be in the United States and happened to be open on weekdays. I could visit.

Within a few months I showed up in Oakland, California, at what looked almost like a vacant lot. But as I approached, I could make out some milk crates full of books and the garden beds growing beans and peppers. An abandoned building, stucco walls covered with bright murals, and a locked chain-link fence defined the perimeter of the space. A library neighbor named Sue came by with her large dog named Blue. She told me that eventually someone with the combination would show up and unlock the gate. Probably, she said, it would be Omar. He'd be riding a bike and wearing a hat. She was right. An hour or so later he arrived, opened up the gate, and about a dozen people ambled in to work in the garden, sit in the mismatched chairs and chat, and look through the books. While I was meeting with the folks who built and used this library, a donated truckload of manure was delivered, and I shoveled poop as part of my library volunteer work that day. It was meant to fertilize the gardens, but it also helped grow my own understanding of what a library meant to a community.

Once I started googling and talking to people about these "libraries of protest," I quickly learned that there were hundreds of these kinds of spaces, and information began pouring in from all directions. Between 2014 and 2018, I interviewed librarians from protest libraries around the world. I am enormously thankful for the grants from my institution to travel to some of these sites. Because of the nature and pace of academic funding, though, I usually did not get there until the occupation was over. I was able to tour the sites where the encampments had taken place and meet with people who had created and run the spaces. In the summer of 2016, an encampment emerged in Paris after I had made plans to visit Kiev, so I was able to adjust my layover and actually visit BiblioDebout while it was in full swing. And of course I also cyberstalked all these places, following dozens of social media accounts and reading as many real-time first-hand accounts as possible.

I found, after following so many different libraries, that the unexpected, highly visible materiality of a protest library book collection stems from a history of anarchism and direct democracy, distinct from the industrial, capitalist history of American public libraries. That is, more simply, the romantic notion of public libraries that most Americans entertain stems from, relies on, and is embedded in capitalism, most notably because of our Carnegie library legacy. Protest libraries emerge and function as a foil to this legacy. They are the spaces of opportunity and resistance that American public library rhetoric can only promise. For these reasons, their stories need to be preserved. The activists involved have told their stories on their own, in large part through social media. I hope this book will help to amplify their voices. They have caused me rethink my fundamental assumptions about what a "library" is and what we should expect from our public libraries. I hope it will do the same for you.

There would be no such story to tell were it not for all the librarians, book lovers, and activists who have been engaged in the work of building, sustaining, and reinventing libraries all over the world. To all of you who have shared your stories with me: your work is inspirational, and the world is a better place because of you. I have tried to do justice to the libraries you have created. Specifically, thank you to Zachary Loeb, Jaime Taylor, and Mandy Henk from the Occupy Wall Street People's Library in New York; to Jaime Omar Yassin, Maura, Susan, and the rest of the collective at the Biblioteca Popular Victor Martinez in Oakland; to Martin Zeke Ochoa, Mercedes del Valle, and the rest of BiblioSol and the Tres Peces Tres collective in Madrid; Anastasiia Makarenko and Viktoriia Kolesnikova from the Maidan library in Kiev; Astrid and Ana from BiblioDebout in Paris; and Damon Williams, Kristiana Rae Colón, Lydia Wong, Frank Bergh, Cherisse Jackson, Onyx, and the rest of the #LetUsBreathe Collective in Chicago. Additional thanks to those who documented and shared your photos of these libraries and occupations, specifically Zeke, Michael Oman-Reagan, Tres Peces Tres, Sarah-Ji Young, and David Shankbone. Also, thank you to those who provided translations of texts and interviews: Natalia Knoblock with Ukrainian and Russian sources, Kathryn Belliel with Turkish sources, and Zeke with Spanish sources.

Thank you, Saginaw Valley State University, for the extensive financial and professional resources that this research required. Specifically,

I appreciate the support of the SVSU Foundation Resource Grant Program, the English department, Deborah Huntley, Marc Peretz, Pat Graves, and Melissa Woodward for helping me find time and money. Additionally, I thank Anita Dey, Ashley Blinstrub, Scott Mellendorf, the Zahnow Library team, and my extended network of professional librarian friends for sharing your thoughts on libraries, for letting me bounce so many ideas off you, and for your help in finding and procuring so many different sources and documents.

Thank you, Brian Halley, Amanda Heller, Rachael DeShano, University of Massachusetts Press, and the external reviewers for your enthusiastic support of this project and for your feedback on all matters, large and small. Thank you, Arthur and Marilouise Kroker and the editorial board at *CTheory*, John Ganim and *Pacific Coast Philology*, and the New Urban Languages conference organizers for editing and publishing articles leading up to this book, and for allowing parts of those articles to be included here. Marta Albalá Pelegrín and Hilary A. Haakenson, thank you for the opportunity to present some of this work and talk over related ideas at Cal-Poly Pomona. Thank you to the BABEL Working Group for including the panel "Liminal Spaces of Protest Libraries" in the 2015 conference, making space for our protest pop-up library, and financially supporting some of the librarians' costs in attending.

For such detailed and thoughtful feedback on the multitude of drafts, thank you so much, Zachary Loeb, Nicole Roberts, and Nicola Imbracsio. To my various accountability partners, Emily Cox Pahnke, Sher Ratnabalasuriar, Natalia Knoblock, Sara Beth Keough, Rob Drew, and Warren Fincher: you have kept me motivated, on track, and sane. Thank you, Geof Carter, Emily Beard, Elizabeth Rich, Karen Horwath, Sara Jacobs Carter, Jennifer Jenkins, Diane Gatzke, Tara Schultz, and Karin Van Zeist for brainstorming, pep talking, draft reviewing, offering to do draft reviewing, getting me off the couch to exercise more than my brain, and messaging in the middle of the night as I sought human contact amid too much word processing. To my mentors Victor Vitanza, Wolfgang Schirmacher, Carolyn Guertin, and Janna Jones, thank you for the ongoing inspiration, professional guidance, and academic opportunities.

And to Stephanie and Gus Roberts, who I think would have loved this book, thank you for leaving me in a place where writing professionally could become possible. Nicole Roberts, Bob Wall, and Kelli Leventhal, I feel fortunate every single day to be part of your lives, and I thank you for visiting libraries with me every time we travel together somewhere new.

LIBRARIES AMID PROTEST

INTRODUCTION

The national press coverage of New York City's destruction of the Occupy Wall Street (OWS) People's Library in Zuccotti Park provided my first encounter with a "protest library." OWS activists had taken over the park on September 17, 2011, and within a couple of weeks it had become a tiny model of a robust city. Comprehensive, organized, and mapped, the space included areas for essential services like kitchens and first aid, and spaces dedicated to common, necessary tasks such as infrastructure, outreach and signage, and child care. Remarkably, this camp also included a library with several thousand physical books. Eight weeks later, on the night of November 15, the New York Police Department seized most of the book collection as part of the overall eviction of OWS from the park. They tossed hundreds of books into Dumpsters, rendering them unreadable as a result of water damage and torn pages. Much of the collection disappeared, and the books that were eventually returned to the librarians were mostly unusable.

The fast rise and fall of the People's Library signaled in many ways a loss of hope—not only for those directly involved with the library, but also for like-minded and sympathetic book lovers across the United States. The actions that the police took against the People's Library were an affront to the common modern American narrative that a public library is, and has always been, a reflection of the unfettered freedom and opportunity represented by the American dream. Images of books ruined at the hands of police, who had cleared the park in full riot gear, shocked the library's Twitter followers and the audiences of major media outlets like the *New York Times* and *The Rachel Maddow Show*. Years later, New York City settled a lawsuit with OWS, and the People's Library received monetary compensation for the loss of its collection, which it then donated to other activist causes.[2] The narrative is dramatic and fast paced, and if American readers have ever heard of a protest library, it is probably this one.

But the People's Library was not the first documented library of its kind. That recognition belongs to BiblioSol, a protest library that had emerged a few months earlier in Madrid as part of the Indignados movement. BiblioSol would set the standard and serve as inspiration for over forty subsequent protest libraries around the world between 2011 and 2016. The waves of Indignados, Occupy, and Nuit Debout encampments across the United States, Canada, and Europe included multiple libraries in dozens of locations. Movements as diverse as EuroMaidan in Ukraine, the Gezi Park protests in Turkey, and the #FreedomSquare protest in the United States would also include libraries within their occupations.

The first time I read about a protest library, it struck me as a curiosity, as a little treasure hidden within a much larger, more serious political movement. The second time I saw protest libraries mentioned was also surprising. But by the third time, a wider landscape began to come into focus, revealing patterns and raising questions. While these libraries have emerged from within different political occupations all over the world, they share several features: They are mostly outdoor spaces that usually last between one and six weeks. They include makeshift shelves, seating, tarps and canopies, and thousands of donated physical books. They have volunteers functioning as librarians, cataloging systems with free access to thousands of books, and guidelines for borrowing by the general public. Library patrons can borrow a wide array of literature and nonfiction, well beyond political philosophy or propaganda.

These spaces seem to be, unquestionably, libraries. And yet, despite the clear identity markers, almost everything about protest libraries defies logic. They are labor-intensive, temporary installations in parks and city squares, poorly protected from the weather, at odds with security forces, and destined for eviction. Where does the drive come from to take on a project like this, simultaneously so lofty and so heavy? What happened during this five-year window to generate so many of them—such a massive, unexpected, and labor-intensive anomaly—within political occupations? And since the end of their five-year history, post-2016, what have they evolved into—or have they simply died out, having filled a contextual, timely purpose that now no longer calls for such amenities?

As I began researching the answers to these questions, two parallel purposes developed. First, I wanted to help document and preserve the histories of these protest library. Their nature by definition is temporary, and their footprints within the larger political movements are relatively small. While some documentation does exist, much of it is digital and is slowly eroding as social media accounts are deleted and websites expire. The documentation that does exist in print form addresses only a single library or two at a time, and often includes them only as asides or footnotes to larger political narratives. *Libraries amid Protest* situates protest libraries as the primary common thread among multiple political movements between 2011 and 2016.

The second purpose of this book is to analyze the patterns generated by the reproduction of protest library spaces around the world. The consistent predominance of a print collection of books rather than a digital collection is a crucial aspect of a protest library. The physical spaces these libraries form draw out a common community of librarians, contributors, and readers within each of these very different yet in some ways similar political events around the world. The community emerges within a certain kind of appropriation of space (i.e., the boundary of the library within a larger political camp) and with the aid of specific things-as-objects (i.e., stacks of books). Ultimately, the materiality of these libraries generates a community identity that endures well beyond a collection's short physical existence.

In looking for patterns through a series of protest libraries, I've found that the shift in context from an individual library to a collection of libraries is risky. It places the libraries in the spotlight, and one might argue that in the grand scheme of movements like the Arab Spring and Occupy, the libraries were not *that* important. On occasion, friends have argued (gently) with me that those activists who chose to volunteer in the libraries fetishized print books and were distracted from what they saw as the "real work" of the occupation: that of effecting political change. After all, during many of these protests, laws were created and/or broken, governments changed hands, and people were harmed and even killed. It would be silly to say that the libraries were more important than any protester's life, and I do not mean to diminish the gravity of the radical occupations in which they are embedded or the significance of the changes the movements made. I also do not claim that protest libraries could have happened without the tremendous force exerted by the wider network of protest activities. Certainly a protest library needs the landscape of a larger form of resistance.

The libraries, though, support their own kind of "real work," different from—but aligned with—the work of the occupations. This work is important in the effort to understand our human relationship with the sharing of books, space, and freedom of information. The library is both within and beside the bigger occupation, coming into focus not only as an object of study but also as a sovereign thing in itself which has strong enough rhetorical agency to affect, and permanently alter, the people in its wake. This book takes a close look at how the parts of a protest library fit together in various ways, first to produce each specific library and then to form a definition of a more enduring protest library concept.

To define the concept has been challenging, and in documenting the libraries and identifying patterns, I have necessarily been drawn into also defining and documenting "regular" libraries, specifically public libraries in the United States. Most of the time people have no idea what I mean when I say I study protest libraries. As I explain, I can see their expression change, first to one of surprise and then to one of nostalgia, and inevitably we slip into a discussion of their experiences in public libraries. These conversations often lead to the sharing of childhood memories and to extolling the virtues of a neighborhood's modern public library resources. I love these conversations and the chance to hear about how books, and spaces filled with books, have acted as powerful catalysts to change someone's relationship to learning, to telling stories, to sharing space and resources, and to becoming part of a community. The idea of a library forms a shared memory that connects a large swath of the American public. The library, we tend to believe, is the cornerstone of a democratic community, and it embodies the values of freedom of speech, uncensored access to information, and a desire to use public space in a way that benefits all the members of society. Without a doubt, a protest library is built from the same stuff as a "public library," and people draw natural connections between the two. The idea of a library, its essence, seems indisputably positive. In all the research I have done on libraries around the world, I have yet to find anything arguing against the concept of a library. Libraries, both public and protest, are just, very simply, good.

If the perceived benefits of a library are consistent, their implementation is not. The American public library has been around for about 150 years, but it has evolved. At different points in our history, "library" has meant paid memberships for access to private reading rooms. It has meant spaces above retail shops that offered books. It has meant expanding spaces for children and also sometimes filtering children's content. And more recently it has meant full-blown tax-funded institutions that provide not just books but an array of social services. Today, American public libraries are largely focused on reinventing their spaces by moving out their print collections and replacing them with technology and digital information, "maker spaces," and various other services in partnership with government and industry. While local communities usually support these changes, it means that public libraries are moving away from precisely that which makes protest libraries so noteworthy. So while this book makes the case for the importance of libraries within a community, it is with several caveats: the library is hardly a static institution; not all changes benefit the longevity of a community library; and we must be mindful to separate library rhetoric from library reality and ideology from implementation.

In telling these library stories and working through the arguments just described, I include the background and context of the larger political and governmental events precipitating the formation of each library. For this reason, it seemed logical to begin with the first protest library and work my way chronologically through the five years when this type of library proliferated. Each chapter cross-references other libraries in order to highlight similarities and differences, whether or not they happened before or after the example at hand. But the dominant traits and changes from library to library do not always follow a cause-and-effect logic. Each library emerges in response to a specific political context, the particular space available for use, and the barricades (literal and legal) presented by local law enforcement.

Part one of the book, "Definition of a Protest Library," identifies the genre of protest libraries and addresses how these libraries came into being. The general concept of "library" (and specifically the American public library) comes into better focus as this type of outsider library is described. A library is more than a space with books. But must a library be *at least* a space with books?

Chapter 1, "Origins," addresses the birth of the protest library and begins to tell the story of BiblioSol. Spain's Acampada Sol occupation, part of Movimiento 15 (15-M), named for the day the protests began (May 15, 2011), provided the petri dish in which BiblioSol, the protest library prototype, coalesced. It explains the meaning of prefigurative politics and shows how the interpretation of the concept in Spain created an openness to the magnetic force of a pile of books, as well as an openness toward letting these books accumulate and become a library. The quantity of material books aggregated and reached a critical mass, crossing the threshold from a "pile of books" to a "collection."

Chapter 2, "Materiality and Virtuality," continues with BiblioSol as the primary example. It addresses the importance of the library's identity and of the material book collection. The development and durability of a protest library after its emergence in a prefigurative environment depended on two critical factors. The first was the ubiquity of social media, which allowed for a unique library voice to emerge and persist within and beyond the larger identity of the political occupation. And the second was the presence of the physical pile of books. As it grew, its pull became stronger, drawing people toward it and creating a shift in identity from activist to librarian, or from protester to reader. Despite the reliance on the Internet for identity development, the libraries did not rely on the Internet for the development of a digital collection of books and files. Electronic documents were incorporated into these libraries to varying degrees, but it was always as a complement to the primary material collection of books. The libraries thrived because physical books drew people to them and because social media accounts preserved their identities.

Because of their heavy emphasis on material space, the libraries within occupations sometimes became a focal point for conflict with property managers, security, and police. Chapter 3, "Behavior in Space," looks at Occupy Wall Street's creative use of "privately owned public spaces" (POPS) to better understand the significance of the OWS People's Library physical footprint and its effects on the behavior of people within it. The claim of space by the occupations, and by the book collections of the libraries, led authorities to focus on questions of legally acceptable behavior in such spaces and on changing the laws to make library installations difficult, if not impossible. The materiality of the libraries called attention to the importance of a physical footprint and the visibility of books to drive the use of public space.

Chapter 4, "Visual Spectacle," recounts the raid on the OWS encampment that destroyed the People's Library. Resistance emerges within the local community, and often witnesses invoke the rhetoric of freedom of information and information as freedom. The destruction of books seems inevitably to lead to the battle cry "Libraries are democratic institutions and cannot be tampered with."

Once the book collection amasses and crosses a threshold into a cohesive "thing," and once space has been claimed for the purpose of a library, any move toward dismantling the collection seems like an act of aggression. This includes any removal of books from the original space of the library, whether by destroying the books, permanently removing them, or just moving the books to a more distant location. Chapter 5, "Library as a Democratic Institution," makes an explicit comparison between the People's Library and the New York Public Library's main branch in order to view both as "real" democratic institutions.[5] In this case, the city proposed moving a significant portion of the public library's collection to a remote site. While they wouldn't be destroyed, the books would become a little less accessible and a little more invisible. In exchange, library officials wanted to install more technology and electronic options. The general public responded to the destruction and disappearance of the two collections in remarkably similar ways.

Chapter 5 concludes the first section of the book by underscoring the many similarities between these outdoor, temporary spaces and public libraries in the United States. But because these libraries are created in such a different way from public or institutional libraries, questions emerge from within and without the libraries and occupations: Are these protest libraries "real" libraries? If not, why not? How does democracy function regarding protest libraries? These are the questions I take up in the second part of the book, "Libraries and Undercurrents," which reveal fundamental conflicts between the origins of a public library system and the ideology of the country in which the system develops. Since protest libraries are international in nature, their origin transcends any one country's politics and reveals bibliocommonalities within the commons.

Chapter 6, "Carnegie's Influence," opens part two of the book by introducing the Biblioteca Popular Victor Martinez, known to those involved as "the Beeb." This protest library emerged in the side yard of an abandoned Carnegie library building. This chapter addresses the American general public's notion of a public library, which is largely influenced by Carnegie's legacy. This funding propelled the rapid development across the country of a particular type of library, one with an orientation toward the dissemination of information for the purposes of helping people better themselves as workers, citizens, and community members. Carnegie was much more focused on funding the library buildings than on the books and other content within the buildings, as if the physical attribution of space for material books in itself held power. This led to a troubled history with regard to the types of content and the funding of libraries for affluent versus immigrant and minority neighborhoods. Chapter 6 addresses the many ways in which US public libraries have been complicit with capitalism and corporate America since their great expansion at the turn of the twentieth century.

Considering this connection to big business and funding motivation, chapter 7, "Library as Social Space," questions how well the rhetoric of libraries as "free to all" delivers on its promise. Modern US public libraries are more and more frequently providing social support services outside the original function of making books available. Together with the services, however, also come policies designed to ensure library patrons are productive and on-task with library-relevant activities. That is, patrons may read, attend classes, and make things, but they should not wash in the bathrooms or sleep at the tables. In these ways, libraries practice a type of information-grounded gentrification. This is not to disparage the librarians and the people inside the buildings working within the institutional structure, but money mutes and diverts the calling of individuals as it does in so many other institutional endeavors. Every instance of removing physical books and replacing them with other things furthers this silencing. Through the continued example of the Beeb, one can see not only the possibility of revolution through a library-inspired land grab but also the benefits of creating support services run by and for the local community.

As 15-M and Occupy spread, encampments began to expand to other protests in places from Turkey to Hong Kong to Ukraine—places that had very different histories with public space, libraries, and freedom of information. Chapter 8, "Borders and Barricades," moves us from the United States to the occupation of Gezi Park in Istanbul. This conflict began over a political fight about space, the environment, and public access. The use of space and repetition of patterns reveal fundamental similarities despite differences in nationalities and ideologies. Specifically, a library like the one in Gezi Park presents itself as a democratic institution even when it is behind a barricade, when the perimeter is clearly articulated, and when it is meant to exclude an oppressive government. But while the Carnegie legacy makes collaboration with corporate interests suspect, the Gezi Park library owes its origin to the business world. Specifically, it was a Turkish publisher that provided the initial boxes of books and made the call on social media to other publishers to support the library as an act of resistance.

Chapter 9, "Engaging in Nation-Building," takes as its primary example the Maidan library, the protest library that emerged in Ukraine during the EuroMaidan protests. This example further complicates the relationship between protest libraries and institutional authority because of the protesters' collaborative relationship both with Ukrainian publishing houses and with the owners of the building they were occupying. In this case, corporate interests and protest libraries became allies against governmental actions and military violence.

Finally, part two wraps up with chapter 10, "A Library without Books," a detailed look at the legacy carved by Lenin in contrast to that of Carnegie. This chapter describes the controversy over the Library of Ukrainian Literature in Moscow, which has been subjected to the disappearance of the majority of its collection. The building itself was reassigned to the Department of Sports in what the *New York Times* described as an "Orwellian" move. By the end of this section, we will have seen what it means beyond the American sense to call a place a "public library," to confront the mythology embedded within this definition, and to consider the roles of circulation and borders in containing information and controlling behavior. The comparison of libraries in the United States, Turkey, and Ukraine provides some perspective on the government's long-term influence on the public perception of library spaces.

The last section of the book, part three, "Reinvention," addresses the ways in which protest libraries reinvented themselves after experiencing the five-year history recounted in parts one and two. Chapter 11, "The New Shape of Space," discusses the example of BiblioDebout in France. By mid-2016, countries around the world had passed laws and regulations that severely limited the use of public space for occupations and political activity. When the Nuit Debout movement began in Paris and spread across and beyond France, activists made a conscious choice to occupy their parks and plazas primarily at night, leaving the spaces empty during the daytime. These library sites were thus nomadic from the very beginning, and their organizers were self-aware: they knew about the now five-year history of other protest libraries.

Part three also describes the libraries' responses to the changes made to public space, or rather to the behaviors permitted in public space. Chapter 12, "Phases of the Protest Library," summarizes the major stages in the lifespan of a protest library. This chapter looks at the internal rhythm of the individual library, which can generally be broken into three distinct lifecycle phases, and then at the larger global pattern that these libraries, taken together, create, a pattern that 2016 seems to punctuate the end of.

Chapter 13, "Reinvention as Collective," helps us see how books feature prominently before, during, and after the lifespan of an occupation and how a library within a collective constitutes the most logical final phase of a protest library. The example of Freedom Square in Chicago provides the last documented protest library to emerge during the summer of 2015. These activists had coalesced into a collective called #LetUsBreathe as the Black Lives Matter movement was gaining traction across the country. Their collective used books as part of various community outreach programs, and in 2016 their Freedom Square occupation featured a library.

Chapter 14, "Circling Back," returns to the story of BiblioSol, the protest library with which we began in chapter 1. BiblioSol demonstrates that what we perceive as the end of this pattern may only be an interruption. I argue that if we keep in mind all the possible variables, and if we maintain an open stance toward their repetition, we can see the protest library continue. This chapter looks at what has happened to the protest libraries since their emergence and gestures toward the future of this kind of space as well as the influence of radical politics on the librarian profession—and vice versa.

The unexpected, highly visible materiality of a protest library book collection stems from a history of anarchist and prefigurative politics, distinct from the industrial, capitalist history of American public libraries. This materiality carries its own rhetorical weight, one that generates a predictable public outcry when physical books are destroyed or removed. As public libraries slowly shift to online systems and digital information, removing physical books to make room for collaborative work areas and maker spaces, the invisibility of the collection becomes a risk. Ultimately, protest libraries are emerging and functioning as the spaces of opportunity and resistance that the rhetoric of the American public library can only promise. A study of protest libraries offers the potential to generate connections with the global commons in a way that American public libraries, because of the heritage they bring with them, likely cannot. Protest libraries help us see that while the heart of a library is found within its community, it takes a book collection to form its spine.

PART ONE

DEFINITION OF A PROTEST LIBRARY

CHAPTER 1

ORIGINS
BiblioSol, Madrid

On May 15, 2011, Spanish activists known as the "Indignados" entered a large popular city square in Madrid called Puerta del Sol and prepared to occupy the space in protest of the austerity measures taken by the national government, including deep cuts to social services and tax increases. They quickly coalesced into a micro-village with designated areas for things like sleeping, cooking, first aid, child care, and public relations. Some of the activists also wanted to make sure that the funding reductions to Spanish libraries were not forgotten among the myriad budget cuts under protest, so a few of them brought a handful of books to the occupation as a visual aid. As they would later explain on their blog, they did not intend to build a library in Acampada Sol.[1]

But something about that little stack of books spoke to the other activists and visitors, compelling them to donate their own books to the pile, and then more books, and then more—in fact, around two thousand more within the first week alone. In response to the growing piles of books, several activists spontaneously took on the role of "librarian" and dedicated their volunteer efforts to organizing what fast became a proper physical library with a robust general collection of reading materials.[2] The library soon had a dedicated space in the square with its own tarp, its own shelving and seating, and its own reputation as a place not only to borrow books but also to linger and read, play board games, and hear performances, lectures, or music. The library would last about a month, and in that time it would name itself BiblioSol, grow a physical collection of around four thousand books, and develop a durable online community. In mid-June, less than four weeks after it began, Acampada Sol would be peacefully dismantled, all the tents, supplies, and signage cleaned up, and the library collection boxed and transported to a nearby squat for storage while everyone decided what to do next.[3]

BiblioSol and its sizable collection of books represents a particular type of outsider library called a protest library.[4] This is a temporary physical library that emerges spontaneously within a political occupation or encampment. These occupations take place when activists and community members want to visibly resist national politics, preserve and amplify cultural histories, and emphasize unique local demands, and the development of the occupation often leads to something that resembles a miniature city with areas for first aid and child care, signage and building supplies, religious and meditative spaces, and so on. While each protest library is occupation-specific, from camp to camp around the world the libraries themselves are strikingly similar. They are all physical spaces with boundaries defined by stacks of books, shelves made of found objects, and tents or tarps. Their book collections begin with a handful of volumes and usually grow to several thousand within a few days or weeks. The collections themselves include a wide variety of general reading materials and are not restricted to political texts. Activists, many of whom have professional library training, though just as many do not, are drawn to the books and take on the persona of "librarian," helping to define and name the library, create systems of organization and lending rules, create stamps to mark the books, and collect equipment to store, display, and protect the volumes. The libraries become dedicated spaces within the camps for conversation and activities like poetry readings, music, and chess.

BiblioSol was the first protest library of its kind and provides a springboard into addressing some of the most obvious questions: Why libraries at all when there was so much other work to be done within the occupations? Why put so much effort into an aspect of the camp that had no direct impact on the protest, something that was only obliquely related to the main purpose of the resistance activities? To address these questions, the protest library story begins with the prefigurative orientation of the Indignados and the 15-M movement.

THE INDIGNADOS AND 15-M

Puerta del Sol, the public city square the activists took over in Madrid, accommodates a large flow of pedestrian traffic and consumer activity. The spacious brick plaza has an irregular shape closer to a half moon than a square. It marks "kilometer 0," the place from which Spain's original network of roads emanate. The oldest, most imposing, and most infamous building facing the plaza is the Real Casa de Correos, built in 1768 as the Royal Post Office. The building has primarily served as a location for various legislative offices since the nineteenth century, but while Generalissimo Francisco Franco's regime ruled the country for the middle third of the twentieth century, it was home to the Dirección General de Seguridad.[5] On a visit in 2015, several Madrileños pointed out to me that the building's basement had a long, sordid history of torture during this time. They said the period from 1957 to 1965, under the direction of Carlos Arias Navarro, whose nickname was the "Butcher of Málaga," was especially brutal, and it was not uncommon to pass through Puerta del Sol and hear screams coming from the Casa de Correos.

Franco died in 1975 and was succeeded by Prince Juan Carlos. Under this new leader, Spain held its first elections in 1977 and began passing more democratic laws. The government's stranglehold on culture was also loosened. Today, Franco's dictatorial fascist government has been replaced with a constitutional monarchy. Spaniards democratically elect a congress, which chooses a prime minister to run the national government. All areas of Spain have municipal governments that manage city services and local regulations, although some regions have been granted more autonomy than others.

Franco's legacy remains complex, however, with many officials even in the 2000s still refusing to denounce his regime. According to Almudena Escobar López, this transition reveals a "hypocrisy of the

Spanish democratic ideal and the traces left by Franco's dictatorship." She writes that the transition away from a "repressive police state" and toward democracy "was a quiet process. It was a transition without justice, in which the perpetrators of the totalitarian regime were assimilated into the newborn constitutional monarchy. This meant that, in contrast to other countries that endured fascist regimes, such as Germany and Italy, there were no trials of former regime members and collaborators. Spaniards who suffered repression during the regime had to keep their mourning quiet within the walls of their homes."[6] A politically active student in Spain identified as "Y" interviewed by an anarchist zine called *Mutiny Zine* in 2013 said: "It's very important to remember, that here in Spain we had a dictatorship that lasted for more than 35 years and only ended in 1975. Most of our parents were born when that dictatorship still existed. We're all influenced by that. There is still a strong current of fear of, or respect for, authority, especially for people over 40."[7] While the public no longer fears speaking out against the government, many still choose their words carefully.

The grave political history of this space is notched and grooved by the flow of modern economics, providing the perfect landscape for the coming community of 15-M activists and catalyzing the other political movements around the world between 2011 and 2016 that also spawned libraries.[8] As with so many public urban areas these days, consumerism has taken over the Puerta del Sol. By 2011, the Real Casa de Correos was flanked ignominiously by a Kentucky Fried Chicken on one side and an apartment building on the other. The opposing edges of the plaza are lined with souvenir shops, ticket kiosks, currency exchanges for the many tourists, flagship storefronts for cosmetics and cell phone companies, and restaurants and bars. Back in 2011, however, underneath the rapid flow of buying and spending ran a deeper current of financial hardship making the wares for sale in the Puerta del Sol out of reach for many Spaniards.

Activists flooded the square on May 15, 2011, to protest the abysmal economic state of Spain, which suffered the highest unemployment rate of all seventeen Eurozone countries. Spain's rate of 22.8 percent was double the average unemployment rate of 10.3 percent, and a demographic breakdown reveals that among Spaniards between sixteen and twenty-four years old, the jobless rate was a breathtaking 48.6 percent. Every other young face you looked into was someone unable to find work, living with family or crashing with friends, and anxious about his or her future career opportunities. The housing industry was in crisis as well as a result of overinflated construction costs during the previous decade, an increase in subprime lending, and home repossessions that had risen by 32 percent in the previous year.[9] When the government took an austerity stance and proposed severe budget cuts to resources and services, Spaniards—particularly the youth, people like "Y"—were outraged. Between twenty thousand and fifty thousand participated in the May 15 march. The march became a sit-in blocking traffic on a major road and resulting in the arrest of approximately two dozen activists.

At the end of the day, somewhere between thirty and one hundred people—angrier than ever and dissatisfied with the day's outcome—decided to spend the night in the plaza. They had not arrived with a predetermined plan to stay. Initially they were angry, and they were marching. But soon after, the idea was hatched that they would remain there for a week, until the upcoming local and regional government elections on May 22. Once this decision was made, the number of people camping in the square grew daily, and they began to organize themselves into a small city. Acampada Sol began.

THE LIBRARY

I did not learn about BiblioSol until months after the occupation was already gone from the square, and by the time I arrived in Madrid to talk with the librarians and activists, what remained of the BiblioSol book collection had been incorporated into a new social collective called Tres Peces Tres.[10] It was here that I met Zeke Ochoa for the first time in person. He was one of the original activists who helped build and organize the library, and he remained deeply involved with BiblioSol for many years. He and several other BiblioSol librarians showed me the new space and guided me through the 15-M and BiblioSol archives. They have done a remarkable job of preserving the realia of their brief history. Walking into the L-shaped space, visitors are greeted at a reception desk where volunteers sell snacks before events, where it is possible to buy shirts and other items with the Tres Peces Tres logo, and where a warm welcome is provided along with the answers to any questions you might have about the calendar of events. The night I arrived, the other wing of the space had been set up for a movie night, so a large screen had been placed at one end, rows of folding chairs set out, and some of the other regular seating moved out of the way. The walls were lined with books, and a large, colorful papier-mâché shark hung from the ceiling. In the back room, extensive archives were maintained about 15-M, the Indignados, the occupation, and the histories of the other groups that had joined BiblioSol to create the collective.

Supplementing this physical archive, the library's story had also been documented online, more or less in real time. In their blog *Sin Bibliotecas No Hay Paraíso*, the activists describe the work of building their physical, temporary outdoor library. The blog, whose title translates to "Without Libraries, There Is No Paradise," paints a utopian image, proclaiming, "Our efforts were aimed at creating awareness, to open a continuous debate in a public square, to build a visible structure to work, learn, advance."[11] The pictures uploaded here and on their other related social media accounts record a vibrant space full of motivated, thoughtful, diverse people who are not just *surrounded* by rows of books but *enveloped* by them. The books provide photo backdrops. They cover tabletops. They frame faces and activities. Ad hoc shelving of boards and cinderblocks defines the perimeter of the space, and handwritten signage signifies the different categories into which the books have been organized.[12] A tarp overhead keeps the bulk of the sun and rain off the weather-sensitive texts and often casts a blue shadow over the readers and the pages in their hands. In some photos the feeling is almost claustrophobic, with shelves very close to one another or towering above the photographer. In others the perspective widens, and more tarps become evident in the background behind BiblioSol, blurry, expansive, covering a large portion of the plaza in shadow. The camp extends as far as the horizon of the camera's viewfinder.

Figure 1. Martin Zeke Ochoa working as librarian at BiblioSol, Madrid, May 2011. Courtesy of Martin Zeke Ochoa Archive.

The visual spectacle of a stack of books, even an initial small stack of three or four, generates a gravitational pull that affects people passing by. The librarians describe BiblioSol's rapid emergence within the larger occupation in exuberant tones. "The first week of BiblioSol, the second of the camp, people kept arriving with plastic bags, shopping carts, backpacks, out of which came books and more books: 100, 200, 1000."[13] As the librarians from Occupy Wall Street joked later that year in New York, where there is a pile of books, a librarian is not far behind. As the number of donated books increases, the force of attraction becomes even stronger for some people than for others. Some librarians said they didn't even know they had the drive to work with books until they were confronted by the piles. As the book collection grew to several thousand volumes within the first week, the space took shape and the work of formalizing the library began. A blog post conveys the breathlessness of the project: "And there were tables. And there were chairs. And we made a stamp bookplate. And armchairs. And 2000 books. And we put in a newspaper library." While it was all very exciting, it was also rough on the volunteers, most of whom did not have any construction expertise or library experience. A librarian named Gonzalo says it was an exercise in patience as much as anything else.[14]

Working groups formed the organizational foundation of Acampada Sol, the larger occupation in which BiblioSol existed. Acampada Sol had been created by the still larger political occupation called the Indignados or the 15-M movement. To accommodate the rapid influx of reading materials, the volunteers requested more shelves and building supplies from Acampada Sol's infrastructure working group. "'Economy,' 'Art,' 'Immigration,' 'Education,' 'Environment,' 'Legal,' 'Thinking,' 'Action,' 'Music,' 'Theatre,' 'Spirituality.' Every day new groups are born," writes activist and blogger Oscar ten Houten. Working groups were assigned their own areas within the boundaries of Acampada Sol, though some, like "Extension," reached beyond the camp, organizing assemblies and gatherings in different neighborhoods around Madrid.[15] The camp even had an "Internal Coordination" group to help the other working groups collaborate and manage meeting spaces, and maps were available to help visitors find their way around the crowded square, which swelled at times during the day to 25,000 people. Protests like this one and, later that year, Occupy Wall Street were "attempting to create, in miniature, the kind of society that they wanted to live in—a society that took care of all its members' needs for food, clothing, shelter. The encampment gave them a sense of community and family."[16] The more shelves they added, though, the faster new books and readers arrived. In fact, the infrastructure working group itself was inundated with book donations in addition to other materials like wood and canvas. Briefly, books were routed to the media/archives group, but by May 20 a vote was passed to formalize the library as its own working group. The identity of the library and the librarians tending to it began to solidify.

Zeynep Tufekci, author of *Twitter and Teargas* and a writer with firsthand experience in several of these occupations, asks, "Why do so many protest camps set up libraries?" Her answer focuses on the type of community that activists were committed to creating. Emphasis on community was key, she says, writing that libraries "express a set of values that are aligned with the deeply held values of the protesters." Activists were seeking a sense of belonging, and the work of building the camp brought with it a sense of joy. Tufekci writes that "the environments that demonstrators are quite deliberately fashioning are a major part of what makes participation in protest worthwhile."[17] Building the shelves, deciding on a system of organization, and doing the "work" of the library is a bonding experience. As Jaime Taylor and Zachary Loeb write regarding their experience in the OWS People's Library, "Professional or not, many ended up in the library working group in order to have something concrete to do; the library was one of the sites where there was always work."[18] And while the work was physically demanding and unpredictable, it was also deeply rewarding. BiblioSol librarian Bárbara writes that those who help build these libraries will pass through, looking at all the books on the shelves, perhaps picking one off the shelf randomly: "It is possible that you open it with curiosity and read the dedication written on the first page: To the indignant of 15M, forever, with love, and signed by Eduardo Galeano. Most likely, at that moment, you will close it and bring it to your chest for a while. You will surely breathe, knowing that it is safe, you will say proudly looking at the rest of the shelves: I have loaded these books. I have taken care of these books."[19] This was the work of creating and maintaining a space for a book collection that gave voice to a surrounding community longing to be part of the radical politics represented in the larger occupation.

PREFIGURATION

15-M's focus on community was grounded in prefigurative politics, which generally means an attempt to create right here and now the kind of world we want to live in, rather than setting that world as an idealized goal and working to achieve it in the near (or distant) future. David Graeber, an American anthropologist and anarchist who was heavily involved with organizing OWS and other encampment sites, writes that prefigurative spaces are

> zones of experiment in leaderless direct democracy. These new forms of democracy were not, exclusively or even primarily, products of

Europe or North America; they were, as we liked to call it, part of new insurgent civilization, planetary in its scope and ambitions, born of a long convergence of such experiments carried out in every part of the planet, from the forests of Chiapas and Brazil to the villages of Karnataka in India, squats from Lisbon to Quito, with substantial inputs from feminism, anarchism, and traditions of non-violent civil disobedience; a repertoire of terms, tactics, gestures, endlessly nurtured and elaborated in [a] thousand local variations, that was to explode in public squares across the world a decade later, from Tahrir to Syntagma to Zuccotti Park.[20]

As Graeber notes, "prefigurative" signifies a repertoire of terms, tactics, and gestures. One important aspect is anarchism, which has a history of valuing libraries. It comes in a variety of flavors, but here, anarchism means a society in which relationships are based on choice rather than enforced by government or systemic hierarchies. These relationships based on choice are sometimes described as horizontalism.

Argentina provides one of the strongest, most widespread examples of prefigurative politics in action. After the Argentine government collapsed and five new governments had come and gone in just two weeks, the general population took matters into their own hands in late 2001. Some of them occupied various empty buildings and created small communities to support neighborhood people. Others took over the factories where they had been working, and as a team they redesigned the production and management of the resources. The actions they took were grounded in the prefigurative notion of here and now, and in the notion of horizontality: everyone's voice was meant to be heard equally. They held assemblies where they discussed and made decisions, and everyone involved was offered a seat at the table. The system was not without its problems, but it worked, and it did so in a radically different way from any kind of traditional politics.[21]

The 15-M activists' practice of prefiguration, critical to the way they chose to physically occupy space, was not explicitly articulated until the Occupy movement began, and writers like Graeber started to make clear the connection between Occupy-style camps and prefiguration, anarchism, practices of horizontality, and occupational peaceful resistance. According to student "Y," the connections may have been less clearly articulated in Spain because of the fairly recent history of fascism and a lingering reluctance to use that particular vocabulary. "Y" says: "The repression of the dictatorship and post-dictatorship years helps to explain why 15-M was so successful socially. But it also explains why 15-M doesn't use words like 'communist' and 'anarchist.' For many years, these words were taboo. So 15-M has a strong anti-system view, but doesn't use the names of the ideologies that developed that kind of view."[22]

This prefigurative foundation would be carried through for the duration of the protest library's history. Immediately following Acampada Sol, OWS would implement similar ideas. Within the borders of the People's Library was the idea that "free access to knowledge was in, while vertical and authoritarian organizing structures were out."[23] The working group seated librarians and maintenance and support staff next to one another at the discussion table, for example, giving all working group members an equal voice in a nontraditional way, fostering new communities in space and in language. In 2016, five years after BiblioSol, the BiblioDebout library would emerge as part of Nuit Debout in France. BiblioDebout, according to the librarians there, "does not seek to save the actual democracy or the liberties we have, but more to build democracy from a perspective that does not refuse utopia."[24]

Similarly, in Chicago, where the very last of the documented protest libraries was created by activists of the #LetUsBreathe Collective as part of the Freedom Square occupation, the activists do not use the term "prefigurative." But their own description of their goals is very much aligned. Kristiana Rae Colón, one of the co-founders of the collective and one of the organizers of the Freedom Square encampment, describes its members as abolitionists, devoted to dismantling the institutions and systems that are based on and perpetuate inequity in the United States, specifically when it comes to African Americans and other people of color. Americans, she says, "are investing huge sums into more police and more guns and more surveillance and more militarization, and we see that when we invest in violence, it begets more violence. We are proposing a divestment from those systems and an investment of that capital into the systems that actually keep us safe and into the communities that they have historically pillaged from. Our work is the work of imagining and embodying what that looks like."[25] Freedom Square exemplified this work, and the encampment developed and functioned similarly to other prefigurative spaces. Rather than writing letters and lobbying for change, activists in all of these spaces instead took up residence in a public place and built a camp that reflected the world they wanted to see. Colón goes on to say, "We were building what we're in favor of, not protesting what we're opposed to." Though the language is quite different, and not all the protesters and political movements discussed in this book use the term "prefigurative," the common orientation simmers under their surfaces.

The 15-M movement was not the first to ground an occupation on prefiguration or anarchism, but when this orientation converged with the particular history of post-fascist Spain, the Indignados displayed an openness toward letting the books amass and toward seeing them as a potential collection. As the books became something more substantial than a "pile," they also became something that would prove valuable and worthy of the labor they would require. In taking over a public square and creating a new community from scratch, one that was meant to reflect the world they wanted, the Indignados in Madrid shifted their focus as a movement away from any specific demands to which the Spanish government could respond. Once we turn our gaze to the here and now, and once we build a space based on the ideas of prefiguration, the libraries do not seem so surprising a development. After all, what good is an ideal community if it does not include books, as well as knowledge and all the other symbolic values that a library brings with it?

But this openness only begins to answer why libraries began to appear in occupations in 2011. The relationships between material and virtual books, and material and virtual identities, also played a key role. In the next chapter, we will take a deeper look at the case of BiblioSol to understand how protest libraries emerge through the convergence of prefigurative politics with material book collections and social media identities. I will address the question of why the libraries consistently focus on *material* book collections rather than digital ones.

CHAPTER 2

MATERIALITY AND VIRTUALITY
BiblioSol, Madrid

At Acampada Sol, the prefigurative orientation discussed in the last chapter provided the catalyst for creating a library, opening up the possibility of helping a like-minded group of people find one another and work together toward building the world they wanted to live in. For them, this included without question a library. But two other factors were just as critical: the development of the library's identity via social media and the concurrent development of a material book collection. Protest libraries emerged when they did because these specific factors were present simultaneously.

This chapter demonstrates how the emphasis on materiality and the easy accessibility of social media combine with the underlying politics of prefiguration and anarchism to make the kind of protest library heralded by BiblioSol a unique and timely type of space. By the time BiblioSol left the plaza, the volunteers and activists had taken on a new kind of librarian identity, a hybrid identity that included librarian, activist, and community member. It was an identity that many of them had not recognized in themselves before the donations began to arrive. The protest-librarian-as-activist-as-other emerges in response to the pull of the initial stack of books, and the library develops as various types of donors continue bringing books. The voice generated by the library via social media proves just as loud and powerful as the physical collection that began it all. The activists' new identities and voices persist longer than the library itself, even after the library has been evicted, the books boxed and made inaccessible, and the librarians scattered.

SOCIAL MEDIA

Occupation as peaceful resistance has been "rebooted" in the early twenty-first century as activists have woven their occupation of physical space together with the networking power of the Internet and social media. The occupations that preceded Acampada Sol under the umbrella label of the "Arab Spring," which began in late 2010 and inspired a wave of occupations and protests around the globe between 2011 and 2016, are often credited with effective utilization of this strategy. Manuel Castells traces these connections explicitly in his book *Networks of Outrage and Hope: Social Movements in the Internet Age.* Tunisia was the site of the first occupation, the catalyst for the entire Arab Spring movement.[1] In this case, Castells writes, "the connection between free communication on Facebook, YouTube and Twitter and the occupation of urban space created a hybrid public space of freedom." Less than two weeks later, activists in Egypt's Tahrir Square "planned the protests on Facebook, coordinated them through Twitter, spread them by SMSs [short message services], and webcast them to the world on YouTube."[2] Despite the government's order to shut down the Internet, Egyptian activists were able to maintain communication and spread information about what was happening. From there, occupations buoyed by social media channels spread across the Middle East and North Africa. According to Castells, this communication autonomy changed the balance of power between the protesters and the governments they were opposing: it provided a way to send their messages out to the global public without suppression or censorship by the authorities. Neither were they beholden to established media outlets to pick up, and possibly mediate, their stories.

The same innovative strategy holds true specifically with regard to protest libraries. For the libraries, the proactive use of networked technology fosters a new working group, the nascent library microcommunity. Social media provide a platform for a library's unique voice, making possible an identity that can be preserved as distinct from the conversation of the larger political occupation. The easy accessibility of social media lets the protest librarians distinguish the library from the occupation as a whole, speak directly to other librarians and book lovers, make and maintain external relationships, and generate an archive of the library experience that revolves around the material needs of a physical book collection. BiblioSol maintained its own blog and Twitter feed, and several active members also shared information through their personal Facebook pages. The library cohered in real life, and the librarians redistributed their collective voice into their own dedicated accounts. Without the power of social media to distinguish the voices of the librarians, the documentation of the libraries would exist primarily as a subset of the larger story of the occupation or movement. And because they emerged as part of a larger political resistance movement, they did not have to fight alone against censorship or government shutdowns. They were able to collaborate and support the larger cause both within and alongside it.

But just as prefigurative politics alone were not enough to spur the development of the library, neither were social media alone enough to spur the development of the library. While the Arab Spring occupations pioneered the use of social media to affect political revolution, before Spain there was no library like BiblioSol. On January 25, 2011, Egyptians descended on Tahrir Square in Cairo to protest the corrupt regime of Hosni Mubarak in the first major occupation of the Arab Spring. They filled the square with tents, stood their ground, and occupied it for just over two weeks, until February 14. They quickly developed support systems for serving food, for keeping the area clean, and for cohabiting the public space. But there was no library. Their protest was predicated on specific political demands, and the activists faced a much different regime than did the activists in Spain or the United States. A few months later the Indignados would emerge, and Spain would quietly integrate anarchism with prefiguration. Once that happened, a library made perfect sense. Every major occupation site after this included a library. Later that year, in July, Egyptians again occupied Tahrir. This time they were protesting the slow response of the military to their demands to hold new elections and bring Mubarak to justice. On Friday, July 8, a day the activists call the "Friday of Determination," they retook Tahrir. By July 11, in a firsthand account of the new occupation reported on CNN, a participant mentions a library tent. Only once the movements had been filtered through the Spanish site did libraries begin appearing regularly.³

DIGITAL BOOK COLLECTIONS

Given the importance of the Internet in developing the identity of the library as distinct from the overall occupation, an emphasis on collecting electronic texts would have seemed logical. In fact, one common question I hear when talking with people about protest libraries is "Why didn't they just build a digital library? That seems a lot easier." Material book collections in protest libraries almost sound like an amenity, even a luxury, because they require so much ongoing attention and labor. The sheer brute force that it takes to move even a few hundred books is obvious, and these large collections in outdoor spaces required high levels of care, especially during inclement weather—and as my conversations with so many librarians made clear, it seems like *any* weather can be considered inclement when it comes to books. Despite a physical book collection's weight and size, the collection is at heart quite vulnerable. It needs protection from park security, and it needs rapid mobility in case of emergency evacuation. Even if we concur that an ideal community should have a library, a physical library seems, at least on the surface, to be more trouble than it is worth.

The librarians did consider digital collections but eschewed the idea for a variety of reasons. With BiblioSol, they decided to focus on materiality because they just did not have reliable Internet access or electricity for recharging batteries. In the Maidan library in Kiev, Ukraine, librarian Anastasiia Makarenko says: "We liked that we didn't have a computer or anything. It fit the situation." She notes that at one point, people did suggest electronic books because they were already using Kindles or downloading pirated texts off the Internet. But the Maidan librarians knew that Ukraine publishing houses were losing a lot of money and were in rough financial shape. "So we wanted it to become fashionable again to get a physical book. We talked about it. We liked the idea that people would get a physical book."[4]

In the case of the Occupy Wall Street People's Library, in addition to facing the problem of accessing reliable Internet connectivity and electricity in a public park, the librarians actively debated the role digital texts should play, documenting on their blog the deliberate and thoughtful process they went through to reach their decision. They considered cost factors such as proprietary software requirements, and subscription and licensing fees. Mandy Henk, a librarian at the OWS People's Library, directly addresses the relationship between protest libraries and digital texts on the People's Library blog. "For many of us," she writes, "doing business with companies whose structure and management reflect the exact opposite of the world we want to see, is anathema. We can't change the world, rebuild it into a place of justice and equity, if we can't reflect the values we support in our internal dynamics and operations." She draws attention to one of the most important benefits of focusing on print books, the doctrine of "first sale." First sale "protects the primary activity of libraries, lending books and other materials." Thus, "when an entity purchases an item they are free to use it as they wish." That means once you have a physical book in your possession, you can do anything with it: share it, give it away, copy it, cut it into pieces. By contrast, "digital items are controlled by private contracts, contracts that determine what can and cannot be done with the item."[5]

Meanwhile, many electronic files have digital rights management (DRM) restrictions embedded within them, so not only is it problematic to share them, but also even the authorized reader can access the files for only a finite period of time before they lock themselves and will not reopen. Or the files may be bundled together in what is commonly referred to in the library industry as a "Big Deal" package. These bundles "make traditional collection development impossible," says Henk. Instead, this approach "transfers that role to publishers who can add and remove titles at will." On top of all this, often digital files must be read through a proprietary interface, which either is not free or restricts the ability to print or copy and paste text. And when a company like Microsoft decides to deactivate an e-reader service entirely, the books "will stop working."[6] Of course, a company's claim of terms and conditions does not mean that users will necessarily respect them, and some restrictions may be hackable or ignorable. But for these kinds of reasons, it turns out that for protest libraries, digital files, not physical books, were more trouble than they were worth.

MATERIAL BOOK COLLECTIONS

The attention demanded by a large quantity of material books is not only *not* a detriment; it is actually an asset. The physical properties are precisely the thing that defines the books' worth, calls the space of the library into being, and generates a drive that literally pulls people off course and attracts more and more books. Once the activists at BiblioSol were oriented toward creating the world they wanted to see in that moment, it did not take many books to catalyze this drive and generate a library. They began with only three or four books, and these books attracted more books.

This origin story of a pile of books appearing and becoming a library, suddenly and without much human intention, is repeated in many of the other protest library narratives. For example, from the beginning of the OWS occupation (which I address in greater depth in the next chapter), books had been piling up in New York's Zuccotti Park. According to the Writers for the 99%, the catalyst consisted of "a few dozen books, magazines, and pamphlets [that] had been collected by one of the occupiers."[7] He stacked them up and put a simple handwritten sign on them that said "Library." Then he moved on, shifting his efforts to other projects and becoming heavily involved with the Occupy archive initiative.[8] But the tiny collection he had gathered—now untended and on its own—remained intact long enough to be noticed by other people. In the words of Jaime Taylor and Zachary Loeb, two activists who were deeply involved with the library, the People's Library as most people remember it "started with a pile of books. Really." It began to grow as strangers brought more books and left them on the pile, as if the books themselves had adopted the Occupiers' claim "We are our demands" and were claiming a space of their own, beyond any particular political agenda. Say Taylor and Loeb, "Maybe it was mitosis or some other unseen process, but the pile of books kept growing."[9]

One of the last libraries to emerge, BiblioDebout, reflects a similar experience. Lionel Maurel, one of the BiblioDebout founders, writes, "One day when we arrived late compared to the schedule we had announced, we were surprised to see that people had already started to leave books on cartons under a sign 'BiblioDebout' that we had forgotten to take down the day before. BiblioDebout had thus reproduced itself, without our having to intervene. It was fascinating to watch it work 'by itself' because passers-by began to pick up and drop books." He goes on to say, "In a way, having seen BiblioDebout reborn without us that day was perhaps our greatest reward, as it provided evidence that people in the square themselves felt that they 'needed' a library and they rebuilt it with this simple gesture."[10]

In a talk at a conference about books, BiblioSol Librarian Zeke Ochoa described the kind of force emitted by books as magnetic, and if the books themselves acted as magnets and "people's attention is made up of iron filings." He went on to say that part of "the influence this critical mass of books may have on people in the encampment" is that their "pattern seems to align people's attention."[11]

With digital texts playing supporting roles at BiblioSol, the material collection of books was free to function as the hub around which everything else revolved. From this perspective, the development of the library was due to the books, not the activists. That is, rather than stating that the libraries were built by activists through their desire to create community, one could say that the books came first. It is as if the library's "thing-ness," to use a term from Jane Bennett's work, sends out a call and generates a drive in people to respond.[12] The inception of a protest library hinges on the power of a stack of books to attract more and more books, placing an increasing emphasis on the material underpinnings of the library.

THE GENERALITY OF THE COLLECTIONS

When I describe BiblioSol to friends and colleagues, they often first imagine a collection of books specifically dedicated to educating visitors about the movement's politics and history. Or they presume that the collection is composed of books that no one would want to read, and that the value has more to do with creating a physical footprint in order to claim a space. But neither of these assumptions is the case. The book donations come from a variety of sources: people who live nearby and are curious to see what is going on in the square or park; supporters who are themselves not able to actively "occupy" and are seeking other ways to demonstrate their solidarity; friends of the activists, and friends of friends; sympathetic organizations; and, in many cases, professional publishing houses. These books form a general collection with no particular theme or ideology, and they are well used during the protest library's physical lifetime.

The BiblioSol librarians estimate that the largest percentage of donations came from people who wished to support the library and bring pleasure to the readers. Librarian Mercedes del Valle says that when she was volunteering in the library, more often than not the books she saw on the shelves were ones that BiblioSol patrons were eager to read. She clarifies that this often meant new literature and recently published books, rather than dense political or historical texts.[13] In some cases, according to the BiblioSol blog, patrons would make requests for a specific book, and then a contributor would actually bring that book.

Some contributors focused more on sharing personally meaningful or valuable texts with a wider audience rather than on donating texts that the readers themselves wanted to read. Del Valle recalls, "In the early days, some people would bring books and tell you it was a good idea for the library to have them, and they would tell you all the benefits of reading these books. It was a little funny."[14] But this also included limited edition texts, books signed by the authors when they visited the encampment in a show of support, and original works produced for the library. Librarian Gonzalo says he thinks the book most emblematic of BiblioSol is *The Book of Embraces* by Eduardo Galeano, who personally brought signed copies of a couple of his books to the library

MATERIALITY AND VIRTUALITY   35

in solidarity with the activists' cause. The inscription reads "To the Indignados of 15-M and to those of always, in Madrid and wherever else they may be."¹⁵

Protest libraries also provide a natural venue for counter-national histories to be newly encountered. BiblioSol was gifted entire and partial collections of one-of-a-kind materials from related historical political groups and organizations. Many of these archives given to BiblioSol had been banned at the time they were published. "We had the chance to receive some extremely rare publications like handwritten diaries or magazine collections from different Union and anarchist Spanish associations of the seventies," says Ochoa, who views this as a "sort of inheritance" and an asset for BiblioSol.¹⁶ While they did not always provide the kind of light reading or flights of fantasy that readers requested, they were a tremendous resource, a "special collection" for the new library to tout that could not be found anywhere else. When we consider the ideological solidarity among unions, anarchists, and the Indignados, then the donations can clearly be seen as a reasonable way to carry on these "family" histories.

In some cases the giver is not an individual but a publishing company. Publishing houses often have a relationship with local protest libraries, and they have directly donated a significant number of remaindered books to several library sites. In Spain, according to Ochoa, a local publisher donated books, carts, and other supplies on the condition of anonymity. It was the Taksim Gezi Park library in 2013, however, that would receive the most recognition for publisher donations because it was a Turkish publisher who put out the call to start the library, and these donations formed the basis of the collection there. Similarly, several Ukraine publishing houses provided resources to the Maidan library.

WORTHLESS BOOKS

Uncurated, unconstrained collections such as these are vulnerable to accumulating less than stellar texts. Ochoa says that a sizable number of contributors brought books "simply because they have no use for them."

For the contributors, the primary purpose of this type of donation is to clear space to round off their personal collection, and in such cases, these books represent an unneeded excess. In other words, nothing will be missing if these books are removed from someone's private shelves. BiblioSol provided an appealing alternative to the repugnant idea of throwing books away. As Ochoa points out, "There seems to be some kind of superstition on throwing books in the garbage."[17] Besides, libraries like BiblioSol—libraries built solely on remainders and excesses from other collections—are not inclined toward exclusion. The protest library is driven by the collection, a glaring inversion of the usual model of library building.

While this type of donation is not a pervasive problem for protest libraries, librarians at several sites have had to consider how to define these leftovers and what to do about them—if anything. BiblioSol accepted all donations, although Ochoa admitted that on occasion some materials may have found their way into the trash.[18] In a post on his blog *S.I.Lex,* BiblioDebout librarian Lionel Maurel refers to bags or boxes full of old, damaged, or useless books (for example, a 1995 medical dictionary) as "toxic contributions." But even when it comes to useless books, "it is extremely difficult to refuse 'toxic waste' at the time of the gift, as this would imply a value judgment or censorship, which our group preferred to avoid. Besides, for a person who brings texts in good faith, to reject the donation on the basis of a quality criterion may be something quite violent." BiblioDebout, Maurel says, provided "in some sense an incentive for owners to abandon books, giving other users the right of 'cultural gleaning.'" Too many contributions like this, however, threaten to diminish the value that the community might find in the overall library collection. "Indeed, these books are heavy; they occupy space; they require unnecessary handling; they tend to accumulate without leaving, and their presence devalues the rest of the collection." Despite these concerns, the Paris team decided that they would not reject these donations. As Maurel writes:

> It soon became clear to us that we should not abandon these books in any way and [should] show them a certain amount of respect, because even the most useless works can still find takers. We usually place them at the end of the evening in boxes with a sign "Help yourself!" And we

found that they go quickly, sometimes even in ten or twenty minutes. And it is also an interesting phenomenon: the same books that no one would have taken when placed among the other works in the collection are still recovered when they are abandoned as "waste." Sadly, people in need such as the homeless or migrants, who are numerous in the square, probably do not dare to approach BiblioDebout while we are there.[19]

BOOK STAMPS

According to Anastasiia Makarenko, the Maidan library also had to deal with these kinds of donations. "In the beginning, [the books] were really good," but over time the quality diminished a bit. Eventually the librarians made some requests through their Facebook page asking that patrons not bring so many books about Soviet heritage, biographies of Lenin, or religious pamphlets. Like BiblioSol and BiblioDebout, however, Maidan never rejected donations. "We took everything," says Makarenko. Their solution was to create a special area in the library for the unusable books with a sign that read "Please take one if you would like to have a souvenir." People were delighted to have a remembrance of the library, complete with a Maidan library stamp inside the front cover.[20] In this way, having been a part of the collection imbues the book with new value, and marking it with the stamp cleverly converts it from an unwanted remainder to a desired piece of the new whole.

Most of the protest libraries utilized some kind of labeling system, even when they did not require that the books be returned. Maurel from BiblioDebout writes:

> Labeling and tagging are simple ways to signify that the act of individual appropriation "does not erase" the passage of the book in the BiblioDebout, but it does not express in itself the idea of an obligation of reciprocity contracted in return. As a result, we have changed the text of the label so that this idea is formulated more clearly. Our labels now say, "This book has been given to us. Take your turn so that it remains a common good." By this we meant to suggest ... that the right of use in the object should continue to take precedence over exclusive appropriation; by encouraging the "sampler" to put the book into circulation afterwards ... the initial intention of sharing having presided over its entry in BiblioDebout is prolonged.[21]

Zachary Loeb from OWS felt that once a book had been tagged as part of the People's Library collection, it would symbolically keep the library alive wherever the book ends up. He wrote in his blog in March 2015 that "there were thousands of books that were distributed to library visitors, thousands of books which now make their homes on thousands of bookshelves and that is wonderful. It may seem a bit naïve to make this claim—but I still feel that the People's Library is out there alive and raising hell as long as people have books on their shelves labeled OWSL."[22] I have to agree with him. In 2016, five years after the People's Library had been evicted from Zuccotti Park, I visited BiblioDebout, the protest library in Paris. Zachary had given me a box of books from the People's Library with "OWSPL" marked in black on the spines, and I brought these with me. These books were put out on the table right away, and the librarians tweeted a picture. They became instant "celebrity" books. The material book collection, from the special collections to the toxic volumes, gives rise to the identity of "the library," and this identity becomes strong enough to generate value external to its original community.

The Acampada Sol activists had taken up residence in Madrid's Puerta del Sol in mid-May 2011, and about three weeks later they voluntarily ended their occupation. They wanted to leave the square of their own volition and without any violence, so they made a conscious decision to vacate the plaza peacefully on June 12. The librarians knew that without a larger political encampment in which to embed themselves, they would have to make a choice about what to do with their collection. While accumulating the books had happened piecemeal over the course of three weeks, moving the hefty collection of four thousand books out of the square was another matter entirely. It was going to require some planning.

Via their blog, the librarians asked for input from the public. Some of their options included giving away all the books, gifting the collection to another nonprofit organization, or taking them to the Biblioteca Central, Madrid's public library. They ultimately opted to keep the books and find a new location to reestablish the library. On June 13,

2011, the day after leaving the Puerta del Sol, the librarians posted this message: "Thank you for letting us dream that one day there would be a library with the sky as a ceiling and the letters as walls, with users who are not, with librarians who do not know what that means, with people arriving with writing that leaves you excited. Thank you, see you, we will read. This has been only the prologue."[23]

We temporarily leave BiblioSol here, returning in the final chapter to look much more closely at how it carried on for several years after leaving Puerta del Sol, transforming itself over and over again. As we will see, the evolution that seemed so surprising at the time becomes a traceable pattern in most protest libraries. The creation and building of a protest library is a process shared equally by the books themselves, the librarians, the readers, the contributors, and the space in which they all come together. Once the library has come into being, it does not end with a fixed identity. It continues in motion, evolving and devolving. As part of this process, we have seen that the collection of a pile of books reaches a critical threshold and becomes a collection, taking on more power to affect activists and visitors within the occupation. In the next chapter, I address one more factor critical to the development of a protest library, the accessibility of public space, in order to understand the differences between public and private space, the types of behaviors that are acceptable in those spaces, and who manages those definitions.

CHAPTER 3

BEHAVIOR IN SPACE
Occupy Wall Street People's Library, New York

The Occupy Wall Street occupation began in New York's Zuccotti Park on September 17, 2011, just a couple of months after Acampada Sol vacated the plaza in Madrid. OWS activists renamed the park Liberty Square, and the People's Library emerged there within a few days, officially becoming a "working group" on October 2, 2011. Like BiblioSol, the People's Library experienced the magnetic effect of material books, and the collection grew to several thousand books in just a couple of weeks. But while BiblioSol left the Puerta del Sol in a planned and strategic move, by contrast the story of the People's Library includes midnight raids, hundreds of destroyed books and the mysterious disappearance of thousands more, lawsuits, and diatribes about elected officials. The library became a highly publicized aspect of OWS when, just a few weeks into the occupation's existence, park security and the New York police confiscated the books, most of which were then destroyed or lost. The stories and images of Dumpsters full of waterlogged, ruined books made their way into mainstream media and provoked passion and anger from book lovers across the country, even people who were otherwise apathetic toward the larger Occupy movement.

The People's Library calls attention to the physical space of the library itself in a more urgent way than did BiblioSol because of the ongoing conflict with police and park security, the behind-the-scenes political discussion with property owners, and the lack of clarity in existing legislation regarding who can use a given space and for what purposes. The development of the OWS People's Library reinforces what I have already discussed in terms of prefiguration, social media, and physical book collections, and it also addresses the issue of physical space required by the necessary presence of books and people for the development of a protest library. Space must be available to the library at least long enough for the initial selection of books to aggregate into a pile and for the momentum to begin.

THE CALL TO OCCUPY WALL STREET

The Canadian-based *Adbusters* made the initial public call to action in a notice that urged people simply to "flood into lower Manhattan, set up tents, kitchens, peaceful barricades and occupy Wall Street for a few months." It closed with the appeal to "screw up our courage, pack our tents and head to Wall Street with a vengeance September 17."[1] The announcement sought to provoke people who were disillusioned by the 2008 banking crisis, the subsequent bailouts, disparities between "Main Street" versus "Wall Street," and a slew of other inequities that had recently come to light. On her MSNBC show Rachel Maddow said of the encampment in Zuccotti Park in November 2011: "What they're imagining is a permanent or semi-permanent presence. They're imagining some sort of long-term physical commitment to their space." When she asked her guest Jeff Sharlet, a co-founder of OccupyWriters.com, "Is that intrinsic to the message?," Sharlet responded: "I think it is. There's that slogan that sort of made the rounds, 'We are our demands.' What are your demands? We are our demands, the fact of their presence."[2] In other words, physical bodies require space and material care. Physical bodies cannot be ignored or kicked around like a political action object (although the occupiers who were arrested or manhandled by security would disagree).

The Occupy Wall Street camp that ensued was a raucous affair, filling the outdoor space with constant sound from the drum circle and drawing so many people into Zuccotti Park that the fire marshal intervened. At one end of the park were the personal tents where people took up residence while living in the park for several weeks. The People's Library could be found at the other end, where the larger, military-grade tents, which had been erected more slowly, housed various working groups to take care of the business of the occupation. And from one end of the park to the other, pockets of people discussed politics and the state of the world around them.

The media reported on the original encampment in New York City with both wonderment and disdain, recounting with surprise the large numbers of participants and their also surprisingly vague and contradictory demands.[3] For the general public, one of the most confounding aspects of Occupy was the lack of a clear-cut list of demands. Many of us watching the spectacle unfold on TV and through social media wondered how so many people could find the time and energy to be in that space for so long without asking for anything in particular. Within the context of measurable outcomes and quantitative results in which so many of us operate, we wondered, how would they know if their occupation had been successful?

Within the encampment itself, the goals were clearer. It was a movement in the spirit of direct action, which the anthropologist and activist David Graeber defines as

> a certain ideal—in its purest form, probably unattainable. It is a form of action in which means and ends become, effectively, indistinguishable; a way of actively engaging with the world to bring about change, in which the form of the action—or at least, the organization of the action—is itself a model for the change one wishes to bring about. At its most basic, it reflects a very simple anarchist insight: that one cannot create a free society through military discipline, a democratic society by giving orders, or a happy one through joyless self-sacrifice. At its most elaborate, the structure of one's own act becomes a kind of micro-utopia, a concrete model for one's vision of a free society.[4]

This is a variation on the idea of prefigurative politics introduced in chapter 1. In fact, the OWS protesters were directly inspired by Acampada Sol, and their encampment manifested itself in many similar ways. They incorporated in it the concept of the general assembly and the working group model, as well as an organizational approach based on horizontality and prefiguration.

THE PEOPLE'S LIBRARY

During the first few weeks of the encampment, the ever-growing group organized itself and developed its collective voice. In order to get anything done, people needed to attend a General Assembly meeting and propose their ideas. If the group approved of the idea, then often an ad hoc committee called a "working group" was formed to carry out the plan. It was not a perfect system. When different demands were made, sometimes voices of contention found ways to promote constructive conversation so that disagreement would not hold up an entire working group over a single sticking point or pet issue. On occasion, this approach caused consternation rather than consensus. For example, Zeynep Tufekci recounts the experience at an Occupy Atlanta assembly in October 2011, when Congressman John Lewis attended and requested the opportunity to speak. Despite overwhelming approval from the crowd, one person chose to block the request. Those gathered discussed the request, and ultimately Lewis was not allowed to speak.[5] Nevertheless, despite incidents like this, overall the approach worked, and the philosophy of "we are our demands" remained a strong undercurrent that carried the movement as a whole forward.

Within the library, some of the activists began to devote time to organizing the growing stacks. In any protest library, one could find volunteers who were formally trained as librarians, some who were college educated, some who had worked professionally in the field, and some who had done none of those things. The only consistent factor: they were above all book lovers. As donors were bringing books to the occupied space, these volunteers stepped forward to take on the obligation of tending to the growing collection and to provide service. This drive was already within them; it took only the arrival of the books to help call it forth.

Some People's Library documentation includes the names of the library originators. For example, Betsy Fagin is credited as the person who made the formal request to start a library working group. Jaime Taylor, Zachary Loeb, and Mandy Henk had a relatively high profile through their writing and conference presentations about their experiences and

Figure 2. The Occupy Wall Street People's Library in Zuccotti Park, New York City, October 2011. Courtesy of Michael Oman-Reagan.

because of their professional connections to the library world. Stephen Boyer edited the OWS poetry anthology and was active with the People's Library 2.0 mobile version. But the librarians, not just at the People's Library but at most other protest libraries around the world, emphasize that there were many, many people involved, and they are generally reluctant to name any individual as catalyst. This reluctance is a feature of the horizontality adopted from the Indignados.

When the BiblioSol activists heard about the existence of the OWS People's Library, they sent a "solidarity letter," writing, "What we saw at the pics of OWS was quite impressive, but you couldn't imagine how surprised we were when we realized that OWS has also a library." During their own occupation, they go on to say, "we slept always waiting for the final police riot that would throw everything down. We had time for joy and also for despair. We never knew what we were doing, we only knew that it was right." Even as the Sol activists faced their own unknown future, they celebrated the news about the People's Library as the birth of a new family member. "You don't realize it," the letter says, "but you're making our dream come true."[6] While most of the BiblioSol librarians had never met the People's librarians, they were connected via their social media voices.

By October 2, the books were taking up enough space and energy at Zuccotti Park to warrant creating a formal "library working group." The activists named the library the Occupy Wall Street People's Library, and the collection continued to increase in size very quickly, creating an ever larger physical presence. *Time* magazine's Newsfeed website reported in October 2011, "There are between 2,500 and 4,000 volumes in the park, with more in storage." According to the same article, "the most popular books on offer seem to be what one would expect: leftist tracts on history and politics by authors like Howard Zinn, Noam Chomsky and Naomi Klein."[7] But protest library collections generally do not discriminate, and all manner of politics were represented on the People's Library shelves, said Loeb, including "Milton Friedman and John Maynard Keynes. We have Ayn Rand and George Orwell. We have Sean Hannity, Glenn Beck, Michael Savage, and Ann Coulter." Beyond politics, "we also have Stephen King, William Shakespeare, Dr. Seuss, and a book by the library's star patron [Mayor] Michael Bloomberg."[8] Hakim Bey's *T.A.Z.*, Guy Fieri's *Diners, Drive-Ins, and Dives*, a Harlequin romance called *If the Ring Fits*, and the fiction of Jorge Luis Borges were all also available according to the library catalog.[9] Such a wide variety of books provided reading materials for everyone in the park, but it could also have served the usual cross-section of readers who might visit any neighborhood public library.

Taylor, Loeb, and a slew of other volunteers organized and maintained the People's Library catalog of books, the contents of which were fluid and changed daily, making it difficult to keep an accurate list of available titles. In the three weeks of the library's existence, they used a site called LibraryThing to document an astonishing 5,500 different titles that were donated and loaned out, although one estimate of the total number of books that passed through was closer to twelve thousand.[10] Patrons could browse the stacks of books in the library, ask librarians for help locating particular items, or search LibraryThing for specific titles. They could immerse themselves in a wide variety of texts, all while surrounded by the chaotic atmosphere of the larger OWS experience.

Thanks to the library working group volunteers, the books took on a clear, if esoteric, system of organization. "We performed what I liked to call 'directly democratic shelving,'" says Taylor, which meant that "whoever was sorting books was empowered to put items where they thought they best belonged." They did have general categories of fiction and nonfiction, and topics such as "history, economics, poetry, education, women, queer, people of color, non-English," and so on. They developed a "reference section" with books that they asked patrons not to remove from the library. This included "traditional reference materials such as dictionaries as well as copies of our most popular books."[11] Everything else was fair game for borrowing, though "borrowing" was loosely interpreted, and there were no penalties for late returns. In fact, nothing was ever late because there were no due dates at all. Patrons were welcome to keep the books they borrowed or to pass them along to friends or other libraries.

BLOOMBERGVILLE

Clearly, New York City had known that Occupy was coming. The *Adbusters* call to action was hardly meant to be kept a secret. But Wall Street is a city street, and city streets are public property. Public property includes spaces owned by city government and designated specifically for use by the general public: not only streets and sidewalks, but also city parks, government buildings, and public libraries. Public property is beholden to laws that respect the First Amendment, prohibit discrimination, and adhere to a variety of common rules. Public property is regularly closed overnight, festivals and events must obtain permits and limit their size, and issues of public health and safety may mandate sudden and unexpected closure. While Wall Street was the obvious location for the initial Occupy convergence because it was a location symbolic of the unchecked greed of neoliberal capitalists, it was ironically and problematically located on public property. Thus it was no surprise when in September, on the designated Occupy day of action, supporters arrived to find that Wall Street itself had been blocked and was teeming with police. In terms of occupying Wall Street proper, the action was over before it even began.

Activists and members of the New York City General Assembly were aware of these limitations. A few months before Occupy, several groups of New York activists had collaborated on an occupation in front of City Hall, which lasted from June 14 to July 5, "to protest the draconian cuts and layoffs proposed by Mayor Michael Bloomberg."[12] Calling themselves New Yorkers against Budget Cuts, according to the *Huffington Post*, "they dubbed their city Bloombergville, in honor of the mayor's plan to lay off 4,000 public school teachers and close 20 fire companies."[13] Bloombergville also included a library, but it never reached the critical mass of the People's Library because of the limitations of the existing public space.

The steps in front of City Hall had been a contested site since at least the late 1990s, when Mayor Rudolph Giuliani first tried to limit the number of people allowed for a press conference or protest, and then "attempted to close the steps entirely to all protest activity, citing alleged security concerns." The court ruled against the city, which a few months later announced a new policy that events would be permitted only if "they were sponsored by a government official and were limited to 50 persons."[14] Eventually the city regulation "required groups to obtain permits before assembling in front of City Hall and limits the number of participants to 50 on the building steps and 150 in the front plaza."[15] Twenty years later, when Bloombergville formed on the sidewalk in front of City Hall rather than on the steps, this policy was still active. Had the protesters exceeded those limits, the city could have removed them legally.

In anticipation of the city's response, the OWS activists had been researching alternative spaces behind the scenes. They created a short list of options, all of which fell into a peculiar category, the "privately owned public space" (POPS), which was actually neither public nor private. In 1961, as part of an updated Zoning Resolution, New York City began allowing developers to increase the square footage of buildings by adding additional floors beyond what had been permitted by prior zoning guidelines if, in exchange for the extra height, the developer would agree to include a public park or plaza, defined as "an open area accessible to the public at all times." By 2000, New York had documented approximately five hundred plazas, parks, and arcades with

POPS zoning status, covering eighty acres of city space.[16] The use of Zuccotti Park as a backup plan for the Occupy kickoff was no accident. Originally called One Liberty Plaza and privately owned by a company named Brookfield Properties, the park had been created in 1972 as part of the POPS incentive program.

Public *space* is distinct from public *property*, and both are distinct from private property. The parks and plazas with POPS designations exist in a strange liminal space among all three. In 2000, Harvard University professor Jerold S. Kayden partnered with the New York City Department of City Planning and the Municipal Art Society of New York to document the spaces for the first time. According to Kayden, "public space means a physical place located on private property to which the owner has granted legally binding rights of access and use to members of the public, most often in return for something of value from the City to the owner."[17] Because they are spaces within private property that are designated explicitly for public use, they are not subject to the limitations that private property owners may impose on the bulk of their land or buildings. Kayden compares a POPS plaza to an easement, although these spaces negotiated between a business and a city government entail significant differences.

USABILITY

One of the most anomalous and unusual aspects of New York's POPS zoning is the lack of guidelines specifying permitted and prohibited activities, that is, the rights of and restraints on people within the public space. From the start, regulation had much more to do with defining the space and the objects within it than with addressing the anticipated behavior of visitors.

The original motivation for zoning regulations in New York was to make sure that "air and light" were available throughout the city and not completely obstructed as industrial innovation enabled buildings to become taller and taller. According to Manhattan Borough president George McAneny in 1913, there was "a growing sentiment in the community that the time has come when an effort should be made to regulate the height, size, and arrangement of buildings . . . in order to arrest the seriously increasing evil of the shutting off of light and air . . . to prevent unwholesome and dangerous congestion . . . and to reduce the hazards of fire and peril to life."[18] In 1916, New York passed the first comprehensive zoning ordinance in the United States, and it included very specific building and architectural guidelines. Formulas were included to calculate how tall or how far from the street a building should be. Forty years and 2,500 amendments later, the original 1916 Zoning Resolution was comprehensively reviewed. The resulting 1961 Zoning Resolution remained focused on ensuring adequate access to "light and air" at street level. This time, though, the report went even further by creating the POPS incentive plan. "In order to bring more light and air into streets surrounded by tall buildings, as well as to create more usable open space," reads the report, "a bonus device has been established to encourage the setting back of buildings from the street line."[19]

The addition of that one word, "usable," opened a Pandora's box for the city. As Kayden notes, "The concept of 'usable' open space, as distinct from space meant to bring more 'light and air' to the street level, was never elaborated."[20] CWS's unprecedented encampment within the POPS-designated Zuccotti Park pushed the vagaries of the behavior policy to a critical threshold, leaving unanswered the question of who had the power to regulate not the material aspects of the space itself but the ways in which the public might make use of the legally required "usable" space. The city imposed very few other conditions and never defined what it meant for the space to be "usable" by the public. When developers requested a variance in exchange for adding a POPS park or plaza, they simply had to indicate on the plans where the physical space would be located and file the appropriate forms with the city.

As a result, some of the earliest POPS areas were completely useless as public spaces. They ended up being used as passenger drop-off areas, loading docks, and parking garage driveways for the companies that owned or leased the building. Over half of the POPS plazas from this era are ranked as "marginal," which means that not only is the space not enticing, but also it actually "deters members of the public from using the space for any purpose." As a rule, marginal spaces "are environmentally and aesthetically hostile to public use, typically seen by expert, as well as non-expert, observers as barren, desolate, depressing, and sterile . . . Their microclimates are cold, with surfaces frequently untouched by sunlight and sometimes subject to wind tunnels created by the juxtaposition of vertical and horizontal planes." They lack seating and landscaping, and spikes or railings prevent people from sitting on ledges or steps. The most egregious violations of the principles behind POPS plazas are committed by private owners who have "erected illegal fences, walls, gates, and other physical barriers around and in the spaces, allowed adjacent commercial uses to install tables and chairs for private customers, and deployed their building staff to instruct users that the space is private." By the mid-1970s, it had become clear that while many developers may have been following the letter of the zoning regulations, they were certainly not following the spirit of it.[21]

In an effort to ensure that POPS parks were usable, the city started subjecting developers to much more specific regulations. Today, in order to meet the "more usable space" directive, the city formally requires POPS areas to be pleasant and inviting places for the public to use. A POPS plaza must be well lit, easily accessible, and also somewhat removed from the cacophony of the street. The regulations also specify how much seating must be available according to the size of the park, and city guidelines describe the different kinds of appropriate seating in great detail. The park may include benches, chairs, retaining walls, and steps. The seats may not be designed to be uncomfortable, like the seating so common now at bus stops. Spikes may not be installed on retaining walls to prevent people from sitting there. The guidelines even dictate the acceptable degree at which the backs of the chairs may be angled. Notably, a POPS park is by definition open twenty-four hours a day unless the owner files a request with the city and provides a reasonable explanation as to why the park should close at night. Unless this formal request is made, POPS parks must remain open at all times by default. Until Occupy, very few POPS owners had requested such exceptions.

CLEANING THE PARK

Initially, Brookfield Properties claimed that Occupy was welcome in Zuccotti Park. John Zuccotti himself, Brookfield's US chairman at the time and the namesake of the park, visited, though as Sam Roberts wrote in a blog post for the *New York Times*, "nobody recognized him during several casual sojourns he has made to the park from his office at the World Financial Center to survey the scene." Describing Zuccotti as someone "who cuts a judicious, even owlish, figure at seventy four, [and] is no stranger to gracious hospitality," Roberts noted, "As for Brookfield's continued welcome, Mr. Zuccotti said, 'my guess is that we basically look to the police leadership and mayor to decide what to do.'" Relating what he'd seen in the park, Zuccotti told Roberts, "If you go there, you can't tell the protesters from the tourists," adding, "It has a kind of festive atmosphere." Roberts continued, "After his visit on Wednesday, though, he said the park has gotten 'a little messy,'" and "sooner or later we're going to have to get in to clean it. With gas generators and other things there, we don't want anybody to get hurt."[22] In October, when protesters were told that Brookfield wanted to clean the park, they took it upon themselves to do a major scrub-down of the space, temporarily preventing intervention from the company.

But the city wanted them out. Brookfield Properties and the mayor's office spent several weeks wending their way through the court system. The park was private property, so the city needed Brookfield's permission before it could employ NYPD resources. But it was also a regulated public space, so Brookfield did not have the explicit legal rights to restrict activities in its POPS plaza beyond the scope of the Zoning Resolution. Eventually the city claimed the right to evict the protesters from the park on the basis of health and safety concerns. A police raid ensued, along with the destruction of the new world the protesters had been building.

BEHAVIOR IN SPACE

Because of the peculiar POPS spatial designation, the city and Brookfield Properties were in dispute over who was responsible for controlling the behavior of the activists as their OWS camp grew. Who had the authority to maintain order, enforce rules, and eventually evict the activists?

Since behavior itself was a legal gray area, most of the guidelines provided to activists had to do with the objects in the space. For the library, because of the heavy materiality of their space, the guidelines became onerous. Mostly these had to do with the ways in which the librarians were allowed to store the books, and they were in daily conflict with both Brookfield's private security and the New York Police Department over both their basic right to occupy the space and what constituted permissible behavior within the park. They faced variable sets of rules and expectations, as well as varying degrees of force from those applying the rules. The librarian activists struggled to understand what kinds of boxes, tarps, and tents were permissible, because permissions and guidelines changed daily and arbitrarily. They worried over how they could best protect the books from the elements, and they generated contingency plans for disassembly and mobility.

The space grew to include rows of makeshift shelves and bins lined with several thousand physical books, and a certain amount of flexibility was required as the storage plan evolved. "For most of the library's existence," says Taylor, "we didn't have actual shelves. The first volumes were placed on a stone bench at the northeast corner of the park. Then they were put in cardboard boxes. Which melted in the rain. Then they were covered by tarps and put in plastic bins." Sometimes the police prohibited the use of tarps, "you know, because we might be hiding bombs under there," so the librarians used clear plastic sheeting instead.[23] All of this was eventually housed under a large hangar-shaped tent donated by singer Patti Smith, the kind that are described as "big large warm secure army tents that can be used for building institutions and so on."[24] Loeb says that after this, "the OWS librarians affectionately referred to the library tent as 'Fort Patti.'"[25] The library seems to have been targeted by security and police because it was maintaining such a large material presence in the park. It was, however, also due to this sense of permanence, as well as the organized nature of the work at hand and the egalitarian approach toward running the project, that the future of the library seemed "promising, and the park was filled with optimistic talk about weathering the winter."[26] The optimism would be short-lived.

The use of a POPS space shows ingenuity on the part of the protesters, the kind of innovation that, according to David Graeber, "only those who are not bound by the existing legal order can create."[27] Their example give us an opportunity to consider the kind of physical space that generates protest libraries and also the kind of space that protest libraries themselves generate, a relationship that fluctuates constantly. Simply calling a space a "library" is not enough; we have to consider the behavior permitted within that space and the ways in which information about what is allowed is disseminated.

The spatial aspect of a protest library is an individual element with the capacity to affect, and be affected by, the larger community surrounding it. The purpose of emphasizing space in this chapter is not to overlay a linear cause-and-effect logic on the relationship between protest libraries and the spaces that contain them: If an encampment can set up in a certain kind of space, then they can/will have a library. Such a generalization is tempting but problematic, because it risks glossing over too many variations. As we will see, myriad types of space have hosted protest libraries and have demanded from the activists a wide range of behaviors, resistances, and protections. In the next chapter we will consider what happens after the books reach critical mass and become a collection. The removal and deconstruction of a library collection evokes powerful responses, and the Occupy Wall Street People's Library found itself on the front lines in this regard.

CHAPTER 4

VISUAL SPECTACLE
Occupy Wall Street People's Library, New York

The visual spectacle of removing a physical library collection creates a rhetorical frenzy among the general public in a way that removing files online does not, and the slow digitization of library collections puts them in danger of eventually disappearing without any public notice, much less outcry. When we do not see the quantity of texts decreasing, we do not react in the same way, and the gap between the public perception of losing physical books versus the public perception of a shrinking database is tremendous.

But while the books' power comes by way of their physical presence, the power of the voice need not. The social media narratives of protest libraries, and specifically the story of the OWS People's Library, reveal the ability of the disembodied virtual voice to generate public reactions to the destruction of a book collection. This public reaction, in turn, affects the library's community as significantly as the material books themselves.

THE RAID

At around 2:00 a.m. on November 15, 2011, Zuccotti Park was raided by the New York City police and sanitation departments. All of the activists were evicted and their belongings removed. Video taken that night shows police dismantling the larger tents using chainsaws and unceremoniously confiscating the boxes of books at the library site.

The library working group had undertaken planning and preparation for precisely this kind of emergency exit situation, but activists had had only an hour or twos notice, which simply was not enough time to remove their property. Jaime Taylor received a text about the raid and rushed to the park, but she was unable to cross the barricades that had been set up by the police. "It hardly mattered what our emergency plan had been," says Taylor. "Of the five librarians who were inside the park that night, two elected to stay and three others were only able to remove what they could carry in one trip; once they left the park they could not return to retrieve either personal possessions or library materials."[1] Despite their frantic efforts that November night to protect the contents of the library, the bulk of the collection was removed by the police before the sun came up. William Scott, a faculty member on sabbatical from the University of Pittsburgh, who had been living in the park and volunteering his time at the People's Library, wrote in *The Nation*, "To see an entire collection of donated books, including many titles I would have liked to read, thoughtlessly ransacked and destroyed by the forces of law and order was one of the most disturbing experiences of my life."[2]

Mayor Bloomberg had authorized the raid, and in a formal statement he attributed the city's actions to a need to ensure health and safety. The authorities, he said, had to come in and clean the park. At the end of his statement, he made a surprising and seemingly unnecessary rhetorical move away from a logical (though fallacious, the librarians would argue) claim of hygiene to an emotional stance. "Protesters have had two months to occupy the park with tents and sleeping bags," he said, adding, "Now they will have to occupy the space with the power of their arguments."[3] So occupy with argument they did, publicly and loudly, by activating the strong network to which they belonged.

As the Occupy movement fanned out across the country and then around the world, libraries were emerging in many of the encampments. This series of protest libraries served as a primary witness to the People's Library argument. *American Library Magazine* reported: "Along with the movement, Occupy libraries are spreading. There are libraries at Occupy Boston, Occupy Seattle, Occupy L.A., Occupy Portland,

Occupy Dallas, Occupy San Francisco, and elsewhere among the more than 100 Occupy sites in the United States that have sprung up since September 17," providing significant support for the claim that it was "becoming a part of the working model of long-term occupation sites that they have a library."[4] In fact, the BiblioSol blog documents libraries at several of the US sites and also many international sites, all by the end of November 2011. The BiblioSol library in Madrid, and another library in the Barcelona encampment, had inspired the People's Library in New York, which in turn

> inspired the creation of the one in Philadelphia. This was quickly joined by the Occupy library in Chicago and the *Audre Lorde* in Boston and followed by the *Occupy LA* of Los Angeles, the *Occupy DC's People's Library* of Washington, the *Library tent* of Oakland, the *Lending Library* of Delaware, the *Occupy Bloomington Library* of Indiana, the *Library Tent* of Dallas, that of Seattle, Portland, Baltimore, San Francisco, Orlando, and the Eugene Public Library in the State of Oregon. In Europe: the Défense Library in Paris, the Öffentliche Occupy Bibliothek in Frankfurt in Germany, the Star Books in London, the Cork Library in Ireland, the Occupy Amsterdam in the Netherlands, the Toronto Open Library, and the Library tent in Vancouver in Canada, the Sydney Open Library in Australia, and the Occupy Auckland library in New Zealand among others. All of them are our new sisters, offspring who were born looking at our BiblioSol. The silent readings we did at Sol during the month of May have gone around the world.[5]

Most of the Occupy libraries had their own social media account, and most of these accounts provided links or references to the other libraries with which they were in solidarity.

In addition to following the protest libraries' social media accounts, many individuals in New York made use of the People's Library in real life, and many others made book donations. These people were affected directly when the library was removed from the park. And more broadly, there were people all over the world who were following the story simply because they loved the idea of the library, and its destruction brought this sense of connection to the forefront in dramatic fashion. The People's librarians knew that their large social media audiences, their readers-as-witnesses, were watching, and this intensified the visibility and performativity of the events as they happened.

The librarians immediately demanded that the city return their property, which included not only the physical books that formed the foundation for their work and the backdrop for their space but also several laptops, tents, shelves, and other furniture. At around noon on the fifteenth, the New York City mayor's office tweeted, "Property from #Zuccotti, incl #OWS library, safely stored @ 57th St Sanit Garage; can be picked up Weds," and released a picture of relatively neat stacks of books on a folding table with several plastic bins of books underneath.[6] The librarians tweeted back asking where the rest of the books were. By the time they were admitted to the Sanitation Department garage, the vast majority of their collection either was missing or had been thrown into Dumpsters, rendering many of the books unreadable and unusable. Only a fraction of what had been taken, about twenty-five boxes of books, remained. "I went in ready to triage 4,000 books," says Zachary Loeb. "There weren't 4,000 books." Once they'd had time to re-inventory everything, they found that approximately 3,600 documented books had been confiscated by the city during the raid, though they had managed to recover only 1,275. Loeb divided these books into three categories: "lightly damaged or undamaged"; "damaged but reusable," which included "books that had ripped covers, heavy spine damage, light water damage"; and "destroyed," which included "books ripped in half, books that had been warped beyond readability, and books that were more mud than book."[7] Of the recovered books, between five hundred and eight hundred were salvageable.

"It's obvious to me," one of the librarians wrote on the People's Library blog, "that by recklessly throwing the contents of the park into dumpsters, the NYPD and DSNY working under Bloomberg's orders destroyed what we built. And that their claim that the library was 'safely stored' was a lie."[8] On Twitter, they were even more direct: "Hey @MikeBloomberg, you lied."[9] An apocalyptic picture of the ruined books with a damaged copy of Ray Bradbury's *Fahrenheit 451* front and center began to circulate.

CHAPTER 4

RESPONSES TO THE RAID

The story of the raid and the loss of books went viral, triggering harsh words from those who loved the People's Library as well as from those who were simply drawn to a romanticized idea of "the library." On Twitter, one user wrote: "@owslibrary Track confiscated books, bet they incinerated them. @NYCMayorsOffice: Proud trashers of Constitution and Book Burners #OWS." Another wrote, "@OWSLibrary @NYCMayorsOffice Sounds like a Dictatorship." Someone else tweeted: "@RayBeckerman @climatebrad @NYCMayorsOffice @MikeBloomberg @OWSLibrary Of course Bloomberg lied. His legacy is shit, term limit lying pig."[10] And on a *Shareable* blog, Ellis Jones commented: "I do not know of a single case in history when the side destroying libraries has been cast in a favorable light. It is the mark of an unjust action by a desperate force." On the same site, Gabriel Levinson posted, "Congratulations Mayor Bloomberg, your name is now synonymous with the dirtiest word in the English language: censorship."[11] Another user tweeted, "@OWSLibrary @NYCMayorsOffice Sue the bastards for destruction of property."[12]

The materialization of a collective voice intensified and formalized when American Library Association president Molly Raphael issued a statement in support of the People's Library two days later:

> The dissolution of a library is unacceptable. Libraries serve as the cornerstone of our democracy and must be safeguarded. An informed public constitutes the very foundation of a democracy, and libraries ensure that everyone has free access to information. The very existence of the People's Library demonstrates that libraries are an organic part of all communities. Libraries serve the needs of community members and preserve the record of community history. In the case of the People's Library, this included irreplaceable records and material related to the occupation movement and the temporary community that it represented.[13]

Later that week, some of the librarians held a press conference to share their experiences during the raid and publicly document the Bloomberg administration's destruction of the library. Norman Siegel, former president of the New York Civil Liberties Union, who helped orchestrate the event, commented: "History informs us that when books are burned there is almost immediately or subsequently universal condemnation of that act. Here, the Bloomberg administration lost, damaged and possibly destroyed books. That is wrong."[14] Siegel would go on to represent the People's librarians pro bono in a lawsuit against the city. In 2013 the suit would be settled for $47,000, again supporting the notion that the People's Library had monetary value in addition to rhetorical value.

Authors and allies with more clout than the average Twitter user also weighed in. *The Rachel Maddow Show* had run a segment about the library before the raid and then followed up with a post on the show's blog titled "Update: The People's Library Not So 'Safely Stored,'" in which Tricia McKinney asked: "Ummm, Mayor Bloomberg? Do you really want to run afoul of librarians?"[15] On *Countdown with Keith Olbermann*, as part of an eight-minute editorial litany of the many ways Bloomberg had offended democracy, Olbermann asked: "Who else but a human platitude like Bloomberg could have . . . enabled the image of policemen seizing 5,500 books from the Occupy Wall Street library and throwing them in a Dumpster as if the cops were book burners? . . . Michael Bloomberg—no such a figure, no such a living breathing embodiment of all that is wrong and all that is stupid in the establishment of this country could be ordered up from the works of fiction."[16]

AFTER THE PARK

After the OWS People's Library was destroyed, while some people lashed out in anger over the loss of the books or the affront to democracy, others rightly mourned the loss of the space itself. OWS poetry anthology editor Stephen Boyer later recounted, "I read poems to the officers as they hit people with batons and destroyed the beautiful experimental world we had all worked so hard to create."[17] The night after the raid, the librarians returned and set up a "new" library with one hundred books. Within a day, the police and Brookfield employees returned and cleared the park again. William Scott writes: "The NYPD first barricaded the library by lining up in front of it, forming an impenetrable wall of cops. An officer then announced through a bullhorn that we should come and collect our books, or they would be confiscated and removed. Seconds later, they began dumping books into trash bins that they had wheeled into the park for that purpose." As soon as that was done, though, someone came out of the crowd of onlookers with a book to donate. The librarians wrote a new library sign on a piece of paper and the library was again reborn. Scott writes, "A true people's library, after all, doesn't depend on any particular number of books, since it's ultimately about the way those books are collected and lent out to the public."[18]

The library was never able to regain the pre-raid critical mass, however. Many activists and librarians returned the next day, and the librarians brought a box of books with them to try to reestablish their presence, but it was not the same. In Boyer's words, "We were all heartbroken mid-November, when the NYPD came and squashed the park."[19] Jaime Taylor and Zachary Loeb noted that while the library had maintained a steady stream of foot traffic and contributions before the raid, after November 15 visitors to the various versions of the library typically "came with lamentations over the loss of the library proper rather than with book donations."[20] In order to survive, the library had to evolve.

Several new iterations of the library emerged. "It's like if you beat up a hornet's nest and the hornets go everywhere," says Boyer.[21] A video on the blog shows People's Library 3.0, a cart being wheeled around the streets of New York City as Boyer shouts an offer of "free books." The People's Library was present with its "mobile book crate" at Occupy Macy's for "Buy Nothing Day."[22] The mobile library also made appearances on New Year's Eve 2012 at One Police Plaza and later that night in Zuccotti Park. Boyer writes that he had been participating with other protesters in a march around Chinatown, but when police caught up with them, "since I had the People's Library on my back, I realized I needed to stop marching and get the books to Liberty Square. By the time I got back to the park, it was about 10:30pm and everyone had started taking the barricades down. I set up the library."[23]

Meanwhile, the working group continued to hold regular meetings, and in December they posted a call for "current legal reference books" in order to help other working groups involved with "civil rights, housing, finance," many of which were facing legal issues and challenges. Despite the $47,000 in damages the People's Library had won from the city in April 2013, Taylor and Loeb write, "it was never about the money. We asked for money because that's the language spoken by the government and the court system. For us, it was about getting an admission of wrongdoing from the city. And we got that, if expressed in the formal, wishy-washy language of lawsuit settlements." The librarians donated the money to other like-minded organizations and slowly redistributed the library books back into circulation through donations to other libraries—as well as sending several boxes to the Babel pop-up library discussed in the conclusion to this book and providing a box that I brought to Paris to donate to BiblioDebout in 2016. Taylor and Loeb hoped that "the letters 'OWSL' written on the edges of the text will always stand as evidence of what the library once was. And what it can be again."[24]

ACTIVATING THE NETWORK

Reactions to the raid and the destruction of the books were hardly relegated to mere tongue-lashing and lament. People took action. The destruction of the book collection in Zuccotti Park galvanized relationships and heated up the network of communication among all the librarians and their allies. OccupyWriters.com was launched, and hundreds of writers, including Salman Rushdie, Neil Gaiman, Margaret Atwood, and Alice Walker, signed the digital petition in support of the library. The statement is simple: "We, the undersigned writers and all who will join us, support Occupy Wall Street and the Occupy Movement around the world." According to *The Guardian*, Jeff Sharlet, one of the OccupyWriters.com founders, said the website "was already 'stunningly busy,' with more than one hundred thousand visitors a day and a backlog of one thousand writers to be vetted, 'just to make sure they're real people.'"[25]

After the raid, "connecting Occupy libraries together has become one of our primary aims," says librarian Betsy Fagin. In that spirit, the librarians at the widespread sites all worked together to form a coalition and make connections. They considered how to reach out to different constituencies, including educators. Fagin notes: "Books are being published about the Occupy movement, professors are teaching courses on it, and students are studying what we have already done. We mean to be an integral part of these conversations." In January 2012, Fagin was one of several librarians who appeared on a panel at the American Library Association's annual conference to talk about the actions that had been taken. They spoke passionately about the experience, stating, "As librarians we understand the vital role libraries play in society and in a healthy democracy and our library stands as our living commitment to fulfilling that role."[26]

An extended viewing audience responded to the tweeted photos of the Occupy Wall Street raid. If there is one thing that can unite a wide swath of diverse people, pictures of the wanton destruction of books will do it. Libraries draw us to them and whisper to us that they are special. Often in conversation with friends and colleagues, I hear people describe libraries as "magical." Some of us are more susceptible than others to this magic. Laurie Gries, author of *Still Life with Rhetoric: A New Materialist Approach for Visual Rhetorics,* writes that "from a new materialist perspective, things become rhetorically meaningful via the consequentiality they spark in the world." Her book traces the viral life of the "Obama Hope" image, and while the images of the destroyed People's Library book collection did not reach the same levels of exposure as this poster, Gries's reading of "Obama Hope" can be applied to other viral images such as those of the People's Library books. According to Gries, images like these allow us to "theorize how rhetoric materializes, moves, transforms, replicates and, especially, how publics, or I would prefer *collectives,* materialize in relation to such distributed rhetorical activity."[27] This is precisely what happened as the images and the story of the People's Library raid made their way through the networks of people watching and reading. A collective emerged and became galvanized in support as the pictures circulated.

CRITICAL VOICES

Even among those who do not consider themselves "readers," it is rare to encounter anyone who completely disavows the value of a library collection. But amid the solidarity and galvanization of pro-library, anti-Bloomberg allies, and despite the votes of confidence from the American Library Association and the New York Civil Liberties Union, a few critical voices could be heard. Some people feared that overuse of the word "library" might normalize alternate, unvetted definitions. Blogger Stephen A. Matthews, author of the *21st Century Library Blog*, made the claim that the librarians had "affiliated a social protest movement with a 'library' by using totally warped reasoning." Matthews wanted to know "Who assessed the need for a 'library' for the protestors?" and "What is a People's Library? Is that a new category like Public, Academic, School, Special, etc.? Who decided this was a 'library' in any sense of the term?" And one of his readers commented: "Lets all support free access to information . . . information as a fundamental right of a free people . . . democracy. BUT lets be careful about how we throw around the word LIBRARY . . . if WE as librarians are willing to apply it too loosely why on earth should we expect any one else to value the truly great institution that is the FREE PUBLIC LIBRARY."[28] The BiblioDebout protest library faced similar criticism a few years later. Librarian Lionel Maurel wrote, "One day, we were confronted with this criticism when a person came to us and said, 'You are not a library, since we can keep the books.'" For Maurel, this signified that for the critic, "the library grants a right of use, but not a right of appropriation, while our system leads to the opposite effect: to grant a right of appropriation, to the detriment of collective use (the book that is taken can no longer be used for public readings or animations, for example)."[29]

Matthews writes on his blog: "If we concede that building a library—'any library'—would be great and a necessary act, it would only be revolutionary if there wasn't one already! Last time I heard the NYC Public Library, and its 70 something branches, is still up and running stronger than ever. How far away was the closest NYCPL branch—2 or 3 blocks?"[30] One of his readers posted a comment in response: "AS a public librarian, I found their comments and actions to be incredibly dismissive of the excellent work of the hundreds (thousands) of staff of the New York City Public Library. THERE IS A 'PEOPLES LIBRARY' in NYC." The blog *SafeLibraries* takes issue with the endorsement that the People's Library received from the American Library Association, primarily making the case that the ALA had declined to endorse other similar libraries in Cuba and that as an institution, it did not necessarily reflect the will of the individual members.[31]

Coincidentally, at the same time, the New York Public Library, which these critics held up as the library gold standard, was embroiled in its own heated dispute over the removal of books from its main branch collection—several million rather than thousands. And in fact, the same week when Bloomberg authorized the Occupy raid, he spoke at the NYPL's major annual fund-raising gala, held to honor "distinguished individuals who have made significant cultural and educational achievements to increase our understanding of the world around us."[32] Earlier in 2011, Bloomberg had committed $150 million in new funding for a renovation of the NYPL Central Library and was putting forward the public face of a library supporter. As it turns out, this renovation, called the "Central Library Plan," was controversial because it called for the removal of 3 million books from the main branch collection and the closure of a technology-oriented branch library. Bloomberg's support for and allocation of funds toward this plan generated as much controversy as dismantling the humble grass-roots People's Library, providing evidence for the claim that community libraries need physical books: they help to call attention to the disappearance of resources.

Whether books are part of a radical outsider library, a conventional public library, or even a small regional academic library, responses are similar when they are destroyed or disappear: the books symbolize freedom, democracy, and community. Access to information is a cornerstone of American ideology. In the next chapter I address the ways in which an intense, emotional rhetorical response is generated not just by the destruction of physical books but sometimes simply by the threat of their disappearance.

CHAPTER 5

LIBRARY AS A DEMOCRATIC INSTITUTION
NYPL Main Branch, New York

I ended the last chapter with the words of some online critics who took issue with the idea that the destruction of the People's Library should be mourned in the same way that the destruction of a formal public library should be. One tweet after the raid read: "I was momentarily mad about the #ows library being destroyed until I realized that it wasn't a REAL library WTF."[1] The Annoyed Librarian, in a blog on the *Library Journal* website, wrote, "A collection of books in boxes in a park called a 'People's Library' is hardly the same thing as a public library. The 'People's Library' was stocked and managed by volunteers. It belonged to no one and suffered the tragedy of the commons. If public libraries managed their collections the way this one was managed, they would be grossly irresponsible."[2] Annoyed Librarian highlights a distinction here between "the collection" of the books themselves and the idea of a "public library." Neither writer calls into question whether the NYPD was justified in destroying books. Rather, they both question what it means to call something or somewhere a "library."

Is it possible to dilute the meaning of the word "library" by using it too loosely? By using the same word to describe a place that lends books and one that gives them away? Or by calling a place a library that is not officially designated as such by government or other authorities? While the defense of the public library system is admirable, the definitions and categories being used in these arguments seem too static and rigid to be productive in understanding the landscape of libraries today. The librarians themselves were clear that the People's Library differed from the New York Public Library. Yet this is no reason to disregard the place of protest libraries within the larger landscape. Rather than restricting us to thinking of the situation as "either/or," as these critics are doing, the protest library opens an opportunity to think in terms of "and/and." We should not miss the opportunity and the joy offered by protest libraries because of a limited vocabulary.

At the same time the People's Library was building its massive ad hoc physical collection, the New York Public Library's main branch on Forty-second Street was, with some secrecy, preparing to remove theirs. The reactions of the New York public, the mobilization of an extended network of library allies, the rhetoric deployed to save the books, and the values that emerge from the experience are too similar to ignore, forcing the question, how can we *not* consider a protest library to be a "real" library?

BUDGET CONSIDERATIONS IN PUBLIC LIBRARIES

Commentary on public libraries in the United States often focuses on the symbolic value of a library as a democratic institution and as a freely available community resource. In early twentieth-century America, if a community "didn't have a library," writes Wayne A. Wiegand, "somehow you were not supporting culture."[3] A century later, in 2013, an extensive study by the Pew Research Center found that 95 percent of Americans still believed that public libraries "play an important role in giving everyone a chance to succeed," and 94 percent believed that "a public library improves the quality of life in a community."[4] These themes are reinforced in a large proportion of the canonical literature on libraries.[5]

Despite the lofty rhetoric and the public claims that libraries are essential and foundational, funding for public libraries in the twenty-first century is precarious. Public library systems around the United States rely heavily on funding from local governments—city and county, and occasionally the state—through budget allocations, or increases based on taxes, millages, and so on. In 2015, local government funding represented 86 percent of the average public library budget, an 8 percent increase since 1998.[6] The greater the reliance on government funding, the greater the risk of a funding cutback every fiscal year and every election cycle. Local government money is raised primarily via individual ballot measures in each county or city, and each election entails a risk of losing existing funding or defeating new funding proposals. Every time a library faces budget cuts or a publisher changes its pricing structure, databases come and go, and with them the entire archives of multiple publications, invisibly and instantly. Even if we notice, it often feels more like an inconvenience than an outrage. Sometimes it is just a matter of having to wait longer for our interlibrary loan request to be processed. The emotional impact is not the same as the sensation of seeing a physical book destroyed or removed.

At the federal level, too, library services are strained. A draft of the 2018 federal budget proposed the complete elimination of the Institute of Museum and Library Services, to which the American Library Association swiftly responded: "America's more than 120,000 public, school, college and university and many other libraries are not piles of archived books. They're trusted centers for education, employment, entrepreneurship and free inquiry at the core of communities in every state in the country."[7]

In terms of funding, 2008 and 2009 were exceptionally bad years for libraries across the country. "When they were dealt a terrible 'macroeconomic' hand with unemployment, the housing crisis, and the collapse of Wall Street," notes an article in *Library Journal*, "not even the best campaign strategy, tactic, or practice could overcome voter resistance in some places."[8] In 2010, the NYPL reported, "In the last two fiscal years our budget has been reduced by $20 million and our workforce by 300 positions." Libraries across the country echoed these financial woes. According to Scott Sherman, writing in *The Nation* in 2011, the American Library Association reported that library usage by the public was increasing, and yet, because of the troubled economy, "'more than half the states have reported a decrease in funding, with cumulative cuts averaging greater than ten percent.' Library systems of all sizes are under pressure. The Los Angeles County public library system, which serves 3.7 million citizens, faces a structural deficit of $22 million a year for the next decade. Budget cuts have forced the Seattle Public Library, one of the nation's finest, to shut down for a week in late summer."[9] Unlike other public institutions such as museums or national parks, libraries do not generate any revenue by charging admission or selling tickets. The NYPL, and a few other high-profile libraries, have endowments that bring in library-specific revenue, which make their budgets a bit different from those of purely public libraries. But when the economy crashes, so too does the income generated by their financial assets.

The Annoyed Librarian questions whether a protest library might be diverting funds and resources away from institutional libraries that need them more. When the People's librarians returned to the park a few days after the raid to start again, they were almost immediately shut down by the police. Over the next several months, they would reinvent the library in various mobile and nomadic iterations in different places. In February 2012, for example, they set up a library for a short time in Union Square. Why not use this energy to support the existing public libraries, the Annoyed Librarian argued, and have a bigger impact? "The 'people's librarians' were throwing out books as soon as they set them up in the park. If they didn't know that's what they were doing, then they're hopelessly naive, which wouldn't surprise me," she writes in another blog post. She points out that these repeated attempts served to normalize the confiscation of books. Also, she says, "Libraries are one of the few public services that most communities manage to provide for everyone, including the poor. Why try to duplicate something that's already successful when there is so much more that could be done?"[10]

The People's Library is outside much of this discussion regarding budgets. If anything, a library within a protest encampment is a product of austerity measures rather than an institution threatened by them. The low-tech, grass-roots, DIY spirit of the OWS People's Library provides a stark contrast to the slick reinventions that American public libraries are undergoing, and yet it unquestionably embodies many of the community-driven "free to all" expectations that Americans have of their tax-funded public libraries. Protest libraries bring this issue to the forefront, especially when compared to the public libraries that already exist in their communities.

THE NYPL CENTRAL LIBRARY PLAN

Several years earlier, in 2008, and in response to a budget shortfall, the board of directors of the New York Public Library approved a course of action known as the Central Library Plan (CLP). As library president Anthony Marx put it: "In the back quarter of this iconic building are stacks of books that are rarely used . . . To the degree that we can make that space available, and replace books with people, that's the future of where libraries are going."[11] The CLP included three main actions. First, the NYPL would close two branch libraries and sell that valuable property to the highest bidder.[12] Second, it would move 3 million research texts out of the main branch on Forty-second Street and into a storage facility in New Jersey. And third, using the money from real estate sales of the closed branches and the empty space where the books used to be in the main branch, it would construct a "state-of-the-art, computer-oriented library" inside the existing historic main branch location. It would be a library-within-a-library, one with a circulating, lendable collection embedded within the austere and preservation-oriented research stacks. The CLP included cost estimates of $250 million, though this figure eventually rose to $300 million.[13] The library would have to fund-raise a significant portion of the remodeling expenses. But the costs saved from having to manage the two closed branches and the 3 million relocated books would make up for it in the long run.

By 2011 progress had slowed almost to a halt. The plan had been through several revisions since its inception, changing architects and churning through potential buyers for the branch sites. But the CLP engines revved once Mayor Bloomberg committed the city funding. Reporter Scott Sherman brought the CLP plan to light in his cover story in *The Nation*, which appeared on November 30, less than three weeks after the Occupy raid and three weeks after the library's big fund-raising gala. Sherman points out several problematic aspects of the plan. Once the news made its way to the general public, the response was passionate, coalescing in a "letter of opposition" written directly to Marx. The letter was originally circulated as an email written by Joan Scott on April 4, 2002, but eventually it became an online petition that anyone could sign. Ultimately, over two thousand "librarians, scholars, artists, writers, students, and 'ordinary users'" put their names to it, including well-known writers Mario Vargas Llosa, Salman Rushdie, and Colum McCann.[14]

The letter detailed several concerns regarding the CLP. One of the most fundamental had to do with removing the 3 million books, the heart of the research collection. Despite the fact that those books were not frequently used, their relocation to New Jersey would damage the NYPL's nationally esteemed reputation. For one thing, if the books were off-site, they would need to be delivered to the researchers who requested them, which would slow the pace of their work. While the library's stated wait time was two days, the reality was already often longer than that. The petitioners argued that any delay would hamper efforts by scholars who were under time constraints. In order to address some of these concerns, the CLP included changes to the reference policy itself. Some of the reference collection would, for the first time ever, be available to check out and take home. This caused new concerns regarding the time that would be lost waiting, sometimes days, for books to be returned; the frustration felt when those books turned out to be missing; and the danger that irreplaceable books would become damaged. CLP critics wanted the library to remain the caretaker of the books.

People's Library patrons and librarians felt the same sense of protectiveness over their own collection and the same panic and outrage when it was not just *threatened* with removal but *actually* removed by the city. In its short lifespan, the library had accumulated a wide array of one-of-a-kind texts and realia, "irreplaceable records and material related to the occupation movement and the temporary community that it represented." Signed books delivered by the authors themselves, original fiction inspired by the Occupy movement, and artwork had all disappeared. The People's Library was not a "venerable research institution," but its collection, including the Occupy memorabilia, had become valuable enough that institutions such as the Smithsonian were interested in acquiring pieces.[15]

The letter of opposition went on to state, "NYPL will lose its standing as a premier research institution (second only to the Library of Congress in the United States)—a destination for international as well as American scholars—and become a busy social center where focused research is no longer the primary goal." The incompatibility of serious scholarship cohabitating with banal social activities was a complaint echoed by other critics. Certainly the public should have access to public libraries, said author Edmund Morris in a *New York Times* op-ed. "But scholars are people, too, and we are beginning to feel, well, if not threatened, increasingly crowded out." The behaviors in a circulation library are very different, much more "popular," he argued, as he imagined the distractions of a café, squeaky shoes, and tour groups. "I remember," he chided, "when the library elected to spend its budget on the enrichment, rather than the impoverishment, of cultural resources," and he cynically predicted, "You can be sure that what is new and hard and digital will prevail over what is old and papery and transportable elsewhere."[16] Morris's letter was taken by some as an elitist tirade against the general public and the middle class, but his point stood: swapping out 3 million books for computers would definitely alter the feel of the space.

Meanwhile, the American public's perception of what a library should offer its patrons has been changing. The American Library Association's 2018 publication "The State of American Libraries" reports that "as many as 44 percent of voters (up from 35 percent in 2008) view the library as a place for people in the community to gather and socialize. They increasingly see this as an important role for libraries."[17] Faced with this shifting public expectation as well as budgets that are contingent on the will of taxpayers to support funding, public libraries understandably often choose to focus on relevance and efficiency and to position themselves as leaders in making new, exciting resources available. In practice, this means that rather than increasing their old-school physical book collections, they are more extensively incorporating digital information, "maker spaces," and private partnerships. These are ideas that usually garner excitement and enthusiasm among the general public.

The patrons of the People's Library fall into the "popular" category. The People's librarians, however, were also mindful of the ways in which their space would be used, and the physical collection of books without a doubt prevailed over other variables. "Occupy is often thought of as a digital movement born of a hashtag and promulgated in news feeds. But Occupiers treasured their physical books, as they did their print newspapers, colorful posters and abundant handbills," noted a report on Al Jazeera America.[18] After all, it was the gravitational pull of a small mass of material books that had drawn the library into being in the first place. Sacrificing books for the sake of computers, or even for the sake of people, would have run contrary to the existing dynamic.

DEMOCRATIC IDEALS AND THE LETTER OF OPPOSITION

Related to the question of research libraries versus popular libraries, the letter addresses a litany of problems the branch libraries were facing after years of budget cuts. Branch libraries traditionally bring books into immigrant and non-affluent neighborhoods, while central libraries tend to be seen as centerpieces and showplace architecture for the city. Branch libraries reach deep into a community, catering to its various demographics and needs. When city government cuts services to a branch library in a particular neighborhood, sometimes it is perceived as slighting that ethnicity or economic class. Sherman asked NYPL president Marx directly "whether a significant portion of the $250–$350 million designated for the Central Library Plan should go instead to the eighty-seven branch libraries. I could see the annoyance in his eyes as he replied, 'I won't sacrifice what those branches can do for the opulence of Forty-second Street.'"[19] But the CLP appeared to some to be privileging a certain kind of library over another. The Central Library Plan got its name because the goal was to close branches and consolidate resources at the main branch. Critics were concerned this would come at the expense of non-affluent community members, echoing concerns that have been documented extensively throughout the last century of US library development.

The letter of opposition did more than refer obliquely to the needs of New Yorkers served by branch libraries. It addressed head-on the pledge of democratization as a goal of the plan: "One of the claims made about the CLP is that it will 'democratize' the NYPL, but that seems to be a misunderstanding of what that word means. The NYPL is already among the most democratic institutions of its kind. Anyone can use it; no credentials are needed to gain entry. More space, more computers, a café, and a lending library will not improve an already democratic institution."

The rhetorical disconnect between Bloomberg's approach toward the People's Library as compared to the NYPL was too much for the OWS librarians. They posted on their blog: "Mayor Bloomberg clearly prides himself on his deeds and actions as a philanthropist, and it is likely that he had a lovely evening on November 7 at the event honoring the Library Lions. Yet his actions on November 15 make clear that when it comes to supporting the democratic ideals behind libraries, Bloomberg is just lying."[30]

DISAPPEARANCE

Book collections, whether they are part of a spontaneous outdoor protest library like the People's Library or part of a formal collection in an institutional or public library like the NYPL, carry heavy symbolic value. Books make this claim of value especially when the pile reaches critical mass and we are inclined to start calling it a "collection." And when it begins to function as a unified whole, it suddenly seems wrong, like some sort of breach of trust, to break it apart or parcel it out. This is true of a wide array of library collections: not only those found in public and institutional libraries, special collections, and our own personal private libraries, but also those found in other, less expected places. Protest libraries are one such example. Like the People's Library, they have several unique qualities that differentiate them from public libraries, but their foundational element—a large collection of books—has a positive effect on people that taps into our general feelings of goodwill and warm nostalgia toward libraries.

Deleting digital books and electronic files does not have the same effect on a community for several reasons. For one thing, we assume that the book is still available somewhere. Deletion does not equal destruction. Despite the distribution restrictions put in place by publishers for economic reasons, digitized texts still exist in a libidinal economy. There is no limitation of resources preventing publishers from printing as many copies as they might choose. Additionally, digital files are often aggregated and presented through an interface that smooths out the differences among books. When we search a database, each result is flattened into a text entry about the same size as all the others. The markers of a physical book are absent, at least until we click on the link and can see a scan of the original cover and a PDF that includes the original font and layout. These qualities of aggregation, smoothing over, and a mediating interface make it hard to notice when books go missing.

And they do go missing. The OWS librarians decided to catalog the contents of their collection on the LibraryThing website, and this catalog is still available to view, but it is hardly a substitute for the books themselves. BiblioSol also created an electronic spreadsheet to catalog its book collection, even putting out a call on its blog for people to help crowd-source data-entry all of the titles. Unfortunately, this file was lost during one of the library's many moves in the years that followed, a loss that drew little fanfare or outrage.

Are there any times when it is acceptable to destroy a book? The librarians in the Freedom Square protest library in Chicago confided that on occasion they did use books as kindling in their communal fire pit. But only a few times, they emphasized, and only in an act of artistic, spectacular defiance, using books that were especially repugnant to them and their organization's message. As one of the librarians pointed out, they had limited shelf space. Why should they waste it on books by people who had harmed or worked against their cause?

OWS librarian William Scott writes, "With public libraries around the country fighting to survive in the face of budget cuts, layoffs and closings, the People's Library has served as a model of what a public library can be: operated for the people and by the people."[21] More precisely, though, I would say that a more effective public library model would be one *visibly* operated for and by the people. The changes that modern

American public libraries are undergoing in their slow shift away from books are reducing the volume of the public's response. And here the issue with public libraries moving away from print and toward digital becomes acute.

In the years since the occupation of Wall Street, Occupy has permeated American political rhetoric and activist culture, but opinions vary on the overall "success" of the movement. At a conference in 2015, Zachary Loeb pointed out that "now that more years have passed than months were actually spent occupying Zuccotti Park . . . the gaze cast backwards on Occupy primarily finds its faults," and part of the "ongoing discussion hast turned to . . . why did Occupy fail?" Yet, he continued, there were also "aspects that people seemingly remember pretty fondly," which of course included the library.[22] These fond library memories are grounded in tactility: in moving one's head from side to side to take in all the titles; in the sensation of heat or rain hitting a reader in mid-chapter; in the color of the light filtered through the tarp and touching the page. And if these are not actually our own memories, if we were not physically there but rather witnessing online and through different media outlets, nonetheless we experience a punctum when we see images of these things and make connections to our own memories of public and school libraries from our own past.[23] Protest and public libraries converge very clearly in this fashion.

Meanwhile, we do not feel the same way scrolling through the immense list of the OWS People's Library titles still available on LibraryThing but now referencing a material book collection long gone. How are we to understand the importance of the physical book collection as the instigator but not as a necessary, durable part of the library? And if a protest library can persist even after the collection is gone, then why does it matter so much that a public library is shifting slowly into digital holdings? The answer has to do in part with the type of space in which these libraries develop.

The general public's collective romantic memory of "library" usually seems to be grounded in the rhetorical claim that a library serves as a cornerstone of democracy and as a community resource. Protest libraries emphasize much more clearly than traditional libraries the connection between "library" and alternative political stances, or more specifically between "library" and its revolutionary power. The references to democracy often reinforce the library's connection with the circulation of institutional hierarchy and power. Public libraries rely more on an inherent critical tension between, on the one hand, institutional desires for indoctrination and control and, on the other, the "freedom" of information. In a public library, one may find the seeds of revolution within the books. In a protest library, one finds the seeds of revolution simply by crossing the threshold into the space itself.

The preceding chapter ended with a claim that the protest library was not a "real" library while the NYPL was. At this point it seems clear that they are both libraries and share several core values. The question becomes, if the People's Library as a primary example of a protest library is a democratic institution aligned with the expectations that the public has of public libraries, then can we consider protest libraries, across the board, democratic institutions as well? They did spring from very different origins. Part two, "Libraries and Undercurrents," explores the significance of these differences.

PART TWO

LIBRARIES AND UNDERCURRENTS

CHAPTER 6

CARNEGIE'S INFLUENCE
Biblioteca Popular Victor Martinez, Oakland

As the wave of Occupy branch libraries moved across the United States in the fall of 2011, variations on the protest library began to emerge. In Oakland, California, an "Occupy spinoff" took place quite literally in the shadow of Andrew Carnegie's legacy (or at least in the shadow of an abandoned Carnegie building). It was called the Biblioteca Popular Victor Martinez, and it operated outside the circulation of capitalism and economics generally embedded in our day-to-day social space. It also operated explicitly outside the uniquely American Carnegie library legacy.

All libraries incorporate political ideology, even if that ideology is broadly described as "free information for everyone." The 2,500 libraries that Carnegie funded within a thirty-year period beginning in the late nineteenth century has had a lasting impact on the way Americans view their public libraries. Librarians typically hold a strong belief that all people, including immigrants and the working classes, have the right to free access to information. This is particularly true of the librarians in the early days of library development during the Carnegie era in the United States. Carnegie, however, and the institution of the library itself were not always aligned with the beliefs of the people inside the buildings.

Part two of this book asks what it means to label a place a "public library," to confront the mythology embedded within this definition, and to consider the roles of circulation and borders. I compare libraries in the

United States, Turkey, and Ukraine to gain some perspective on the government's long-term influence on the public perception of library spaces.

CONTEXT

In 2012, Occupy activists and community members in Oakland began an occupation of the abandoned Miller Library, which had been built in 1917 with a Carnegie grant. They would name their occupation Biblioteca Popular Victor Martinez after a California author who had died the year before. This library-based squat persisted for several years despite ongoing conflicts with local government and law enforcement. The conflicts specifically involved the occupation of the library building versus the occupation of the grounds outside. This story highlights the ways in which the early development of American public libraries can be viewed as problematic. While libraries were ostensibly meant for everyone, in practice they were only really meant for the "right" everyone, a definition that varied from place to place and was contingent on economic circulation and institutional power. The Biblioteca Popular reveals that this undercurrent is not so much in the past as the general public would like to think, and it shows us how circulation and flow impact a library. Slowing down is disruptive and powerful, not only literally, as in sitting down to read a book, but also in terms of slowing down both the process of indoctrination into institutional libraries and the process of building a community. To better understand how the Biblioteca Popular grappled with this tension between Carnegie and librarian, institution and revolution, law and permission, stasis and flow, I begin with a look at how the Miller Library made it onto the map in the first place.

By 2011, the building at 1449 Miller Avenue had been vacant so long that most people who lived in the Oakland neighborhood didn't know the building had ever even been a library: it had not operated as one since 1976. Some folks remembered it as a school in the eighties and then as a job training center for a short while in the nineties. But for the most part, they knew it as empty. Although it was owned by the City of Oakland, it was clear that the property had effectively been abandoned

Figure 3. The outdoor Biblioteca Popular Victor Martinez on the grounds of the abandoned Miller Library, a Carnegie-funded building. From left to right, the Casita de Libros with "Our Principles" posted, the water collection system, and the gardens. Oakland, February 2015. Courtesy of the author.

for at least ten years. A chain-link fence ran along the perimeter of the grounds, and from outside, the predominant features were the grossly overgrown lawn, broken windows, and piles of trash. Inside the building, weather, pests, and vagrants had taken a toll. Water damage had ruined parts of the ceiling, and the whole place smelled of mold. Surprisingly, the original, mostly undamaged library shelving still lined the walls of the reading rooms on either side of the main entryway, and many plaster and woodwork features remained. Rusty filing cabinets sat in the basement, locks popped, spilling their paperwork and photos of past job seekers across the floor.[1] Built in 1917 with $35,000 from a Carnegie grant, 1449 Miller was included in the National Register of Historic Places and was an official Oakland City Landmark. Despite this pedigree, the decay of the quarter-acre corner lot weighed heavily on the already economically depressed neighborhood.

The building initially came to the attention of activists from Occupy Oakland as a possible site for their encampment in late 2011, but they ultimately decided to use the plaza in front of Oakland's City Hall, about three miles up the road. During their occupation, the activists struggled with internal conflict over how much they should engage in aggressive tactics. One contingent wanted to reach consensus with police and city officials through peaceful protests, occupation, and discussion. Another felt that direct confrontation, "black bloc" tactics, and property damage were more effective ways to generate change.[2] This division led some activists to seek out alternative actions that were deliberately nonconfrontational, and a small group began brainstorming how they might use the large abandoned library as a site for some kind of positive concrete effort to benefit the community. Jaime Omar Yassin, one of the Occupy activists who would remain involved with 1449 Miller for years, refers to these as "Occupy spinoffs," which "took the tactic of occupation and had some real specific victories ... A lot of these people have been activated by Occupy, even if they didn't agree." These spinoffs cropped up around the country, not just in Oakland. Zachary Loeb notes "that the community space (with a library) that I was working on helping set up in Astoria [in Queens, New York] was also an Occupy spinoff."[3] Ultimately, this group of Occupy activists, together with other interested people living in the neighborhood, decided that 1449 Miller should be "reopened" to once again serve the neighborhood through its original purpose: as a free public library.

So on August 13, 2012, activists and community members entered the unlocked abandoned building with cleaning supplies and books. As work commenced, word spread among local residents. By the end of the first day, somewhere between one thousand and two thousand books had been donated and shelved. A handmade sign was hung on the façade renaming the building "Biblioteca Popular Victor Martinez" (Victor Martinez People's Library).[4] To those who worked in the space for a long time, it would eventually become known as "the Beeb."

The activists, familiar with police confrontation, were not surprised when police showed up and evicted them from the Beeb before the sun went down on the first day. Oakland police had a notoriously rocky history with Oakland's communities of color. Oscar Grant, a young African American man, had been shot by police at the Fruitvale BART station a few years before, in 2009, and tensions remained high. The 2011 Occupy Oakland camp had been under police scrutiny because of a fatal shooting near the encampment and because of the aggressive tactics of some of the activists there.[5] Additionally, the raid on the OWS People's Library in New York had taken place fairly recently, and it had been only one of several raids on Occupy locations across the country. It was later revealed by the *New York Times* that eighteen city mayors, including Oakland's Jean Quan, had taken part in conference calls that, according to Mayor Sam Adams of Portland, Oregon, were meant "to share information about the occupying encampments around the country." But, the mayor continued, "we did not talk about what any mayor was considering in terms of any action or inaction."[6] The activists, however, speculated otherwise.[7]

At the Beeb location, not only did dozens of officers arrive within hours, but also they closed off the surrounding streets and maintained a perimeter of several blocks throughout the first night and the week after. Even in the context of Occupy Oakland, this extensive police presence in such an otherwise overlooked area was remarkable. According to Yassin, "the city's exaggerated police reaction—which shut down the entire neighborhood from 16th st., to 23rd avenue, to International and 24th avenue—was widely condemned by all who witnessed it."[8] Oakland's citizens were already disproportionately affected by racial and economic segregation, as evidenced by public school graduation rates, home foreclosure rates, placement of security cameras and streetlights, and even the overall levels of air and land pollution.[9] In the Beeb neighborhood in particular, police presence was perceived as minimal and ineffective. Officially this was the San Antonio district, but it was known locally by many names, one being the "Murder Dubs," and it had a reputation for high levels of drug-related violence.[10] The streets were full of troubled people, some with drug addictions or mental illnesses, and others without permanent homes or stable jobs. One of the Beeb's "biggest supporters" was an ex-felon who "berated police on the day after the raid, recounting all the times he had shot heroin and received blow jobs in the building under their nose."[11] It was in this context that many activists, community members, and media noted the heavy-handed, seemingly disproportionate reaction to people who were simply organizing books.

After being evicted on their first day, the activists and neighbors quickly returned and went right back to work. Prevented from entering the building proper, they lined the sidewalks with books that soon stretched down the entire city block, rehung their signs on the fence, and started digging garden beds in the side yard. "The enthusiasm from the community only grew and was perhaps even greater, because the entire collection was visible and accessible from the street," writes Yassin.[12] But police again cracked down on the occupation, mostly complaining that the books were obstructing the public sidewalks. Finally, the Biblioteca relocated exclusively to the side yard of the building: still on the official city library property, but not inside the Carnegie building and not impeding sidewalk traffic. This was the outdoor space in which the Beeb was able to thrive for almost five years.

CARNEGIE, BRANCH LIBRARIES, AND THE WORKING CLASS

Between 1890 and 1920, Andrew Carnegie funded approximately 2,500 library buildings across the country. Although he required cities to prove that they could provide adequate land and taxes to support the building, beyond that they could manage the libraries as they saw fit. The grants covered only the buildings themselves. This was the case for almost all Carnegie library grants; the books and the staffing were left to the community to arrange.

Minority groups faced hurdles and barriers from the municipal governments responsible for requesting and allocating funds in the early 1900s. As Cheryl Knott points out in her book *Not Free, Not for All*, once local officials met Carnegie's financial prerequisites, "those officials had the right to follow local customs, even to the point of refusing service to some residents." As a result, some Carnegie libraries—especially those in the southern United States—have a history of segregation and discriminatory practices. For example, Charlotte, North Carolina, and Guthrie, Oklahoma, both built whites-only libraries with Carnegie money. Houston, and New Orleans, which already had whites-only libraries, received Carnegie funding to build separate libraries for African Americans.[13] These facilities were at a disadvantage, however, because even when they were able to erect a building through grant money, their collections usually were not as robust as those of the whites-only libraries.

Carnegie-related libraries were not the only ones that took a segregated approach (and African Americans were not the only ones fighting for equal access to books). Knott asserts that pre–Carnegie era private libraries could remain selective by charging fees and requiring membership. The rise of taxpayer-funded public libraries "made it necessary for racist whites to devise a new method to keep blacks out of libraries . . . Segregation would be that method." This meant that "inequitable access did not disappear with the transformation of libraries from private to public; it merely shifted from an economic basis to a racial one."[14] The Carnegie name is frequently invoked today in reference to the remarkable period of library expansion at the beginning of the twentieth century. But despite the romantic rhetoric surrounding this legacy, United States libraries have not been free to all from day one. Their history has been deeply influenced by systemic problems of racial and economic inequality, just as the history of so many other public institutions has been.

TAINTED MONEY

Most often during this era, writes Abigail Van Slyck, a city's central library was run by trustees who were "ambivalent about public access to culture" and "continued the nineteenth-century practice of reserving a palatial central library building for upper-class use." But Carnegie was also interested in using libraries to "help create a disciplined work force," and he focused almost exclusively on funding branch libraries rather than central libraries from 1908 on. In contrast to the trustees, many people actually working in the library professions at the time—librarians, elected board members, and other managers charged with running the facilities—were committed to putting books in the hands of the non-elite. These people, says Van Slyck, "had a vested interest in emphasizing the library's power to change lives."[15] Branches were an important departure from the existing central library model because they moved book collections into proximity with immigrant and poor neighborhoods, something both library professionals and Carnegie were keen to do.

An important underlying difference existed between Carnegie and those working on the library front lines, however. Van Slyck writes, "Professional librarians of a Progressive bent were more sympathetic to Carnegie's goals, but rarely shared his deep-seated distrust of working-class readers."[16] Carnegie is often lauded for his opinion that a free library is "the best gift which can be given to a community," and for resolving "if ever wealth came to me, that it should be used to establish free libraries, that other poor boys might receive opportunities similar" to those he had received. No doubt he wanted to get books into the hands of everyone. But he qualifies "everyone," stating:

> In bestowing charity, the main consideration should be to help those who will help themselves; to provide part of the means by which those who desire to improve may do so; to give those who desire to rise the aids by which they may rise; to assist, but rarely or never to do all. Neither the individual nor the race is improved by alms giving. Those worthy of assistance, except in rare cases, seldom require assistance. The really valuable men of the race never do, except in case of accident or sudden change.[17]

This notion of "helping oneself" is problematic, to say the least.

"The branch library was more than a place to learn to read," notes Van Slyck. "It also served as a training ground in middle-class behavior, preparing working-class readers to fit in at school, at work, or at church. In a sense, Carnegie's brand of reform did not serve to eradicate poverty per se, but worked on eradicating its outward appearance."[18] Members of the working class in some communities were not pleased about this, especially given that Carnegie's fortune had been built on the backs of the working class. During the Homestead strike of 1892, Carnegie, his associate Henry Clay Frick, and the notorious Pinkerton security agents had dealt violently with a union walkout in Pennsylvania, and this was still fresh in the minds of many.

Some cities experienced long delays before accepting offered grant money. This was the case in San Francisco and Detroit. In 1901, Carnegie offered each city $750,000 to build a Carnegie central library and several branch buildings. In Detroit, public opposition was fierce and lasted almost ten years. As a 1904 headline in the *Detroit Evening News* read, "DETROIT SPURNS CARNEGIE'S GOLD—Aldermen Couldn't Bring Themselves to Accept 'Tainted Money.'" Van Slyck explains, "The animosity towards Carnegie's offer was fueled by concerns that the institution would be shaped by the cultural agenda of the elite."[19] It was not until 1910 that Detroit formally accepted the money, and the building itself did not open until 1921. In San Francisco, the standoff continued until 1912 for similar reasons. Organized labor opposed Carnegie, "who had acquired his fortune through the ruthless exploitation of working people, and had used lethal force against them when they struck for improved work conditions."[20] The city did build five branch libraries during that time, but they were constructed without Carnegie money. Finally, in 1912, voters approved the use of the funds.

In some cases, cities were so divided over Carnegie money that even when they had already been approved for a grant, they could not get the voters to accept it. These were the circumstances surrounding a 1903 proposal for a library grant by city leaders in Wheeling, West Virginia. The board of education had been in contact with Carnegie, who promised to commit the money if Wheeling approved a tax levy to support it. Most of the city council were in favor of the offer, with the exception of one member who recommended that Carnegie instead "give his proposed $50,000 to the widows and orphans created by him on the banks of Monongahela" a bitter reference to the suppression of the Homestead strike.[21] The Ohio Valley Trades and Labor Assembly also spoke out against the library proposal, and union members actively campaigned to reject it. The "workers were persuaded that the fight against the library represented a defense of their dignity and manhood, a declaration of independence cast against the encroaching power of a new feudalism," according to labor historian Nelson Lichtenstein.[22] The vote failed. City leaders tried again several years later, and again the vote failed. Wheeling never managed to win approval, and the city never built a Carnegie library.

For his part, Carnegie was not sympathetic to labor's cause. He declared in his essay "The Gospel of Wealth" that the system in which he had made his own fortune was the best there was and that "able men soon create capital." He believed it was natural and reasonable that the best, most talented people should find success. In fact, he wrote, one of the "laws upon which civilization is founded has thrown [wealth] into the hands of the few," going on to say that "whether the law be benign or not, we must say of it, as we say of the change in the conditions of men to which we have referred: It is here; we cannot evade it; no substitutes for it have been found; and while the law may be sometimes hard for the individual, it is best for the race, because it insures the survival of the fittest in every department." And how should society respond to such laws? "It is upon us, beyond our power to alter, and, therefore, to be accepted and made the best of. It is a waste of time to criticize the inevitable."[23]

All of this is not to say that overall Carnegie did not positively influence the modern American notion of what a "library" should be or that the history of American libraries would have been better off without him; but his influence is more complex than most passing references to Carnegie acknowledge. Poor, working-class people who crossed the threshold of a public library in the early twentieth century were subject to a certain kind of industrial, capitalist indoctrination meant to infuse people with the knowledge of how to be better citizens and more productive workers. Individual librarians did not necessarily push this agenda. By and large it was driven by the nature of the library institution itself. As Knott writes, "It was there, in the enclosed space of restricted access, that a burgeoning print culture intersected with a deteriorating racial climate."[24] These were the right kinds of library patrons, those whom Carnegie perceived as wanting to help themselves, and who would no doubt find the most success in the world.

THE EAST OAKLAND BRANCH

California's library system had begun thirty years before Carnegie began his philanthropic campaign. In addition to central libraries, many California cities already offered branch libraries and reading rooms. Most of these, though, were in "inadequate storefronts, upstairs lodge rooms, and city hall basements."[25] In Oakland, according to the city's library system, "the precursors of our modern branches began in 1878 ... These reading rooms provided no circulating books, but provided newspapers and magazines to be read on-site."[26] Oakland received a Carnegie grant in 1899 (the second such grant in the state) to build its central library and a few years later sought funding to build permanent dedicated spaces for some of its ten branch libraries. In 1914, Carnegie granted $140,000 to the City of Oakland to be used for four branch libraries.

Branch library grants frequently incited meaningful public debate and discussion within a community about whom a library was meant for and what a library was meant to do. At the end of the day, a new branch library was an additional desirable resource for a district. Once a city successfully applied for and received a grant, previous arguments for rejecting the money were left behind, and new arguments began over how the city would best use the money now that it had decided to accept the funds. Disputes at this stage usually revolved around where to situate the new library, and Oakland was no exception. The library board of directors decided to place the branches in the Alden, East Oakland, Golden Gate, and Melrose districts.[27] As soon as the board announced these four districts would receive the funding, neighborhoods began arguing over the specific location of the buildings within each district.

Site selection for the East Oakland branch "seems to have been the most problematic of the four," according to the narrative of the National Register of Historic Places registration form for 1449 Miller. The argument boiled down to how far and in which direction from the existing East Oakland branch library the new building should be, but movement in any direction changed the demographics of the population that would be served. Should the building be put in an established, "fully built up" but poor neighborhood mainly populated by working-class immigrants? Or should the city invest this resource in a newer, more middle-class neighborhood a few blocks in another direction? The East Oakland district could never come to an agreement. After two years of squabbling, the board members threw their hands up and walked away from the neighborhoods of the East Oakland branch completely. Instead, they accepted a land donation in the area of the next-closest branch, much farther south than any of the neighborhoods that had been part of the ongoing disagreement.[28]

The donated site was part of a large parcel owned by a man named Henry Root, described in the National Register narrative as "a railroad man and large local landowner with an interest in enhancing the amenities of the district."[29] While he did care about enhancing amenities, he was interested in libraries only so far as they served his financial motivations. His brother-in-law J. R. Talcott also owned a lot of land in the area, and he had a considerable reputation in Oakland due to his involvement in several public controversies and scandals. Together, Talcott and Root had been wheeling and dealing to influence the location of a different branch library, the Melrose location. Melrose was a newer area of Oakland that was "being developed for distinctly middle-class residential use." Talcott and Root's donation of jointly owned land in this part of town, says Van Slyck, "seems to have been another way to improve the amenities of the new neighborhood, without the inconvenience of personal investment."[30] Two years later, when Root donated a parcel of his land to the city to resolve the East Oakland quagmire, it came with similar motivations and included the condition that the city would pay for a road that Root wanted to build through it. The city agreed to the deal.

Root believed that he could make money by buying land that streetcar companies would need for transportation routes; he wrote in his autobiography that he had purchased the land in order to "open new streets and improve lines of travel." Yet because of consolidation and ever-changing plans at the transportation companies, this did not work out as Root had expected. "On the whole," he acknowledged, "my scheme there was not the success I had hoped for." But, he continued, "I feel that if my investment there has not been profitable as a money making scheme, it has been a benefit to the public and a lasting one in the opening of these two libraries."[31] The street that the city built on Root's conditions was called Foothill Boulevard. It served as an extension of the existing scenic Foothill Boulevard, which ran through

Talcott's property. After a few years it was renamed Miller Avenue, and this is where the Carnegie building would soon be constructed.

Today, this road created by the city at the request of a railroad man with the failed purpose of making money off public transportation is not what one would call "scenic." It is, however, still embedded in issues of circulation. Approximately 75 percent of the complaints regarding the site logged by the city between 2007 and 2013 had to do with illegal dumping of trash, mattresses, appliances, furniture, and shopping carts. One of the standard questions asked with each complaint, according to the documents, was whether or not the trash posed an immediate threat to pedestrians or vehicle traffic.[32] The Miller building's history of circulation is oddly consistent, and it seems that one sure way to prod the city into attending to this property over the years has been to obstruct the flow of vehicles and pedestrians. The question of pedestrian traffic had a hand in shaping the Beeb, too.

The Beeb's location, literally in Carnegie's shadow, becomes a perfect metaphor for the relationship between protest and public libraries. The Beeb is both within and beside the public library history. As the building crumbles under regulations, codes, and budgetary constraints, the Beeb thrives, closer to the land and the community. In the next chapter I will look at the roles of productivity and social services and the ways in which these play out differently between public and protest library settings.

CHAPTER 7

LIBRARY AS SOCIAL SPACE
Biblioteca Popular Victor Martinez, Oakland

While protest libraries find their roots in prefiguration, American public libraries are grounded in the philanthropy of capitalism. Their history is informed by our uniquely American Carnegie legacy and an ongoing public tension between institutional authority and personal freedom. Although Carnegie's grants spurred the building of an unprecedented number of libraries and helped books make their way into communities at a rapid pace, the money also brought with it the implied values of Carnegie himself; libraries were to be "free, ubiquitous, and accessible to those who shared his own character traits: industry, ambition, and eagerness to learn."[1] In other words, public libraries were meant for everyone, but only a certain kind of "everyone." Communities sometimes perceived the grants as tainted money, as a problem because of the ongoing tax commitment required, or as too limiting in terms of permissible building usage. "If the building itself was a welcome addition," writes Abigail Van Slyck, "the conditions of a Carnegie grant were more problematic."[2] And beyond that, many Carnegie libraries have a complicated history of racism, segregation, and softer exclusionary tactics toward certain groups of people.

In the first few weeks after the eviction of the Biblioteca Popular Victor Martinez, police frequently patrolled Miller Avenue. This caused anxiety for some of the Beeb volunteers because of their history of conflict with law enforcement or their immigration status. Sometimes the police would run everyone off, and sometimes the volunteers would engage in shouting matches with the police. But no major confrontation occurred, and the Beeb steadily took root, both figuratively and literally. Volunteers erected a structure to house books which they dubbed the "Casita de Libros," and they planted vegetables and flowers. California was experiencing severe drought that year, and the Beeb did not have access to running water, so volunteers used found objects and salvaged trash from the neighborhood to build an irrigation system. The garden carved a large enough footprint in the landscape that it could be seen on Google Maps satellite photos. The Beeb offered yoga classes, language instruction, and community barbecues. Local artists created a large mural on one of the cinderblock walls bordering the back of the property.

The books, which had acted as the catalyst to draw people to the building, now filled the little Casita de Libros. Milk crate shelves sagged under the weight of a few hundred volumes. The collection, just as with other protest library collections, was not thematic or driven by any particular ideology, although sometimes requests were made for certain kinds of works. Over the years, Facebook posts on the Biblioteca Popular page have asked for donations of adult books in both English and Spanish, general interest books that are "relevant to our community," and specific genres such as graphic novels or radical histories about Latino, African American, and Asian/South Asian people, preferably written by authors of color.[3] Biblioteca librarian Jaime Omar Yassin says that when his patrons are asked what they actually want to read, they usually request things like romance and fantasy fiction.[4] Some of the individual patrons said they had made their own personal requests, too, for more science fiction and more copies of J. R. R. Tolkien's work. But overall, the collection was a generic mix of romance novels, science fiction, travel books, children's stories, and so on. Beeb patrons told me that sometimes volunteers would come in and arrange the books or create a system of categories. At the very least, they tried to keep the children's books on the bottom shelves. But usually the organization did not last long, and no one maintained a running catalog of titles; there were just too many people adding to and taking from the collection on a daily basis. There was also a Beeb regular, they said, who liked to dis-organize the books as much as other people liked to organize. He would come in on occasion and knock the books off the shelves for no good reason. But whether or not the books were meaningfully arranged, it was easy enough to visually scan the shelves and find something interesting. The Beeb also boasted a "community exchange box" hanging on the outside of the fence, where passers-by could leave (or take) books and other items without entering the Beeb itself.

A list of "Our Principles" was posted on the side of the Casita de Libros. The document states, "We want to have a wide range of people using and supporting the library" and "This means we need to make the library a good place to be, no matter what a person's identity is." The philosophy at the Beeb was that community members could become leaders by creating and sustaining initiatives and relationships. This included tending to the books and plants, mediating disputes, and ensuring that the space remained safe for neighborhood children. Several local children, too, took ownership of different aspects of the Beeb. During my visit, three young boys were working to fertilize the vegetables with a truckload of donated soil and manure. Another child, Yassin said, "has grown up in the library, she's learned to walk in the library, and one of the first things she learned to do was take care of plants. She has an encyclopedic knowledge of gardening at the moment."[5] In this way, the Beeb was enculturating its younger participants to continue the work as if the Beeb were permanent and could count on its future. Within the space, explains Yassin, people are able to assume long-term responsibility in ways they cannot on the city streets or in a public park.

The city's official rationale for the Beeb eviction was unusual. In light of the targeted police response that the OWS People's Library had faced in New York the year before, it might have been reasonable to assume the books had provoked Oakland's response too. As chapter 1 addressed, books themselves have unique material power, and collecting and distributing books can be seen as innately radical and political acts. Libraries can be seen as threats to local power. But when interviewed by a local newspaper about the eviction, Deputy

City Administrator Arturo Sanchez did not make any of these claims. Neither did he make the more logical—and perhaps valid—claim that the building itself lacked seismic upgrades and was not up to code as a result of damage from the 1989 Loma Prieta earthquake.[6] Rather, as Mayor Bloomberg had done in his statement about the New York raid, Sanchez moved into the rhetorical realm of emotion. He argued that there was a "right way and a wrong way to do things," and "the organizers hadn't asked for city permission before they went in."[7] The city, it seemed, was taking the stance that the problem with the Beeb occupation was one of permission and not of law per se.

This may sound like a pedantic distinction, especially given the very real violence that the librarians and activists faced during other occupations. But Sanchez's argument gets at one of the most significant and precarious aspects of protest libraries in general: the balance between the permanent and the temporary. Had Sanchez focused on issues of trespassing or building safety, he would have provided an argument grounded in law, a word from Old Norse that means "something laid or fixed." This would have tied the discussion rhetorically to the permanency and responsibility of maintaining a brick building, to the stasis of law, to the regulation of taxpayer-funded public spaces, and to the slow-moving legacies of civil discourse. Meanwhile, "permission" comes from the Latin *per* + *mittere*, which means "to let go through" or "to give leave." A request for permission is a request for flow and movement. From this perspective, the argument is deeply embedded in the rhetoric of circulation—of books, certainly, but also the economic circulation of goods and services, the movement of people in space, and the general fluctuation that happens between what is potential and what actually materializes.

EXPECTATIONS OF PRODUCTIVITY

Social spaces are designed to keep us moving at a certain pace and spending at a certain rate. For example, the restaurant industry utilizes several documented techniques—bright colors, loud music—to cause diners to eat and drink faster, allowing the restaurant to turn over tables more quickly, seat more people, and make more money.[8] Some businesses track success by how long people stand in line or how long it takes them to find what they are looking for. And in some spaces, any attendance level above a certain capacity signals that there is a profitable flow of people into and out of the space. Cultural institutions like museums, national monuments, and state parks are no different.

Libraries, which are sometimes pointed to as one of the few public places where you can still go and not be expected to spend money, also exact a toll: they demand that we maintain a type of movement measured by our rate of productivity. It is generally expected that while in the library you will be awake and researching or reading or collaborating or creating something in one of the "maker spaces." People, especially those who appear to be indigent, may not camp out in the library all day long if they are not doing anything productive. The public library system in Houston, for example, prohibits certain behaviors including "sleeping or putting your head on a table" and allows staff to remove people on the basis of "offensive bodily hygiene that constitutes a nuisance to others."[9] Houston wrote its policy into law in 2005 by passing an anti-odor city ordinance. Although Houston claims the policy was due to complaints about heavy perfume, one city councilwoman decried this as a thinly veiled attempt to discriminate against the homeless.[10] Public libraries in San Luis Obispo, California, and in Chicago have posted policies similar to Houston's.

Public libraries have a long history of "dealing" with the homeless, so the fact that protest libraries and the enveloping larger encampments deliberately invite people in who often have nowhere else to go and nothing else to do is a notable difference. Libraries within occupations provide something to do and a place to be, and one of their biggest benefits is that they allow, even encourage, lingering and loitering. In this way, protest libraries counter the notion that when people are in a public place, they must maintain a certain level of productivity or be actively engaged in learning something new. People using protest library space are not required to work or take on responsibility, though the opportunity is available. Even with these opportunities, the space of a library is not conducive to the indoctrination of people into becoming more productive workers—quite the contrary. Protest sites are full of people occupying space in order to deliberately thwart productivity and disrupt the flow of commerce.

Another benefit of the protest library is that it opens a productivity-free zone, but not in terms of laziness or apathy or of deliberately "not working." Nevertheless, sometimes this resistance to productivity is misunderstood as laziness. Jaime Taylor and Zachary Loeb write that one stereotype was that Occupy Wall Street "was supposed to be a bunch of dirty stupid hippies who needed . . . to get a job, to grow up, and be responsible for ourselves."[11] What this kind of description misses, though, is how the productivity-free zone of the protest library opens a heterotopic space, which could also be described as a space of exception. Heterotopic space provides an opportunity for productivity to be viewed as a creative act rather than as labor. As David Graeber writes, "The traditional justification for spaces of exception is that they can become places of creativity: after all, only those who are not bound by the existing legal order can create new laws."[12] The creativity he mentions here is not the same thing as using a 3D printer in a public library's maker space to create a new cell phone case or to print models of cells or solar systems for a school project. This kind of creativity has to do with a deeper change to our fundamental state of being as productive members of society.

Protest libraries are not devoid of work, but when they do facilitate productivity, it is of a bottom-line, grass-roots, internally generated nature. For example, at BiblioSol, students in the encampment had expressed a desire for a place where they would be able to study and to do academic work in addition to physical work. In response, a reading room space emerged. "The grand reading room is still the space that attracts the most students, and is the most popular space to study on campus," says Guylaine Beaudry. "Working in silence in a public space looking at others and being looked at while doing work provides a positive impression of being part of a community and offers encouragement to get things done."[13] Comments on some of the Facebook photos bear this out. For example, Facebook user Tea Lobo wrote, "Qué horas felices he pasado en ahí . . . cuanto me ha llenado el depósito" (What happy hours I have spent there . . . the collection has filled me).[14] At the Beeb, Yassin writes: "It's been remarkable to watch people facing homelessness and addiction self-organize to minimize their negative impact and create some level of stability for themselves and has really altered my baseline of what's possible . . . But there's one intangible benefit, perhaps significantly more important than the rest—they are allowed the space and access to do good things in the midst of whatever it is they are going through in their lives."[15]

Entering the space of a protest library brings with it a sense of safety and continuity absent in the surrounding streets, and also the sense that a different, slower pace is acceptable. Similar to the power of the visibility of books described in part one is the power of the visibility of a community.

GENTRIFICATION VIA OUTREACH

Beeb volunteers did not want the city to implement outreach initiatives that they feared would be disruptive and insensitive, even if they were done with good intentions. Examples of these kinds of initiatives can be found in public libraries across the country, as these spaces have begun to adopt institutional policies geared toward the integration of social support services. Some public libraries, such as in San Francisco and Washington, DC, have allocated resources since 2014 for in-library social workers and psychiatrists to reach out to the disenfranchised who seek shelter within their spaces.[16] The Brooklyn Public Library has a Library Outreach Department, which includes services for older adults such as technology classes, books by mail, and outreach programs at "senior residences, nursing homes, hospice care and more." For immigrants, they offer citizen preparation, access to legal services, literacy programs, and career assistance.[17]

Many more libraries across the country hire staff to visit shelters and offer guidance on gaining job and technology skills, host panel discussions about homelessness to facilitate sharing of information between librarians and social workers, and aggregate information for easy access by patrons in need. The American Library Association has published a document for professional librarians called "Extending Our Reach: Reducing Homelessness through Library Engagement," which provides details on essential library services and ways to implement programs.[18]

Kristiana Colón co-founded the Chicago collective called #LetUsBreathe, which supports political action and community outreach. As we'll see in chapter 13, #LetUsBreathe organized the Freedom Square encampment in 2016, which included a library space, and in reflecting on that experience Colón says, "I think public libraries have become spaces of refuge for vulnerable communities in Chicago," even meeting needs as basic as "I need a place to sit. I need a place to rest. I need a quiet place. I need a cool place. I need a place with heat. Any of those things."[19] For Colón, the work of the collective serves a purpose similar to the work of the library, and the services are valuable whether coming from a community-based group of activists or a public library.

These policies reflect an important and laudable shift for traditionally defined library services, and protest libraries certainly align closely with this newer, more progressive approach. And yet these programs still reflect an underlying Carnegie-aligned assumption that people should be working hard to achieve more in life and that the library should be teaching them how to do this. As Yassin writes:

> Admittedly, not all of us like what goes on in front of the garden and community center. But the reality is that much of what city and state institutions consider rehabilitation is based on a model that people can and want to change the way they live. We have learned that is not necessarily the case for some people; breaking up camps and congregations like this with the fig leaf of "outreach" is simply a way to do the brutal work of monied interests while lying to oneself about the goals and outcomes. Some people can move on, some people can't and may never be able to. And if that's the case, there is no point in simply herding those that can't move on to another place in the interest of illusory peace of mind. The reality is that there are generations of trauma here, and they have been exacerbated in recent decades. Our goals should be to reduce and nullify the trauma for future generations while acknowledging that for some today, that trauma has already done its work.[20]

Another problematic aspect to these institutional services is that they are often implemented and run by people with professional experience and education rather than by people whose biggest (and perhaps only) qualification is that they grew up in the communities being served. The Beeb emphasized horizontal practices, avoiding hierarchy whenever possible and keeping the external community at bay, regardless of the good intentions expressed by that community. The volunteers emphasized that neighborhood residents rather than well-meaning outsiders should be the ones taking ownership of the space. "One of the basic ideas," says Yassin, "is that no one who is not a historical member of this community is allowed to have any leadership role in the library, because that would open it up to issues of gentrification. And pretty soon, without meaning to, white and more affluent activists would naturally take a larger role, because they have more control over their environment, and they know the system a little better."[21] Despite the good intentions of the librarians and policymakers, and despite the good work that they are doing through their outreach programs, social service policies can be read as a continuation of the Carnegie legacy—newer and more liberal, to be sure, but still grounded in an institutional hierarchy that values productivity, effectiveness, and demonstrable positive results. For these reasons, it was critical that community members themselves take the lead in developing the Beeb, no matter how many tries it took or how bumpy the path.

And the path was indeed bumpy. The ups and downs continued throughout 2016, and for a while it was difficult to know—from outside Oakland, at least—what the Beeb's status was. The Biblioteca Popular Facebook page posted a notice in September 2016 that the space would be shutting down—not because of city intervention, but because many of the key players needed to focus on other aspects of their lives at that time. But then, in February 2017, a new post appeared: "The Beeb is back, but it never left. As a community of neighbors and lifelong neighborhood residents, we are revesting the public space we reclaimed from the city and gave life to." By March, it appeared that momentum was again growing. "Its [sic] definitely not what has been envisioned in the past," says the March Facebook post, "but it is an example of a community dealing with its issues on its own, without intrusion from authorities that are often more likely to use violence than one on one problem solving."²² The tone was optimistic and confident, and the post also mentioned several ways that would be appropriate for people external to the Beeb to help out. If the Beeb could adapt to the last five years of challenges and changes, it was poised to succeed indefinitely.

And then, devastating news. In April 2017, almost five years after the Beeb began, fires broke out on two occasions inside 1449 Miller. Both times they were caused by squatters, most likely trying to cook meals, and not by anyone affiliated with the Beeb, whose volunteers were still respecting their permission to use the yard but not the building. Much of the interior of the building was destroyed, but the city told Beeb members that it planned to clean up the building and that asbestos remediation would be required. During the second emergency response, one of the firefighters broke his ankle. The fire department blamed the city for the unsafe conditions and demanded that the authorities take a more aggressive role in securing the building to prevent injury and harm.²³ The building was boarded up once again, and a large Dumpster was hauled into the side yard and dropped where the Casita de Libros used to sit. Members of the Beeb had gone to city hall, according to one of the last updates on the Facebook page in May of that year, intending to "make sure that the officials there understand what they are doing in the process of creating a staging ground on top of the work of families and children that has taken five years to create."²⁴ The city collected $1.5 million in insurance money but chose to try to sell the building below market value rather than to use the money for repairs to the building.

REMAINING SIGNS

In February 2018 a third fire erupted in the building, and at that point fire officials declared it "a total loss."²⁵ The *Mercury News* reported that "Councilman Noel Gallo was at the scene, watching the building burn . . . 'This time it's really burning,' he said. 'It will burn to the ground.'"²⁶ The colorful "Biblioteca Popular" sign that had visually signified the competing histories and practices of the Carnegie building and the Beeb continued to hang on the fence up to that point, contrasting with the building's formal street address, 1449 Miller, prominently displayed next to the main entrance. This was the identifier used on city documents and brought with it the history tied to Root and traffic flow, Carnegie and law. There were also several "No Trespassing" signs on display: Do not enter. Do not loiter. But around the corner, the Beeb's own sign, hand-painted in yellow and green on a reclaimed piece of wood, was a reminder that for a long while, people were welcome to enter the space for sitting, conversation, and loitering. It was a reminder of the alternative side entrance, meant to draw people into a space that provided books and seating in the shadow of the Carnegie building. These conflicting identifiers, "1449 Miller" and "Biblioteca Popular," conveyed the complex ways in which people were empowered to move through—or, more accurately, to slow down and stop moving through—a physically bounded space.

In the case of the Beeb, when the City of Oakland chose to engage with activists and community members in the realm of permission rather than the realm of law, an opportunity opened for the volunteers to act on their own behalf and at their own pace. Far from static or fixed, this pace was slower, less linear, and more repetitive than institutions usually allow for, and working in a space closer to permission rather than law made this pace possible.

My argument up to now has been based on this proposition: a protest library relies on the power of a physical book collection, which helps create a particular kind of space in which creativity is fostered as well as the capacity to slow down and loiter. I have also argued that public outdoor space is more conducive to this assemblage than indoor space because buildings themselves embody economic flow. Finally, I have argued that protest libraries are free from indoctrination and nation-building. And yet, the general public's collective romantic memory of "library" usually seems to be grounded in the rhetorical claim that a library serves as a cornerstone of democracy and as a community resource. Protest libraries emphasize much more clearly the connection between "library" and alternative political stances, or more specifically between "library" and its revolutionary power. The references to democracy more often reinforce the library's connection with the circulation of institutional hierarchy and power. Public libraries rely on an inherent critical tension between institutional desires for indoctrination and control on the one hand and the "freedom" of information on the other. In a public library, one may find the seeds of revolution within the books.

Protest libraries create a boundary enclosing a space meant for the generation of nonproductive, potentially creative ways of being. In contrast, US public libraries are complicit with institutional hierarchy and discrimination because their authority comes from the building itself, as a manifestation of economy and power. Despite the vulnerability and danger of building a library behind a barricade, a temporary outdoor space provides more freedom and autonomy in the space itself. Protest libraries differ from traditional libraries because reliance on buildings—as distinct from the space proper—is different. Without a building, the obligation and responsibility are different. In a protest library, one finds the seeds of revolution by crossing the threshold into the space itself. The next chapter looks explicitly at the function of borders and barricades around the libraries.

CHAPTER 8

BORDERS AND BARRICADES
Gezi Park Library, Istanbul

The 2013 conflict in Istanbul is unique in that the protest itself began over space, or rather, it began because of the trees in a space. One of the few public green spaces in the city, Taksim Gezi Park had been targeted for an urban renewal project, which meant the trees would be removed and replaced with a shopping center and apartments, something the neighborhood residents said they could do without. This chapter begins with the story of the Gezi Park protests in 2013 because this conflict was literally about space, about trees, and about leisure. Then it shifted, as these events so often do, across a critical threshold into a conflict over much broader issues.

Gezi Park was designated as public space and protected by environmental regulations, but this did not clearly define who or what controlled behavior within the space, a consideration that is essential to the emergence of a protest library. By creating a boundary, making a weighty, permanent claim to the space, and rejecting structural productivity, the protest library generated particular behaviors within space. And while the violence at Gezi Park, the heavy barricades, and the clear-cut border helped generate and define the protest library, they also exemplified how an authority imposes its expectations about behavior, circulation, and productivity on people converging in space.

CONTEXT

Gezi Park is next to Taksim Square, an urban space similar to the Plaza del Sol but with more streets running through it, more traffic, and more congestion. In 2011, then Prime Minister Recep Tayyip Erdoğan announced the "Taksim Square Pedestrianization" project, a two-part scheme.[1] The first part included building an underpass beneath the square for cars, making more room for pedestrians at street level.[2] The second part entailed razing the adjacent Gezi Park and building a new shopping and apartment complex on top of it "in the style of ornate Ottoman-style artillery barracks" which used to occupy the site between 1806 and 1940, when they were demolished to allow for the construction of Gezi Park.[3] "If we are going to reclaim our history, there was a historic building there. We will rebuild it," pledged Erdoğan.[4] One reason the proposal included this reconstruction, as opposed to a new structure, writes Thomas de Monchaux in *The New Republic,* was so that developers could use "tenuously applicable historical preservation statutes over local ordinances ensuring the protection of parks and greenspace."[5]

Erdoğan, who was subsequently elected president in 2014, had engaged in extensive urban development under the pretext of "preparation of the urban infrastructure for a potential earthquake, development of the economic conditions of people, preservation of the historical-cultural assets of the city, and improvement of poor living conditions and declined physical environments." According to Senem Zeybekoglu Sadri, a professor of architecture at Girne American University in Cyprus, such "motivations [were] only used as guise for transforming the urban land into commodity for investors and city management."[6] Çigdem Öztürk, a Turkish journalist, explained that at the time, the Turkish economy was based largely "on infrastructure. Construction. So many, many buildings are torn down and new buildings are being built. And that means work for the people, but that's totally precarious work."[7]

The Taksim Square project initially received unopposed municipal approval, but when the general public became aware of the plan, they were angered by the attempt to eliminate one of the few green spaces in the city. Gezi Park includes approximately six hundred trees on about nine acres,[8] which is more or less the size of Washington Square Park in New York City. Newspaper articles about the Gezi protest have sometimes described the park as a "small green space," but one observer, Reuben Fischer-Baum, a New Yorker who lived in Istanbul for some time, points out that Gezi Park is much more than a "blip." It's "a de facto gathering point for young people in the city. If New York decided to build on Washington Square Park, which is a similar gathering point, New Yorkers would freak out."[9] A group called Taksim Solidarity was formed in 2012, supported by the Istanbul Chamber of Urban Planners and the Istanbul Chamber of Architecture, to fight the development and to raise public awareness of the plans. They opposed both parts of the plan, but the biggest issue for them was the loss of trees and green space. Even if some of the natural elements were replaced after the construction, the group argued, these elements would be enclosed as a mall or courtyard area. They feared that the green space would be available only to those who could afford to live or shop in the new center. Their campaign and legal challenges worked: by May 2013, Turkish courts had decided to suspend the plan, and on June 6 the court ruled that the plan should be canceled.[10]

On May 27, during the court-mandated suspension period, the bulldozers arrived anyway and began the work of removing the trees. Taksim Solidarity activists showed up almost immediately, chanting, obstructing the equipment, and climbing the trees they aimed to protect. "What they are doing is completely illegal. The thing that the government is doing is illegal," argued one of the protesters. Police were there ostensibly to protect the public from the construction work, but when they could not disperse the activists, they began spraying tear gas into the crowd. The situation intensified. "An illegal procedure is being implemented now without any legal permit," continued the protester, who did not give his name, "and people who stand against this are being subjected to violence as you may see. This is something that is more dangerous than destroying a venue physically since it shows the signs of a despot government. By intervening people with force, they are attacking the people who are trying to defend the green area and trees in here." That night, the activists set up around thirty tents with the intention to remain in the park and keep watch over the trees until the weekend, hoping that more people would be able to join once the workweek ended, and that the movement would grow. "If we resist until the weekend, people may come out of their offices and help us," said Cam Atalay, a lawyer and member of Taksim Solidarity. "We must look after these trees and our public area."[11]

The next night, well before the weekend arrived, two anti-riot water cannon vehicles and a slew of police appeared. "They suddenly began to attack with gas bombs," recounted Atalay, "without even saying a word and without any warning." They sprayed the occupiers with tear gas and with water, and then "they set the tents on fire, right in front of our eyes."[12] News of the attacks on the environmentalists spread quickly via social media, and soon protests emerged across Istanbul and the rest of Turkey to protest the harsh action of police against civilians. Several times that week the police violently dispersed the protesters, who doggedly returned to the park almost immediately.

Though the conflict had begun over trees, now the much broader issue of the government's tenuous relationship with its citizens emerged as a driving force. In a short documentary written and produced by Brandon Jourdan and Marianne Maeckelbergh, a member of the group called Revolutionary Anarchist Action, Ozelm Arkin, says, "This was a protest against the demolition of the park, but it suddenly, immediately, changed its face and it became a protest against the state's terrorism and police brutality." The conflict at Gezi Park was drawing out undercurrents in Turkey very much aligned with anti-austerity movements like 15-M and Occupy Wall Street. "There is a serious neoliberal transformation that the public sector is undergoing," says Sevgi Ince of the KESK Public Worker's Union, speaking in the same documentary. "We've experienced this especially so in the health sector, but it is also taking place in other public sectors too. And this is pushing people toward insecurity. At the same time, both health and education rights of people are being destroyed because of this situation." Ince continues: "Of course, Gezi Park does not just symbolize the struggle for a park for us. AKP [Erdoğan's Justice and Development Party], with all of its policies regarding women, the environment, workers, and all the democratic demands of the public, has enforced suppressive and fascist measures that we are having to face."[13]

In Turkey, there has historically been a split between different religious factions following decades of government propaganda. But the violence galvanized a larger public. Participants in the protests ranged from "little old ladies" who had never before protested against the police in their lives to members of the Çarşı soccer team, who became deeply involved and helped unify the diverse crowd.[14] It was the soccer team's "energy and mobilisation power that drew in hundreds of thousands of people from diverse backgrounds, including religious and ethnic minorities, leftists and groups such as the Anti-Capitalist Muslims," writes Mark Bergfeld, and helped people from these factions begin to understand how much they all had in common.[15]

THE LIBRARY

By June 1, just five days after the initial protesters arrived in the park, they had prevailed and had taken over the entire Taksim Square and Gezi Park area, creating a "police free zone." At this point the encampment began to develop into a prefigurative community reminiscent of Acampada Sol, Zuccotti Park, and the Biblioteca Popular. The Gezi encampment, what the activists called the "Gezi Commune," did not utilize the working group model that defined so much of the 15-M and Occupy movements, but it was divided into "neighborhoods" that reflected aspects of a prefigurative community. Oscar ten Houten, an activist and writer, created a "Historical Atlas of Gezi Park," in which he breaks down the space into three sections: Uptown, the political center of the occupation; East and West Midtown, which was a "mix of residential zones and socio-political [tents]"; and Downtown. "The heart of Downtown," he writes, "was entirely taken up by the central Warehouse, which collected and distributed all necessary medical, food and other supplies that were donated by the people of Istanbul and the rest of the world. Main features of Downtown, aside from the

Victory garden, were the Library, built in the form of a fortress, and the Mosque, made from two party tents."[16]

For two years, BiblioSol, the People's Library, and the extended networks of protest librarians and library lovers had been maintained on social media. By now, the idea of a library within an encampment was no longer a surprise, at least to the people doing the work of building the camps. Protest libraries had been documented across the United States and Europe, and the activists themselves had cross-pollinated with people participating in and helping to organize different encampments around the world. Ten Houten, for example, kept a blog and later published his experiences at multiple campsites, including both BiblioSol and the Gezi Library.

Approaching the fortress of the library, one could see signs hung around the area: "Capitalism Fells Trees; Don't Sell Shade"; "The Trees That Existed While You Were Not Here Will Stand and Salute You When They Are Gone"; "If You Forcefully Stop the Night, Then Love Does Not Fit into the Human Heart." According to Zeynep Tufekci, an author and activist with firsthand experience of several occupations, including Gezi: "Because of tear gas and police incursions, the library had to be moved from its initial location in the perimeter of the park, but in its new location toward the middle of the park, people busily exchanged books, and activity overseen by a 'librarian' in a rainbow-colored wig. The festive atmosphere continued to be interrupted by tear gas and clashes with the police."[17]

At about the same time that the Gezi Park protest erupted, the Turkish company Sel Publishing was embroiled in lawsuits and other legal action brought by Erdoğan's government. They and other publishers had been in trouble for several years as a result of obscenity charges for publishing work by William Burroughs and Chuck Palahniuk. The government's approach seemed to be to impose censorship at the level of publishing rather than at the level of policing a library's book collection. If the books weren't available in the first place, there would be less need to police the library. Sel, to show its support for the occupation and its anger toward the government that had leveled the charges, sent hundreds of books to the park and called on other publishers to contribute as well. "One of the major acts of resistance for protesters occupying Taksim Gezi Park has been to pick up a good book and read it—preferably in front of a police officer," reported the *Hürriyet Daily News*. Indeed, according to Sel, "books are one of the essentials of the resistance."[18]

Once protesters realized that a library existed, books began appearing at a rapid rate. A video documentary about the Gezi Library captures the vibrant spirit of the volunteers and provides a glimpse into the purpose of the library and the way the books were collected and organized. A librarian tells the camera: "Today, basically the Gezi Library was founded here. People want to know about our library. The most important thing for a society's culture is their library. One tweet about us went viral, and spread and spread and spread, and soon publishers and bookstores began to support us, publishing houses began to liaise with us. People coming to the park brought their books to us, a lot of people are bringing books to us." One participant says: "People are even sending us book donations via cargo. From all over, can you believe it?" Another adds, "The delivery guys just leave the boxes here."[19] The more books arrived, the more the library-as-fortress was able to fortify its walls, defined by bookshelves built from boards and supported by bricks that had been pulled from the surrounding streets.

The boundary of the overall Gezi encampment was distinct as well. Initially, the police managed the boundary by bringing in barricades which functioned to exclude: no one was allowed into the park. Once protesters had reclaimed the park, though, they erected their own barricades to protect themselves and the interior space. Specifically, they were protecting the trees from being cut down, but as the levels of violence rose, the barricades soon became protection for the citizens against the police. In addition to bricks and concrete taken from the streets, the activists utilized long wooden beams, metal benches, phone booths, cars, and even some of the metal barricades the police had originally used to keep people out of the area. The perimeter clearly created an inside and an outside with a threshold that could be crossed.

Not all occupations maintained such tightly defined perimeters. Other protest libraries had boundaries formed by shelves and tents, but they were more permeable and organic in nature, very different from Gezi Library's square corners and sharp lines. During Occupy Wall Street, for example, Zuccotti Park remained open to everyone as the encampment developed. The boundary of the park was permeable, and both activists and police could enter and leave until the night of the raid, when police erected barriers to keep people out. Crossing the border into the physical space of an occupation, and then going even farther to cross into the protest library space, however briefly, brings with it a thrill. Jaime Taylor and Zachary Loeb write that in New York, once inside the boundaries and surrounded by the collection of library books, "visitors to OWS were both surprised and then comforted by the presence of the library ... [T]he surprise always preceded the sense of familiarity."[20] In 2014, Hong Kong experienced its own large-scale street protests, which have come to be known as the Umbrella Revolution, and included a protest library in the Mong Kok district. In this case, the occupation filled the streets rather than parks or enclosed, defined spaces.[21] And in Paris's Nuit Debout encampment, one of the last libraries to emerge, the boundaries were so fuzzy that at times it was hard to tell at all where the occupation began and ended.

CHAIN-LINK BORDER

A boundary also played an important role back in California the previous year, where the Biblioteca Popular had instituted its own unusual "security" setup. After the first day, library volunteers and patrons respected the hard line drawn by the City of Oakland preventing anyone from entering the building, but they had easy access to the side yard. And when the city put a large chain around the gate with a giant padlock, they continued to access the yard through a hole in the chain-link fence. Eventually, though, the city fixed the hole. So someone hacked the locked gate by cutting another link in the chain and adding a second, Beeb-dedicated lock. This allowed both the Biblioteca team and city employees to come and go securely. And it meant that the Beeb was "open to the public" only when a Beeb-entrusted volunteer arrived to unlock the gate. This was a self-governing system, and a core group of Beeb volunteers emerged to tend to the space during operating hours, working together to make sure that the space itself was kept clean and safe for those who wanted to be there. This was easier said than done, because even some of the most enthusiastic volunteers faced ongoing struggles with drug and alcohol addiction. It was not unusual for someone to establish a strong track record with several weeks of responsible behavior, only to show up again on drugs, incapable of tending to the space appropriately, or, conversely, to disappear completely for weeks or months at a time. As the "Our Principles" list reminded visitors, "people should not be excluded from the Biblioteca because they are still learning." The Beeb was a place of second, third, and multiple chances.

By 2016, four years after its creation, Beeb volunteers had coalesced into a functional, effective team, but pressure was increasing from neighborhood people whose "use of the building and grounds revolved around their primary objective in life, which was scoring drugs and alcohol." Even with the gate locked, it was still easy enough to climb the fence to gain access to the space, so sometimes people would spend the night in the Beeb engaged in nefarious activities. More and more frequently, volunteers would arrive in the morning to find that trash, empty bottles, and human waste had been left behind. Sometimes their tools were stolen. In 2016 Jaime Omar Yassin wrote: "For about a year, our small collective of families that run and develop the space has struggled with the very real problems of having a sizeable group of people on the periphery who, for various reasons, lack significant control over their lives . . . All of this created many quandaries for local people and families in various stages of politicization who either helped run, supported or used the Biblioteca Popular space."[22] Soon, the area around the fence, the gate, and the locks became a contested border not between the protest library and the city but between these two factions of people from the neighborhood. Instead of the occupation buffering the library from violent governmental aggression, the Beeb as a heterotopic space was embedded within the social space of a troubled, volatile neighborhood community. This made the resolution of conflict more complicated and blurred than the more obvious distinction of activists versus police.

For a recovering addict or a person struggling with mental illness, taking on a new leadership role can intensify an already risky and unpredictable situation, and there are no safety nets or insurance policies in a space like the Beeb. The people who have crossed the threshold into this space are guided by a set of rules ("Our Principles") but have no expectation that the law will provide protection. They are thus exposed to both opportunity and danger. Despite this, Yassin writes, "I rarely spoke to anyone of these folks who didn't feel some level of empathy for the people making use of the area around the Biblioteca fence." In fact, the Beeb space brought with it some distinct advantages.

> We were outside, in a commons that belonged to no one, where we could interact with one another as fellow human beings and life-long neighbors. We made full use of this tool, opening up dialogue as often as possible, and without any specific methodology in mind... None of this was easy. We suffered through some very difficult periods where we wondered if we could maintain the space and if we even wanted to. But over time, and with a lot of very open talk, we reached an equilibrium that respected the rights and needs of those on the margins while acknowledging the fragility and importance of what neighbors had constructed.[23]

One aspect of the Beeb that helped unite everyone—the volunteers and the neighbors outside the fence—was that no one wanted the police involved. Despite the Beeb's growing sense of permanence over the course of the five-year occupation, the city had never extended any legal right to be there. Yassin and some of the other activists had tried to arrange a deal to buy the property, but this did not work out; the city would not sell to them. Instead, the two sides reached what Yassin refers to as a "blind-eye agreement" and left each other in relative peace. In this way, the city granted tacit permission by letting the situation persist for as long as it did, and after several years, it felt reasonable to think of the Beeb as permanent. The *San Francisco Chronicle* reported in August 2015 that Councilman Noel Gallo "and other officials have thrown up their hands... The activists have become the property's de facto groundskeepers. 'At least they're taking out the trash,' Gallo said."[24] Nonetheless, the Beeb space itself was in legal limbo, and the one thing that everyone, individually and collectively, wanted to avoid was attention from the police. Almost everyone was in agreement on one thing: Do not call the police to resolve conflicts.

While a space like the Beeb is imbued with danger and unpredictability, freedom from the government's protection and safety is also liberating. This is especially true for people who may associate the police with oppression rather than security, and who may view social service programs run by outsiders as an unwanted form of indoctrination or gentrification. The human agency of the individuals in the Beeb's neighborhood emerged in a way that states and institutions tend to stifle, and this is the truly remarkable aspect of the Beeb. While all protest libraries provide a glimpse of this emergent potential, it is brief, usually over within a few weeks. The Beeb held it open for a beautifully long time.

TEMPORARY LIFESPAN

"There is something awesome about barricades," writes ten Houten. "It has got to do with the sense of power and determination they convey. And with their romanticism. Nothing is as romantic as a real barricade."[25] Romance promises action and adventure. Of course, romance brings the possibility of danger and violence, too, and the more intense the violence, the more defined the border. As at Gezi, the protesters at Maidan in Ukraine erected barricades, this time made of tires and packed snow. They also burned tires to provide not only warmth but also some protection behind the dense, dark smoke. So, yes, what could be more romantic than a real barricade? Nothing except, perhaps, the library that is protected by a real barricade.

Books can be romantic in the same ways as the barricades protecting them. As I've mentioned, the presence of so many books tends to provoke the authorities. Those authorities may be private property owners, businesses, security companies, police, or government agencies responsible for tending to the public space. The reasons they give may have to do with the failure to ask for permission, the need to clean the park, or the existence of safety hazards. Regardless, a protest library emerges in its unexpected and heavily material ways because of the books, and through the books it lays claim to a public space that feels permanent. It draws some type of border or threshold around itself that signifies inside and outside, the things and people that it does and does not include. This line creates tension between various combinations of activists, government officials, police, property owners and managers, and different cohorts within the local community. These tensions contribute to the protest library's own inevitably temporary lifespan.

For ten Houton, the temporary aspect of the political occupations was problematic. He blogged regularly as events unfolded. During the Gezi protests, he wrote on June 22, 2013: "The common form of occupation which has been tried in Sol, Syntagma, Zuccotti and Gezi had a fundamental flaw, because it was practically unsustainable. After a few weeks the occupations start to degenerate, and after a few months—if they live that long—they turn into a mess. The reason is because they are a physical living space for many people, which causes increasing logistic and social problems over time."[25] And while ten Houton is talking here about the overall occupation, the problem is exacerbated in the library, where the living space is meant to accommodate the books and all the aggregation, organization, and ongoing maintenance that they bring with them. Instead, he writes, "a Community Occupation aims to be a meeting and working space made up of semi-permanent structures, with a limited amount of people actually manning the site around the clock. If it is well organized, it can be turned into a permanent autonomous zone. It's the first step in the transfer of legitimate authority from the government to the citizens themselves."[27]

When ten Houton talks about shifting from a "temporary autonomous zone" (TAZ) to a "permanent autonomous zone," he is directly referencing the notion of a TAZ developed by Hakim Bey in the late 1980s. Bey writes that "anarchISM" was no longer representing the multiplicity of people that it should. "The anarchist 'movement' today contains virtually no Blacks, Hispanics, Native Americans or children . . . even tho in theory such genuinely oppressed groups stand to gain the most from any anti-authoritarian revolt. Might it be that anarchISM offers no concrete program whereby the truly deprived might fulfill (or at least struggle realistically to fulfill) real needs & desires?"[28]

For Bey, the TAZ was a place that would emerge spontaneously, generate a horizontal-style community, and then dissipate before it could be disrupted by authorities or appropriated by institutional hierarchies. Protest libraries and the overall political occupations align with Bey's work.

What is the problem with converting a protest library into something more permanent? Is that not what public libraries represent? I would say no. We should invert the assumption that permanence should be privileged and instead propose that public libraries might consider how to become less permanent.

Nevertheless, while a shift to permanence is problematic, the ability to slow down is a benefit. The stories of the conflicts surrounding these libraries tell us about the importance of slowing down time. In Gezi, the conflict bought critically important time for the organizers and activists in the encampments to build up the number of participants, the publicity, and the clarity of their purpose. Gezi needed to draw out time only until the weekend, but that brief period, combined with the critical shift that took place when the violence quickly intensified, was enough to push the protest across a critical threshold. The Zuccotti Park encampment had been in place for about eight weeks before the authorities could take any significant action because it was legally unclear who had the right to evict the activists and on what grounds, a distinct advantage for the protesters over previous examples like the Bloombergville library earlier that year.

"It is our hope that this library will be more permanent, will stay, there will always be a library in Gezi,"[29] said one of the librarians. But while slowing down time and people within the space can force the emergence of a critical threshold that creates the potential for revolution or radical change, slowing it down so much that the library crosses into a state of permanence becomes problematic. A protest library's identity is always becoming permanent but can never actually become permanent. The corollary is that slowing down time and people also means slowing down the circulation of social space, that is, capital, power, and economy. In the next chapter I address how books affect the formation and lifespan of the library. I will look at the case of the

Maidan library in the EuroMaidan occupation. This is a library that persisted longer than the overall occupation, and it did so for several months without access to books. If the persistence of a library is contingent on the heavy footprint and distinct boundary drawn by the books, how can a library carry on without books at all?

CHAPTER 9

ENGAGING IN NATION-BUILDING
Maidan Library, Kiev

The story of the Beeb highlighted the necessary tension that libraries experience, sometimes between different kinds of spatial, behavioral expectations and sometimes between conflicting ideologies regarding circulation and productivity. In January 2014, a new protest library emerged from among the EuroMaidan activists embroiled in the Ukraine conflict which balanced these issues of space, borders, cohorts, and tensions differently. Maidan library has a more complex relationship with the government than some of the other protest libraries because Maidan was engaged explicitly in nation-building as part of its mission. While Maidan accepted all donated materials, just like other protest libraries, it was deliberately looking to support Ukrainian writers, publishing houses, and existing branch libraries.

CONTEXT

Maidan Nezalezhnosti, a large public square in the middle of a larger commercial area of Kiev, translates to "Independence Square" and is frequently referred to simply as "the Maidan" or "the Square." Standing in the Maidan today, one perceives a sense of forward-looking growth and prosperity. It has been built and rebuilt over a long period of time, and it is currently marked with a monument at each end. At one end are the Lach Gates, which commemorate the city gates of medieval Kiev, a place that celebrates its official beginnings as a city in the year

498. At the other end is the Independence Monument, commemorating Ukraine's 1991 emergence as an independent country after the dissolution of the Soviet Union. During the fifteen hundred years or so in between Old Kiev's founding and the city's more recent incarnation as the capital of the independent nation of Ukraine, this area experienced a complex political history with surprising variations on its relationship with Russia—or, more precisely, on its relationship with the various incarnations of Russia, including tsarist Russia, the USSR, and modern Russia.

The Ukrainian language was outlawed and Ukrainian culture was systematically exterminated in tsarist Russia during the sixteenth and seventeenth centuries, and then again in Stalinist Russia during the first half of the twentieth century. "Under the Soviet system," writes Maria Haigh, "Ukrainian culture was presented as a lesser derivative of the Russian culture, and Ukrainian history was taught very selectively. Even the grammar of the Ukrainian language was modified to make it more similar to the Russian language." Haigh observes that "Stalin crushed most resistance through artificial famines, deportation, and the resettlement of ethnic Russians, and so [by 2007] most in the region speak Russian and look toward ever closer ties with Moscow."[1] Stalin's impact on Kiev became acute when he designated the city as the new capital city of Ukraine. At that time Kiev was on the western border of the country, and what is now western Ukraine was part of Poland. According to the Ukrainian writer Serhy Yekelchyk, making Kiev the capital "was meant to affirm the military strength of Soviet power and its newly acquired confidence in the loyalty of Soviet Ukrainians. It also signaled the turn from the policy of Ukrainisation to increasing Russification and intensified Stalinist purging of Ukrainian society." Thus "'discipline' and 'culture' became the most popular words in the new public discourse, but 'coercion' and 'hierarchy' were more in accord with the tenor of Stalinist social reconstruction. Kiev was being shaped into a model Stalinist republican capital."[2]

As a result of these periods of long-term Russian suppression, most of modern Ukraine is now bilingual, and a person's choice of language signifies a clear political leaning. In 2012 Ukraine passed a bill called

"On the Principles of the State Language Policy" establishing Ukrainian as the official language, to be used in government, education, and most other "spheres of public life." It also designated a number of regional languages, however, including Russian, and stated that wherever native speakers of any given regional language accounted for 10 percent or more of the population in that area, the regional language could be used in addition to the official language. This meant that government documents, ballots, transcripts of official meetings, and so on would all need to be translated into a second language in the relevant area of Ukraine. The bill drew significant dissent, with fistfights breaking out in parliament and demands that the threshold should be closer to 50 percent than 10 percent.[3]

Ukraine is bordered on the east by Russia, and the farther east one travels in Ukraine, the more likely people are to feel more connected to Russian language and culture than to a Ukrainian heritage. On the western side of the country, Ukraine shares a border with Poland, Slovakia, and Hungary. The western Ukrainians generally wished to retain their own language, emphasized Ukraine as a sovereign nation, and, broadly speaking, tended to favor progressive, liberal social policies related, for example, to homosexuality and feminist issues. These differences made for a country that was divided almost right down the middle, geographically and ideologically, regarding hotly contested issues of nationality and nation-building.[4] The question remained how, and how much, should Ukraine honor its history and connection with Russia?

This question relates not only to culture but to economics as well. After independence, Ukraine relied on trade with Russia. In the words of the Ukrainian sociologist Volodymyr Ishchenko, "If the Ukrainian language dominated the state sphere, then in the market, Russian-language cultural products were predominant." Viktor Yanukovych was elected president in 2010 after campaigning on strengthening Ukraine's Russian ties. Meanwhile, others were pressing for Ukraine to enter into an association agreement with the European Union. Free trade with the EU, according to Ishchenko, would put at risk all the jobs and companies that were dependent on trading with Russia but without guaranteeing any new jobs, since the country would not be as competitive trade-wise with the European Union. Many who favored joining the EU "did not have a realistic assessment of a free trade zone and its consequences for the Ukrainian economy," says Ishchenko, and so from this perspective, it made more financial sense to ally with Russia.[5]

About a year after Yanukovych's election, despite the Russia-leaning campaign, his administration announced that it would work toward EU membership. Then the administration flipped again, declaring in November 2013 that it would not be signing an EU association agreement after all. Political scientist Leonid Peisakhin of New York University Abu Dhabi interviewed twenty-two politicians and civil society leaders in Kiev in the summer of 2014. His findings show that "in response to a direct question about the impact of the non-signing of the Association Agreement on respondents' attitudes toward Yanukovych, 53 percent said that their attitude toward the president would not change, 13 percent reported that it would improve, and only 22 percent stated that their opinion of Yanukovych would worsen."[6] Nevertheless, some Ukraine citizens, particularly students in the west, viewed the failure of Yanukovych to pursue an EU agreement as a betrayal of their future and their children's future.

When Yanukovych suspended further discussions between Ukraine and the EU while simultaneously strengthening ties with Russia, Ukrainian journalist Mustafa Nayyem posted a call on Facebook for people to gather for a protest in the Maidan amid the international banks and hotels that surround the square, an urban landscape that reflected an expectation among Ukraine's youth that they would see a future of growth and prosperity. While the monuments in the Maidan celebrate Ukraine's medieval history and modern independence, the Maidan itself sits on top of a large underground shopping mall and supermarket, and glass panels set in the ground allow visitors a peek at all the commerce below them. The major boulevard, Khreshchatyk Street, is full of traffic, and the wide sidewalks provide easy access to restaurants and retail shops. Although rental rates throughout the rest of Kiev generally were among the lowest in the developed world,[7]

Khreshchatyk Street itself was classified by Colliers International in 2011 as "among Europe's top twenty most expensive streets."[8] It feels very much like the Puerta del Sol in Madrid, and so many other big, bustling, prosperous cities across western Europe. For many Ukrainians—particularly the younger generation—"the contrast in the choice between Europe and Russia could not have been greater. Russia represented the status quo. Europe, on the other hand, represented the future."[9]

POLICE BRUTALITY AND THE SHIFT IN PURPOSE

In response to Nayyem's call to protest on November 21, 2013, thousands of young people, many of them students, showed up over the next few days.[10] The composition of the activists in the Maidan was surprisingly diverse. Nor was the crowd dominated by any particular political party.[11] The protests brought together unlikely bedfellows, from leftist/anarchist activists, to neoliberal capitalists, to radical nationalists, in order to fight for the same thing—the overthrow of Yanukovych's administration. In Maidan, the voices of the "left" were fractured and had a difficult time gaining momentum and building networks. These groups, writes Volodymyr Ishchenko. included "a marginal United Left and Peasants party (ULP) fully supporting the Maidan protests from their very start." They were joined by "more skeptical left wing activists aligning with Maidan only after the threat of systemic repression against political freedoms." The Maidan struggle to gain closer EU ties was also supported by Ukrainian big business, as well as by "elites" from the United States and the EU who had "financed 'democracy promotion' in Ukraine for many years."[12]

According to Ishchenko, "the Maidan protests were fueled not only by European illusions and hopes for a fundamental improvement in the Ukrainian state, economy and society but also by anti-Russian nationalism." A notable segment of the activists were "far right Ukraine radical nationalists," many of them so far right that their nationalism tipped them into the category of neo-Nazis.[13] This group fought in Maidan because if Yanukovych was not going to join the EU, it meant he was moving closer to Russia, something they very strenuously opposed. Closer ties to Russia meant a greater threat to an independent Ukrainian national identity.

But fighting side by side with those from the left did not mean the radical nationalists supported the liberal social policies that the left was fighting for. The governments that these groups envisioned as replacing Yanukovych's administration differed dramatically. This temporary alliance was far from providing the foundation for a unified prefigurative orientation highlighted in other protest movements. Previous movements like 15-M and Occupy had been motivated by austerity policies, and their occupations tended to emphasize community- and world-building as much as or more than marches and clear demands. This was not the case in Kiev, at least not during the first week of protests. Initially the protesters' cry was simply "Ukraine is part of Europe," as the diverse group maintained a presence daily for over a week, hoping to persuade Yanukovych to sign the EU association agreement on the scheduled date of November 29.[14] When the day came, Yanukovych attended the meeting with EU representatives, but he did not sign the agreement. Instead he sent police to the Maidan, where they surrounded the protesters gathered there and beat them with metal batons.

News of the sudden and severe response spread, and the protest crossed a critical threshold, mobilizing even more of the general population. The Kiev International Institute of Society conducted a survey which found "that the overwhelming majority of protesters—69 percent in early December 2013 and 61 percent in early February 2014—came to Maidan as a direct reaction to police brutality on Nov. 30. All interviewees agreed that the fact of police brutality against students, who usually keep at a distance from politics in Ukraine, shook the society to its core."[15] Now the issues included not only Ukraine's potential EU membership and an emphasis on distinguishing Ukraine from Russia, but also the government's mistreatment of its young citizens. One protester interviewed for a Netflix-produced documentary *Winter on Fire* said: "People started protesting because they're sick and tired. At this point it's not about European integration anymore. People just want to live in freedom." Another said they had come "to declare that no one will ever hurt children in this country."[16] Some news sources pointed out that while this kind of police brutality might have been expected under Soviet rule or in Moscow, it was not acceptable in modern Ukraine. These protests, which have become known as Euro-Maidan, led to the 2014 Ukrainian Revolution, or what the Ukrainians themselves call the Revolution of Dignity. The violence between the activists and the government would be even more intense than at other sites such as Gezi, resulting in over one hundred documented deaths.

As the occupation in Maidan grew and the different factions of activists became organized, various groups of police tried to force them out. The government sent not only regular police but also the Birkut, which is a specially trained force of riot police. Soon after that, the authorities also sent the Titushki, mercenaries under the Yanukovych regime with reputations as "thugs" and "hired strongmen." The Titushki were free to commit many acts of violence that the regular police couldn't have gotten away with.[17] Since it was violence that had motivated so many in the square to begin with, these efforts only strengthened the crowd's resolve. The protesters held their ground and formulated their demands. They wanted the opportunity to oust Yanukovych through early elections, and also demanded the release of political prisoners who they felt had been unjustly incarcerated by the Yanukovych government.

THE LIBRARY

Up to this point, the Maidan occupation seemed as if it were unfolding in much the same way as had the original Tahrir Square occupation in Cairo back in 2011. The first protesters had been catalyzed by specific governmental actions and began their occupation of the square demanding change from their government. They were prepared to face violence rather than back down from their stance. As the outrage shifted from Yanukovych's political actions to the violence of the police, a different kind of activist was attracted to the protests. This secondary group of people, more closely aligned with the Indignados, expressed outrage at the government's treatment of the first group of protesters. Specifically, this group joined the occupation to condemn the violence against students. Economic ties to EU or to Russia did not matter if the

Ukraine government behaved in a fascist manner. As the occupation grew, different parts of the encampment began to reflect these different purposes.

The people living in the square had created a camp to take care of basic necessities: tents for sleeping, areas designated for dispensing food and first aid. There also was a stage for speeches and music. Winter in Kiev is cold, however, with an average January temperature of 24 degrees Fahrenheit. Because of the extreme weather, as the outdoor occupation went on, it became largely focused on survival in the face of the cold, a much stronger survival orientation than in most of other encampments discussed so far, which began in warmer weather or in warmer climates.

Meanwhile, as the activists camped and fought in the outdoor square, the Birkut riot police had been using the Ukrainian House conference center about a mile away as their headquarters while they tried to quell the Maidan occupation. On January 25, during a night of intense conflict and violence, the protesters took Ukrainian House from the Birkut and began their own occupation of the building. This indoor space quickly became a welcome refuge.

It was here, inside Ukraine House, surrounded by violence, barricades, and unmet demands, that protesters engaged in a transformation of the place. They created a space for culture that was more reflective of the general population rather than the elite, a space in which spiritual renewal could emerge. While the voices of the left were not the loudest in the Maidan, they took the lead in building the Ukrainian House encampment. Owen Hatherley, author of several articles about Kiev, the protests, and the architecture of the city, writes that the Ukrainian House occupation "was always the best part of the recent insurrection: its rotunda enclosed a shelter, library, university and cinema—plus spectacular stained-glass images of revolution above, and a real revolt below."[18]

The main entrance of Ukrainian House opens directly into a cavernous rotunda, which now contained a medical station, a chapel, a space for psychiatric help, and places to sleep.[19] Downstairs in the basement there emerged what would call itself the Maidan library. Books had already been circulating, and writers had been giving readings in the Kiev city hall, a building occupied by the activists in late December.[20] Then, when Ukrainian House was taken over, the formal library developed.

Viktor and Inna Bisovetskyi are credited with having had the idea to start Maidan library. "When I saw that Ukrainian House had been seized I thought it was a good idea to begin thinking about culture," Viktor Bisovetskyi told the *Globe and Mail* newspaper. "I thought we should think about doing something instead of fighting."[21] Just a day later, on January 26, a Facebook page was created called Maidan Library, asking people to contribute.[22] The name and the social media site solidified the new library's identity and opened the space for its unique voice to develop. Boxes of books were delivered, volunteers appeared, and shelving was found. A photo on Bisovetskyi's Instagram account includes the hashtag #DoSomethingNew.

The International Federation of Library Associations and Institutions (IFLA) reported that "Kiev residents voluntarily brought books to this library and it was very popular with protesters and activists."[23] The Maidan library's own Facebook page announced: "The library has acquired ten bookcases . . . and a group of volunteers. It has its own seal and a system of encouragement now—a candy for every returned book." This was a public initiative occurring within the walls of Ukrainian House, a "place of understanding" that was meant to complement the "place of power" down the street in the Maidan and the "place of spirit" in a nearby monastery. The goal was to be "a place on the Square where people read, think, speak and act, and spiritually renew." The Facebook page conveys a sense of great enthusiasm as it announces events and initiatives in the newly developing library.[24]

The particular space in which a protest library emerges determines the immediate needs, features, and opportunities that contribute to each library's particular flavor. Thus, while the Maidan occupation was organizing militarily in the square, the volunteer librarians began their own organization, which incorporated explicitly prefigurative politics reflective of 15-M and Occupy. This splitting of one resistance movement into two physically and philosophically distinct camps offered an advantage for the librarians. They were a bit more ancillary to the umbrella politics, and they operated a bit more independently. They could focus on supporting the occupation by building their library without having to worry about protecting their space and their collection from the elements the way the People's Library did. While most protest libraries around the world are in public outdoor spaces, the Maidan library was fortunate to exist indoors. Because of the unusual mix of activists in the outdoor Maidan and the harsh weather, it seems unlikely that a library would have come into existence at all without a separate, more insulated space.

Anastasiia Makarenko and Viktoriia Kolesnikova were two of the first librarians to respond to the call. Makarenko was working in a Kiev print shop on the day of the announcement. She says: "I collected some books and took them to the library. The atmosphere was amazing. Everyone who brought books to donate ended up staying. They didn't bring books and leave, they stayed." This signified to Makarenko that "there was something good culturally there." The occupation of the square had been going on for two months, Makarenko says, and "it was very cold, and we were tired. Those who were living there on the square had not seen their home for a long time. So the creation of this library was a wish to do something for the people who were braving the cold. There one finds not just physical warmth but emotional warmth." Kolesnikova recalled: "The evening we started, we had only several boxes. The next day, we already had several shelves. After the first week, we had six large shelving units that one of the Kiev libraries donated. We probably had about two thousand books, and more were brought every day." Makarenko added, "The local people must have really liked the idea, because all of the books came from regular people, not organizations."[25]

Local writers contributed copies of their own works, and eventually some publishing houses "brought several carloads." These donations included magazines and newspapers but also more substantial books. These presses were publishing content on Ukraine history, culture, and new literature written by native Ukrainian authors. The publishers provided an important outlet for Ukrainian voices, and the protest library afforded an opportunity for an audience. Similar to BiblioSol's legacy donations mentioned in chapter 1, these volumes found a home in the protest library. Makarenko says Maidan gladly fostered relationships with publishing houses because at that time in Ukraine, local publishers were struggling. The Maidan library activists wanted to help support these companies and see a revival of business for the publishers as well as an increased appreciation for printed texts in general. In fact, the Maidan library began to receive so many book contributions that an official from the Ukrainian House exhibition complex told them it was a fire hazard. Makarenko says they started calling the library a "book barricade" in solidarity with the physically protective barricades down in Maidan.

As Makarenko and Kolesnikova described it, about fifteen people formed the core of the volunteer librarian group, though there were many others who came and went. They kept a sign-in sheet and tried to have volunteers available to help twenty-four hours a day. Two people actually slept in the library with the books for the first few weeks. They created a library stamp to tag the books as having belonged to the Maidan library, and it took significant effort simply to stamp the books and organize them into very broad categories: modern Ukraine, psychology, philosophy, and so on. No formal comprehensive catalog was created. They simply didn't have time. They put in place a checkout system based on the honor code. Library patrons were asked to leave a note on a slip of paper promising to return the book, though there was no penalty for not returning it. Rather, those who honored their promise were rewarded with candy. The system was more for fun than to guarantee book returns, but it did provide the librarians with a way to keep a general count of the books in circulation. They often had lines of people waiting to borrow or return books, and they kept track of these numbers through the little promissory notes, which were kept in a jar on the front desk. According to Makarenko and Kolesnikova, on average, 150 books were borrowed per day; another volunteer estimates there were around twenty-five visitors per hour.[26]

Under the circumstances, the librarians at the Maidan library were swamped with work, while the visitors to the library often had plenty of time. Usually, says Makarenko, when people came in to return or check out a book, they would stay for a while, chatting. So the library organized readings, music events, and chess tournaments to keep people occupied. The library began to grow "from something static into something dynamic." She says the Maidan library was special in this way. Public libraries in Ukraine were dead, she says. "They're too formal. The system is outdated. We had something new and progressive. It only lasted for a month, but it feels like it lasted much longer than that." Perhaps if the conflict had remained primarily about EU membership and economics more generally, this type of renewal would not have happened—or it would not have happened so quickly. But in the broader context of a people resisting their government in the name of ensuring a decent future for their children, culture and spirit will emerge without fail.

Despite the bifurcation of space, the library's story echoes the by now familiar protest library narrative. The key markers of a protest library were all there, and its makers managed to form a new library assemblage in the image of the world they wanted to see at that moment.

UKRAINIAN HOUSE RAID

Unlike at the Occupy Wall Street People's Library, the Maidan librarians did not have ongoing skirmishes with security about what they were allowed to keep overnight. The Ukrainian House management maintained a presence during the occupation but generally did not interfere with the activities in the space. In fact, when the protesters took over the building, they signed an agreement with the curator of the Museum of the History of Kiev on the upper floors to protect the library's collections and archives.[27] The librarians cooperated with the building management during the occupation, developing a working relationship. From this perspective, the Maidan library became much more closely aligned with business and economics than any of the other protest libraries so far described.

Conflict between the protesters and the government reached a peak just under a month after Maidan library emerged inside Ukrainian House. On February 18, the protesters organized a march from Maidan to the seat of government to demand a meeting. Although Yanukovych had agreed verbally to release some prisoners and repeal certain oppressive laws, he had yet to take action. February 18 saw significant violence, and by the end of it, approximately one hundred protesters had died. They are now referred to as the "Heavenly Hundred," the heroes of the Revolution of Dignity.

That night the military forcefully entered and reclaimed Ukrainian House and, in Makarenko's words, "turned it into a garbage dump . . . Lots of books were stolen, they were dumped out of the shelves, and people had walked all over them." The IFLA reports that the Euro-Maidan library "was destroyed by government troops, but was restarted again as soon as protesters took back the Ukrainian House."[28] The librarians and other protesters returned on February 21 to try to restore what they had built and to clean the building. "There was dirt everywhere, and things were covered in dust and debris as if there had been an explosion. We probably had to wash the floor ten times and we still couldn't really clean it," says Makarenko. The Facebook page at this time includes several posts urging participants to be cautious and not risk their lives, because it was still unclear whether the police would return or how the protesters would be treated. They did not know it at the time, but this final day of violence would result in Yanukovych's exile from Ukraine. Soon his government would be ousted, the prisoners released, laws lifted, and a new president elected.

The protesters in the outdoor Maidan encampment ended their occupation at this point. Politically, they had achieved their goals.[29] The librarians did not abandon the Maidan library. They maintained their occupation of Ukrainian House for several more months and continued to provide books to remote public libraries. Makarenko says that during the occupation, management did not have much of a presence. "One woman's job was to chase people out. Then . . . a director came in and was harsher. He managed to get everyone out. His policy was to get people out of there. [Ukrainian House] became its old self." Management let the librarians stay until July 2014, when, after seven months,[30] they finally insisted on taking back the last of their occupied space. Even then, though, Ukrainian House worked with the librarians as they continued to seek a permanent space for their collection.

The building today is a large conference and event center with a slick corporate website that on normal days touts the space as the perfect place for "product launches, banquets, award ceremonies," and even just "great days out."[31] Makarenko calls it "a big marketplace. They sold fur coats, they rented the space out as offices, and they hosted cat shows." Makarenko and Kolesnikova believe that Ukrainian House is supposed to be a community resource for the Ukrainian people. It should reflect Ukrainian culture and history, and it should be accessible to the average Ukrainian. For them, and for many of the activists who occupied the building, the official activities seem too focused on high-end corporate events. They and the other librarians used Ukrainian House not just for protection from the weather and from the riot police but to carve out an entirely new, alternative space for culture and community. Claiming and reinventing it as part of the revolution seemed perfectly reasonable. "For the first time in the history of that exhibition center called 'Ukrainian Home,' it really became a Ukrainian home," says Makarenko. "Everyone who wanted to bring to life some kind of idea, they managed to do that."

CHAPTER 10

A LIBRARY WITHOUT BOOKS
Library of Ukrainian Literature, Moscow

Ukrainian House was built in 1982, when Kiev was still part of the USSR, to house the Lenin Museum. The large, imposing concrete building exudes impenetrability and stability, and it embodies a complex historical narrative very different from that of the Miller Avenue Carnegie library. Ukrainian House has been described as looking like a "reactor," "a squared-off late-Soviet version of Frank Lloyd Wright's Guggenheim," and "an early 80s, stripped-down classical building."[1] Writer Alex Kleimenov says that "when it was newly built, adorned in white marble and red granite, it was a dream location for Kiev's youth to be inducted into the Young Pioneers, a Soviet version of the Boy Scouts."[2] Less than ten years later, in tandem with the dissolution of the USSR, the numerous Lenin museums across the former Soviet Union would begin to close and their spaces became repurposed. Trevor Smith writes: "As history transformed Lenin from a deified cult leader into an antichrist, his shrines became unwelcome reminders of the Soviet people's misplaced devotion. Accordingly, monuments and memorials to Lenin began to fall like dominoes."[3] And so it was that in 1993, Kiev's Lenin Museum closed and the building was renamed the International Conference Center, known as Ukrainian House.

Libraries, too, succumbed to the same pressure as Ukrainian House to scrub Lenin's name. Lenin's impact on library development in the early twentieth-century Soviet Union was as deeply pervasive and

Figure 4. Ukrainian House, which was occupied by EuroMaidan activists in January 2014. This is where they set up the Maidan library, later storing their books in the basement and occupying the front steps for various library projects. Kiev, June 2016. Courtesy of the author.

influential as Carnegie's had been just two decades earlier in the United States. As Carnegie was nearing the end of his massive library grant program by the 1920s, Lenin, together with his wife, Nadia Krupskaya, was just beginning to revitalize libraries across the country, placing great emphasis on the value of such institutions to the general public. But in 1992, the Lenin State Library of the USSR became simply the Russian State Library, and, as Smith writes, "library director Igor Filipov ruled that the library was not a political arena and thus should not 'promote one ideology above any other.'"[4]

Like Carnegie's, Lenin's ideology regarding libraries was inspired by his own experiences, and Lenin himself had a documented history of being a frequent library patron. He consistently used libraries during his travels, comparing library systems in Germany, Switzerland, and England, and even borrowing hundreds of books while in prison in the late 1800s. In 1932 Lenin wrote a short text, *On the Role of the St. Petersburg Public Library*, in which he outlined four principles for reorganizing libraries based on practices found in Switzerland and the United States. The first principle detailed the creation of a publicly supported interlibrary loan system that would connect libraries not only within the Soviet Union but also with "foreign libraries." According to Krupskaya, writing in "What Lenin Wrote and Said about Libraries," her foreword to the book, "It was his opinion that the library and reading room would for a long time be the main source of political education for the masses and almost their only school."[5]

In contrast to Carnegie, however, who had emphasized funding the buildings and providing architectural and budgetary guidelines and restrictions, Lenin was much more focused on the books themselves. He was concerned with their content, statistics regarding individual library lending rates, reader demographics, and ways to make books more accessible to the general public. As he cataloged different types of libraries around Russia and assessed library access, he was dismayed at how difficult it was to collect accurate information and hoped his numbers were even 75 percent accurate. To improve data collection, he instituted an annual survey with "compulsory questions" such as the location and opening hour of a library, and optional questions such as the types of improvements a library had recently made. He began requiring regular reporting and accountability from the libraries.[6]

Lenin believed that the proletariat needed better education and easier access to texts, but the lack of material resources in the early 1920s precluded any increase in the quantity of books published. Instead, the new communist state needed to be more strategic with what it had. Both Lenin and Krupskaya believed that a centralized library system was the answer, a system that could more efficiently and evenly distribute books and periodicals around the country. Also, while Carnegie focused his efforts on "those who help themselves," Lenin and Krupskaya cast a much wider net. Their initiatives to increase literacy rates among the Soviet proletariat were so successful that by the 1980s, the Ukrainian region reportedly had a literacy rate of 100 percent. In order to stock American libraries with books, Carnegie had required local communities to levy taxes and fund their own book collections. In stark contrast, Krupskaya wrote in 1920 that the only solution was "to move from individual book ownership to collective book usage," and so "the Bolshevik Commissariat issued a directive to confiscate and nationalize all private book collections with more than 500 books 'belonging to the citizens whose professions do not require books as proletariat require their tools.'"[7]

Almost one hundred years later, Ukraine found itself in an economic bind similar to the one Lenin faced in the 1920s. By the time Ukraine claimed its independence in 1991, library resources had become scarce. With its break from the Soviet Union, Ukraine faced "a sudden cessation of acquisitions from other Soviet Republics" and was no longer able to participate in the by then robust centralized library system. The country did not have the resources to increase its own production of books and reading materials. Additionally, Ukraine's "financial situation was so bleak in the 1990s that librarians (among other professions) did not receive compensation for work for extended periods." The long-term Soviet stifling of the Ukrainian language compounded the effects on Ukraine's libraries, causing them to lag further behind. "As a result," wrote an American observer, "processing Ukrainian language materials poses new issues. For example, there is no Ukrainian language equivalent to Library of Congress Subject Headings. Therefore, libraries processing materials in Ukrainian language often do not include subject headings."[8] At the time of the EuroMaidan protests twenty years later, public and academic libraries in Ukraine were still struggling.

BRANCHING OUT

When the Ukrainian House management gave the Maidan librarians their ultimatum, the librarians decided that they did not want to lose control over the books. By the summer of 2016, they had spent over two years working in proximity to their collection, though for the most part the books themselves were boxed up and inaccessible. Librarian Anastasiia Makarenko recalled: "The occupation lasted until July. We came every day. We worked in Maidan library. The library existed for a while and was supporting the cultural aspect of the protest. Then we boxed everything up and we kept it." All this time, the stored collection helped them maintain a focus on the hope these books represented, preserving and spreading the idea of the Maidan library around Kiev and the rest of Ukraine. Handing them over to the convention center seemed like too much of a risk. What would management do with all these books? There was a chance that they would continue to store them or even put them on display and make them available to the general public, but more than likely, they would be somehow disposed of: donated, recycled, generally disappeared. The librarians chose to keep the books.

They decided that if they couldn't find a new location for their books, they would at least share their collection with rural Ukraine branch libraries. They also knew of some organizations that would help them get the books to the eastern front, where fighting was still going on in the wake of the Russian seizure of Crimea in 2014. The books could be donated to military personnel. But they did not liquidate the collection right away. It would be another two years, in 2018, before they finally "closed" the library. What do librarians without a collection do in the meantime? These librarians conducted book drives, held events, and participated in outreach programs and art exhibitions. One of the first events they participated in was a festival in April 2014, "one of the main events of Kiev, so we went to the festival asking for book donations," says Makarenko. They wanted to donate to the libraries in the home villages of activists from outside Kiev who had died in the Maidan protests. That event was a success, so "in September we also participated in a book festival," and continued to do so at other events.

That same year, 2014, the city of Kiev solicited proposals for memorials to the "Heavenly Hundred," those who had died during the Euro-Maidan protests. It took the form of a competition, but it included a series of public discussions and panels with experts in various fields and "people coordinating different Maidan initiatives," such as architects, military personnel, and priests, in order to hear from as much of the general public as possible. "Each Tuesday," says Makarenko, "people would come together and talk. One week, we were invited and we talked about the library." The librarians gave the crowd an overview of the library during the occupation and of the work that had continued since then. "We made our point that the library should continue to exist."

On the first anniversary of Maidan, the librarians created an art installation inside Ukrainian House with the books from their collection. Makarenko says: "We put them on little strings. They were hanging in the air, and people could come and read the books. There were video presentations with music, art, pictures." In the pictures, hundreds of books are suspended at eye level, so walking through them, people must take care not to knock their heads, but they can stop at any moment and open a book in front of them to begin reading. The exhibit was arresting and well received. Given the success of this event, they were invited to bring their exhibit to another local museum. This time, in addition to the cascade of books invited people to donate books there. So we were alive for two more months in that museum." Collaborating with the museum's director, they decided that "it wouldn't be just a static exhibition, it would be a platform. Every day there would be different events. Sometimes once or twice a week we had presentations of books, and authors would be invited to discuss their books." The museum was outside the city center, so it took a lot of effort to generate crowds and sustain the events, which eventually came to a close.

Longer term, some of the library-oriented changes seem to have taken root. In 2015, Makarenko says, as part of another competition, this time for grants to improve the city, "there was a proposal for restructuring the library. So they tried to restore a new library in one of the suburban areas of the city. They were hoping to make it a place where people would actually want to go and congregate. Again, from static to dynamic. They did get a grant [for] the city to redo that library. They have exhibitions, so that it became an attraction for people." One of the main effects of the protests, one that helped support this kind of library orientation, is that "civil activity has increased. People have the feeling that they can organize by themselves and actually bring about change. They don't have to wait for the ministry of something or other to pass a bill." Adds Maidan librarian Viktoriia Kolesnikova: "One of the priorities of the Ministry of Culture that we have is to make the local cultural institutions more active. We have no idea how they're going to implement that, but at least they have formulated that as a goal."

While the Maidan librarians and the Ukrainian House management did work together, it was not a perfect relationship. "They did allow us to store our books there," says Makarenko. But it was first in one place, then in another, sometimes in the hallways with people walking back and forth around the boxes. One day she arrived at Ukrainian House to find that "our books were being moved out because someone decided they needed to be relocated. So we started yelling, 'Don't take our books!'" They requested a place where the books could be locked up and were given some storage space in the basement, which Makarenko describes as "very dark, unpleasant." They were given the basement space for only a short time, too, "until we sorted things out," but the librarians were persuasive, and they talked the building management into storing the collection until March 2016. Around this time, Makarenko says, the director of Ukrainian House was "getting more aggressive toward us and told us to get out." Management said that either they could remove the collection or Ukrainian House would continue to store it but that the books would then belong to the convention center.

As we have seen, most of the other protest libraries did not enjoy this kind of relationship with the management of their spaces. Brookfield Properties made a few overtures in New York, and the City of Oakland, too, was surprisingly accommodating, but neither partnered with the activists in the way that Ukrainian House did. The Maidan event indicates the possibility for a protest library to align itself more closely with social space than we previously saw in our discussion of Gezi Park and most of the other protest libraries I have mentioned. In this case, both the protesters and institutions were working toward the development of a stronger national identity, even if their methods and resources differed dramatically, and even if the larger Ukrainian population still was not in agreement on whether that identity should skew toward Russia or the EU. The physical space of Ukrainian House, where Maidan library was able to develop its identity, embodied this clash of desires.

Ukrainian House reflects the desire to push forward into economic security and to drive Ukraine headlong into an environment of global capitalism, as well as the desire to support the development of local cultural distinction, both of which were goals of the factions fighting in the Maidan.

RIPPLE EFFECTS IN MOSCOW

This highly literate population felt the lack of access to books, but even before the break from the Soviet library system, Ukraine's access to books was limited and censored. Tsarist Russia, and then the Soviet Union, and then the Russian libraries all have a long history of forbidden materials that continue today. After the Maidan protests, Russian oversight, accusations, and sanctions at the Library of Ukrainian Literature increased at a rapid pace. "According to the Sova Information and Analytical Center, in 2016 the leaders of Russian libraries have been illegally subjected to sanctions in the framework of anti-extremist legislation at least 281 times. In 2015, there were at least 322 such cases," reports OVD-Info.[9] And in 2015 a *Newsweek* article noted that "the Ukrainian foreign ministry has complained at the treatment the library and its staff have received and asked Moscow to immediately 'cease its stifling of the library's work' in an official statement."[10]

The Library of Ukrainian Literature has existed in various forms since 1918, with its current incarnation located in Moscow. Until recently it housed a collection of 52,000 books. In 2010, according to *The Guardian*, the 'Anti-Extremism Department" of Moscow's Interior Ministry "confiscated about 50 books and a case on inciting ethnic hatred was opened," so from that point forward, the library was required to keep certain books "in a closed 'special collection' so as not to inflame tensions."[11] In early 2015 the library was raided by riot police armed with machine guns seeking "anti-Russian" books, a move that some journalists claim was motivated by the EuroMaidan protests and the subsequent deteriorating relationship between the two countries, which "nosedived after the 2014 revolution."[12] The *New York Times* described this case as "Orwellian" in a 2017 editorial.[13]

During the raid, "officers found several books which, although not illegal in Ukraine, are either written by authors whose catalogues are banned in Russia or contain images pertaining to Ukrainian nationalism, which have been made illegal in Russia since the start of the Ukraine crisis," writes Howard Amos, reporting on the situation in 2016 in an article titled "We Are Worried about the Books" for the *International Business Times*.[14] "'I received information that they were spreading Nazi propaganda in the library... These books create hatred between Ukrainians and Russians and they shouldn't exist,' said Dmitry Zakharov, a municipal deputy for a Moscow district, who lodged the complaint with Russian police that triggered the investigation. He declined to say from where he got this information," says the *Euromaidan Press*, which claims the confiscated books had been planted.[15] An Interior Ministry spokesman said the journals and books that were seized "contained incitement of anti-Russian propaganda."[16] The raid resulted in the arrest of the library's director, Natalia Sharina, who was "accused of 'inciting ethnic hatred' by making certain prohibited materials available."[17]

For several months after the raid and Sharina's arrest the library remained open, but the staff "joke they get more visits from officers of Russia's internal security service, the FSB, than people wanting to take out books or use the reading room," writes Amos. "The number of people visiting the library is dramatically down, and on a recent visit, there were just two people in the almost-deserted reading room. Six staff members have left—or been fired—from a team of about 12 in the last three months. The remaining librarians said they had not been paid since December," Amos continues, quoting a man associated with the library: "We are witnessing the creeping liquidation of the library." Vladimir Krikunenko, the library's deputy director, described the institution as a unique cultural link between Ukraine and Russia. "'We are worried about the books,' he said, gesturing at the library's overflowing bookshelves."[18]

By October 2018 the books had been removed from the Library of Ukrainian Literature. "In fact, the library stopped working a year ago," the *Euromaidan Press* had reported the previous April, "and only the

[name] plate on the external wall remained. Some of the books and documents were sent to the Library of Foreign Literature; some were thrown out or destroyed."[19] The move to the Library of Foreign Literature was seen by Ukrainians as highly surprising They ask, if Russia is arguing that Ukraine is part of Russia, then how can the authorities consider Ukrainian literature to be "foreign?"[20] And what of the library building that had housed the literature collection before its removal? According to the *Euromaidan Press*, "the library building has been transferred to the Department of Sports in Moscow, which plans to open the Center for Tourism Development in Moscow on the premises."[21] Sharina was convicted, and by 2018, all of her appeals had been denied.[22]

The disappearance of the Ukraine collection points to an ongoing struggle within Ukraine to identify and preserve a national identity, making the work of the Maidan library that much more urgent and the invisibility of its collection that much more poignant. As the *Euromaidan Press* notes, "The fate of the library and the librarian represent[s] a regrettable but iconic example of how the repressive policy has triumphed over language, history, and the principles of academic ethics."[23]

Moving away from this legacy of censorship, mistrust, and government reporting has been difficult for the Ukrainian library professions. "The ideological mission given to libraries during the Soviet era had cost them much respect in the eyes of library users and in the eyes of librarians themselves," writes Maria Haigh, and Ukrainian librarians and educators have been actively working to change public perceptions. "Whereas in Soviet times libraries were required to restrict and filter the flow of information, their mission is now to facilitate and expand information usage." The "ideological Marxist courses in the curriculum have been replaced with a new focus on Ukraine," and the "new Ukrainian Constitution guarantees overall democratic principles of intellectual freedom and free and equal access for all to information."[24]

The Maidan librarians had decided from the beginning of their encampment that they would eventually donate their collection to libraries in rural Ukraine, and they had been collecting information on the locations of libraries in the towns the protesters came from. "That project was one of the things we hoped would really help our country," Makarenko says, because many of these libraries had not received funding since Ukraine's independence in 1991. As these smaller libraries received the packages of books, especially if they arrived before the EuroMaidan protests ended, Makarenko says, some of them refused the donation. "They were just too afraid to take something that was sent from Maidan." The raids on the Ukrainian literature library and Sharina's subsequent legal troubles lend some legitimacy to the fears of the rural librarians. Most of them, however, welcomed the donations. They put the books on display with a notice about the Maidan library. "There was this feeling that we're not godforsaken, and someone remembered us," says Makarenko.

Work is currently progressing in Kiev on a Museum of the Revolution of Dignity. For a while, organizers had hoped that the Maidan library would find a home in Ukrainian House. Makarenko acknowledges: "We probably won't be able to work there, but of course we will participate in creating it. A million times we were chased out of that place, we were without [a] location, without [a] space. We always knew there was going to be a museum sooner or later."

Under the leadership of Igor Poshyvaylo, executive director of the national memorial in honor of the "Heroes of the Heavenly Hundred," the Museum of the Revolution of Dignity obtained funding and held a competition in the summer of 2018 to select an architecture firm to create the new building. The museum will, of course, include information and artifacts from the Maidan library. These archives will include a small, carefully curated slice of the library's book collection. The librarians, Kolesnikova says, kept "the books that we think will be interesting for the library in a future museum," like signed copies and special editions. They also saved several artifacts and realia, including the signed "checkout" slips that people left when taking books and the stamp used to tag volumes in the collection. And there was "one more aspect," adds Kolesnikova. "In spring 2014 there were books published that were about Maidan. One of our projects was to collect as much information, including artifacts of the books that were about Maidan. So by the first anniversary in the fall of 2014, we had a collection of over sixty books about Maidan and we have donated those to the future museum."

Since Ukraine broke free of the USSR, it has begun the work of writing its own history. For a building that seems always to have been intended to represent the country's people, Ukrainian House's changing name and the redefined use of its physical space make sense as the country itself is changed. From a surprising oasis in the middle of a revolution, the Maidan library as a named space within Ukrainian House marks a natural progression. Given the early turn of the 2013 protests from purely political and economic in focus toward a broader grievance against the government's treatment of its children and its vision of the future, the Maidan library was actually no surprise at all. "There are some people here who really think aggressively," said the library's originator Viktor Bisovetskyi during the occupation. "That's their business. But we also need to think about some other things, about culture. It's not about force." His wife, Inna Bisovetskyi, added: "What we want is for people to realize what they want to become. That they really can become whatever they want to be. That's freedom."[25] This is what Maidan library embodied during its short physical existence, and it is a powerful homage to the protesters who lost their lives during the Revolution of Dignity.

My argument up till now has been that materiality is critical. Books are the catalyst. But how do we describe what happened in Maidan? What are we to make of a library with no books and no physical location? This evolution helps point out that even if all the libraries discussed up to this point began with physical collections, they can carry on despite the loss of that part. And even if they began as embedded within political movements, they can carry on despite the loss of that part. The libraries and the politics coexist both inside and beside each other.

PART THREE

REINVENTION

CHAPTER 11

THE NEW SHAPE OF SPACE
BiblioDebout, Paris

The state of the protest libraries had changed over five years of emergence across an array of different occupations. During that time, governments had been working to enact policies that would make it easier to disband and prosecute people taking over space for the purposes of protest, resistance, and occupation. Simultaneously, these spaces had been building on five years of history, cross-pollinating activists from one occupation to another, and sharing ideas through their personal and virtual networks. In the creative spirit of the prefigurative encampment as described by David Graeber, as we saw in part one, the libraries creatively evolved to meet the new challenges.

In part three of this book, I seek to identify some of the regular milestones and phases in a protest library's lifespan and then consider how these phases ebb and flow in different locations and contexts. This chapter begins with the library spaces within the 2016 French Nuit Debout movement, whose name translates to "Night on Our Feet."[1] Nuit Debout took place explicitly at night, and these libraries were more readily mobile than any of the other libraries I have discussed. The acceleration of the material phases into mobile and nomadic phases prompts us to reexamine some of the claims in parts one and two regarding the importance of material book collections, borders, and identity formation.

CONTEXT

The idea for a library in the Nuit Debout encampment in Paris stems from an April 5, 2016, blog post, five days after Nuit Debout began occupying Place de la République. A collective called SavoirsCom1,[2] which translates to "Common Knowledge," proposed the creation of BiblioDebout and called for public participation. Their first physical convergence would be in the park on Saturday, April 9. SavoirsCom1 organizers asked participants to bring books, of course, but also boxes, tarps, cardboard, sawhorses, and other supplies to help with the building of the space.[3] This description of BiblioDebout's birth sounds similar to that of other protest libraries, but it emerged after the genre of the protest library had been around for almost five years, making BiblioDebout a product of both its own national political context and, now, the five-year history of global protest libraries.

During that time, the perception of public space and the legally permissible behavior within it noticeably changed, not just in France but all over the world. Governments at national and local levels everywhere were redefining what "public space" meant. This was coupled with legislation that increased control over behavior within the redefined space. The constriction of space required a creative response on the part of the activists before Nuit Debout could even happen. The activists decided they would use the space at night, putting them outside the harsh daylight view of security.

As a result, BiblioDebout was mobile almost immediately, accelerating the usual pattern and milestones of a protest library's lifecycle. This also means that the original catalyst I have pointed to, the piles of books, must have changed. Since books could not accumulate long enough and in sufficient quantity to reach a critical mass, some other catalyst must have emerged instead. This chapter argues that the self-awareness experienced by protest libraries five years into their history functioned in this way.

Once the occupation formed, the library that emerged within it was distinct from previous libraries in several respects. First, the library was explicitly self-aware and led by professional librarians, so it lacked the essential spontaneity and strong magnetic draw of the physical books as catalyst. Second, BiblioDebout embraced digital files more overtly than any of the other protest libraries I have discussed. And finally, since Nuit Debout was never a permanent fixture in the plaza, BiblioDebout was mobile and nomadic from the start.

Differences in BiblioDebout also demand that we step back and reconsider some of the other claims made thus far about protest libraries in general. These evolving characteristics are ultimately a strong testament to the durability of the protest library model, a model that demonstrates remarkable adaptability and resilience.

#NUITDEBOUT

The political movement called Nuit Debout (or just as frequently #NuitDebout) began on March 31, 2016, as people gathered to protest the French government's proposed labor law changes. The Paris event was linked to Nuit Debout actions in twenty other cities across France. At the end of the march, participants were called upon not to go home but to stay through the night. An announcement posted on Facebook said that this would be a moment of invention and a focal point for "hopes and struggles."[4]

The catalyst for this protest was French president François Hollande's labor reform bill, championed by Labor Minister Myriam El Khomri and often referred to as the "Loi Travail," the work law. It addressed reform through "the easing of protections around permanent contracts and dismissal procedures, the role of employee-representation bodies and the place given to company-level agreements." That is, the government wanted to make things easier on businesses by giving them more flexibility in their obligations and responsibilities toward their employees. The bill changed collective bargaining rules, allowing individual companies to make agreements that would override larger union negotiations. This meant that employee benefits such as overtime pay and limits on the number of hours worked, the rights provided to new parents and to workers with disabilities, the "right to disconnect," which had been "designed to avoid burnout," and other related rights were all at risk.⁵ "I want this bill to help my country," El Khomri said. "We can be proud of this bill."⁶ While the government felt that the changes would provide necessary economic stimulus, members of the public—particularly students and several major unions—were outraged. As Sophie Béroud, professor of political science at University of Lyon 2, writes, the Loi Travail put forth "the idea, unprecedented for a Socialist government, of a labour law adjusted to the economic objectives of business and no longer protective of workers."⁷

While Nuit Debout was able to point to this particular bill as something to which the activists were opposed, they did not otherwise formulate a specific list of demands beyond their general opposition to the Loi Travail. Nuit Debout thus aligned with the Indignados and Occupy in seeking to create the world they wanted right now. As Graeber writes: "The organizers of the original march against the new Labor Laws were planning a single day's event. But things almost immediately escaped their control. A kind of mass outpouring of the democratic imagination ensued; libraries, gardens, popular education centers, kitchens, studios, appeared; thousands taking part in general assemblies began cheerfully adopting, and in the process, creating their own idiosyncratic version of the new global language of direct democracy."⁸ Reported France 24: "'Most protests in France, we go in the street, we express ourselves and then each of us goes home. It's a little sad,' one Nuit Debout protester explained on Saturday night. 'But here [in République] something else is being built.'"⁹ The decision to stay through the night would set Nuit Debout apart from other movements in several ways.

France was still reeling from two separate terrorist attacks, which complicated the protesters' ability to engage in occupation. In January 2015 the Paris offices of the publication *Charlie Hebdo* were attacked and twelve staff members were killed. Then the Bataclan concert hall was attacked in November 2015. Bombs went off across Paris that night, causing widespread panic and killing 130 people.¹⁰ BBC Europe correspondent Damian Grammaticas expressed the fear felt by so many when he said: "What happened in Paris on Friday night is exactly what Europe's security services have long feared, and tried to foil. Simultaneous, rolling attacks, with automatic weapons and suicide bombers in the heart of a major European city, targeting multiple, crowded public locations ... Is France, after two major attacks this year, uniquely vulnerable or does the carnage in Paris mean all of Europe faces new threats to our public places and events?"[11] President Hollande deemed the November attacks an "act of war" and declared a state of emergency,[12] which in France gives "exceptional powers to the authorities, including the right to set curfews, limit the movement of people and forbid mass gatherings, establish secure zones where people can be monitored and close public spaces such as theatres, bars, museums and other meeting places."[13] Additionally, Opération Sentinelle, which was begun under Hollande, called for the placement of soldiers in public places, thus keeping the restrictions related to the state of emergency highly visible and even more oppressive.[14] Hollande would renew the state of emergency several times, ultimately extending it and Opération Sentinelle for almost two full years, until after Emmanuel Macron was elected president in May 2017. It was the longest state of emergency in France since the 1960s.[15]

Macron finally lifted the state of emergency in October 2017, only to replace it with a controversial "sweeping counterterrorism law."[16] The Law to Strengthen Internal Security and the Fight against Terrorism (Loi Renforçant la Sécurité Intérieure et la Lutte contre le Terrorisme) caused civil rights groups even greater alarm than the state of emergency because it sought to make permanent many of the temporary emergency restrictions.[17] "The law expands police powers considerably, and permanently, ensuring the continuation of practices that both Amnesty [International] and Human Rights Watch have denounced as discriminatory against France's Muslim population," wrote Nicholas Vinocur for Politico. The law gave "police forces unprecedented powers to raid, question and detain people suspected of terrorist activity, without the need to consult a judge or magistrate."[18]

In terms of the occupation of public space, the first article of the law addresses "security zones." According to the organization Human Rights Watch:

The bill would grant increased powers to prefects, the interior minister's local representatives, to designate public spaces as security zones, limiting who could enter and leave them; to limit the movement of people considered a national security threat; to close mosques and other places of worship; and to search private property. The courts would have no role in approving the use of the first three powers, although there would be a limited right of appeal for orders limiting where a person has to live and for closing places of worship. A judge will have limited oversight of search powers. The lack of time limits and the bill's vague definitions of terrorism and threats to national security exacerbates the concerns.[19]

This new law made public protest and occupations exceptionally risky for activists.

NEW SHAPE OF SPACE

France was hardly the only country to grapple with the issue of large-scale occupations between 2011 and 2016. Governments, both national and local, that had been faced with these events responded by introducing laws and other measures to prevent the occupations from happening again.

In New York, the city changed some of the rules affecting Zuccotti Park immediately after the Occupy Wall Street permanent encampment was evicted from the park. The OWS People's Library librarians returned on the night of November 15, 2011, the night after the police raid, to rebuild the library. William Scott, one of the librarians, writes:

> All night and into the next day folks stopped by to donate to and take from the collection. Because the new rules of the park forbid us from lying down or leaving anything there, Stephen [Boyer] and I stayed up all night to protect the books until other librarians came to take over for us. Frustrated and exhausted, but still exhilarated and eager to maintain the momentum of the movement, we kept the People's Library open all day in the pouring rain, storing books in Ziploc baggies to keep them dry.[20]

Permanent changes were made for all "privately owned public spaces" citywide as well. New York's POPS-designated areas were already uniquely complicated, as we saw in chapter 3. After Occupy, some of the guidelines contradicted themselves or left POPS spaces at best a legal gray area between the rights of the public versus the rights of the property owners. In a trial challenging the trespassing arrests of OWS protesters, the court found that the "unregulated access" required by the existing Zoning Resolution was "inconsistent with the concept of private ownership."[21] This essentially acknowledged Brookfield Properties' full legal rights over the park. Yet the Zoning Resolution also considered the POPS owner to have "legally ceded significant rights associated with its private property."[22] Furthermore, the court affirmed that POPS in general are intended for "passive recreation, rather than for active recreation or sports activities."[23] This approved Brookfield's ban on political speech in this particular park and gave tacit support for prohibiting political expression in all POPS. In deciding the proper use of POPS, the court appealed to the general practices sanctioned by the POPS owners instead of the Zoning Resolution's requirement. This amounted to changing POPS from semipublic to private spaces. In other words, the ruling would allow contentious activities, political speech, and assembly to be banned in the future should property owners choose to do so.[24] Thus, in the effort to clarify the laws, the courts erred on the side of private owners again, making occupation more difficult for future activists.

Across the United States, authorities were working to prevent new occupations. The ACLU reports that "state legislators in nearly 20 states proposed bills in 2017 that would restrict people's right to protest." For example, North Carolina, Tennessee, and South Dakota proposed "hit and kill" bills that "would have immunized drivers who accidentally hit a protester on a roadway."[25] The bills ultimately failed in all three states. In South Dakota, a law passed in 2017 "enables officials to prohibit protests of more than 20 people on public lands in certain circumstances and expands the crime of trespass; enables the Department of Transportation to prohibit protesters from stopping on the highway; and criminalizes protests that stop traffic on the highway."[26] According to Representative Tim Goodwin, who opposed the measure, "this bill is aimed at protesters against the Keystone Pipeline."[27] Remi Bald Eagle, a member of the Cheyenne River Sioux tribe and part of the resistance against the pipeline, argued: "Nowhere in the constitution did it say anything about how many people can assemble peaceably. We also feel that the right of way on roads is for the public, which includes all the freedoms endowed to the public by the bill of rights."[28] Goodwin agreed, saying that while he was "for pipelines," and that he was "sure the governor's intentions are good," nonetheless, "I'm just not willing to give him authority to create safety zones and turn peaceful protesters into felons."[29]

More recently, at the federal level, in the summer of 2018, Occupy ICE emerged in response to Immigration and Customs Enforcement's aggressive separation of families arriving at the US border. While documentation exists showing that the United States immigration enforcement system has long "been plagued by brutality and lawlessness,"[30] the Trump administration implemented a "'zero tolerance' immigration regime," not only making family separations more widespread and cruel but also serving to "radicalize" the entire ICE organization.[31] Additionally, no plan was created to reunite any of the families, making for a chaotic and rushed situation as the Department of Homeland Security tried to remedy the problem.[32] A statement published in June 2018 on the website OccupyIce.org urged: "We are calling on activists across the country to establish their own occupations to abolish ICE. Wherever ICE agents dare to show their faces, they must be challenged and shamed for carrying out this fascist policy."[33] The Portland, Oregon, occupation was the first and largest Occupy Ice encampment site, consisting, according to *The Guardian*, "of 30 tents and a number of other temporary structures. It had dedicated information and medical stations. Signs called for donations and builders. There were mounds of donated food and water, and makeshift barricades at either end of the camp." The occupation was a success: on June 20 the Portland Ice office "temporarily closed as a result of 'security concerns,' and would not reopen until those concerns were addressed."[34] The Portland police cleared the camp the week of July 26,[35] but as of November 2019, the group remained active, sharing news about events and other information via its Facebook page.[36]

In Turkey, the situation for activists went from bad to much worse.

Recep Tayyip Erdoğan, who had been prime minister during the Gezi Park protests in May and June 2013, was elected president just months afterward, and during 2014 and 2015, over five thousand people were "prosecuted in over a hundred cases linked to the popular uprising of spring 2013."[37] New laws were passed in 2015 known as the Domestic, or Homeland, Security Package, which "enhances police powers to conduct searches, use weapons, wiretap, detain individuals without a warrant, and remove demonstrators from scenes of protest." Additional amendments expanded the government's ability "to order the blocking of websites, allowing it to do so based on vaguely defined grounds related to the right to privacy, without prior court approval, though a court had to uphold the order within 48 hours for a block to remain in place."[38] More recently, Erdoğan pushed the national elections forward by seventeen months so that they were held in June 2018 rather than the end of 2019. In response to public protests, "Turkish police detained 77 people who defied a ban to mark May Day at Istanbul's Taksim Square," the plaza across the street from Gezi Park, where the 2013 occupation took place. "Authorities deployed more than 26,000 police officers around the city, cordoned off Taksim Square with metal barricades and suspended public transit and traffic on roads leading to the key transport hub to prevent marchers from reaching the space. Helicopters patrolled the skies above the square."[39] To add a final insult to injury, the original two-part "Taksim Square Pedestrianization" plan, which was halted by the Gezi Park protests, continued to be implemented. The underpass portion had already been completed in September 2013. The second part of the plan, the barracks construction, was never officially withdrawn by the government or prohibited by the courts, and as recently as 2019, Erdoğan was still calling for its completion.[40] The Gezi trees were still not safe.

Spain, the first country affected by the occupations addressed in this book, was one of the last to put in place any comprehensive national laws. The government passed the national Citizen Security Law, commonly referred to as "Ley Mordaza," the gag law, in 2015. Ley Mordaza allows police (rather than a court) to impose exorbitant fines, the equivalent of over $30,000, on "people exercising their right to protest, or simply criticizing the policies of the government," according to an analysis by Almudena Escobar López. It also "prohibits demonstrations or any 'serious disruption of public safety' in front of the Congress building, the Senate, or any of the regional parliaments, even when the buildings are vacant," "penalizes taking unauthorized photographs or video of police," and "penalizes those who prevent government employees from enforcing administrative or judicial orders," which specifically targets grass-roots organizations involved with preventing evictions. "Maina Kiai, UN special rapporteur on the rights to freedom of peaceful assembly and of association, said that "the so-called 'gag law' violates the very essence of the right to assembly since it penalizes a wide range of actions and behaviors that are essential for the exercise of this fundamental right, thus sharply limiting its exercise." In short, writes Escobar López, "the gag law is one step forward in the process of turning the Spanish state into an authoritarian representative democracy with a narrow margin for dissent and criticism. By limiting the use of public space, the gag law defines a unitary space that legitimates government power and makes invisible any attempt at criticism, protest, or social movement."[41] More recently, Spain seemed to offer a sliver of hope for those concerned with the limitations on public space and public expression. In June 2018, Spanish Socialist Workers' Party candidate Pedro Sánchez was elected prime minister and almost immediately announced that his administration would "start work on repealing the most virulent aspects of the Gag Law."[42] Sánchez then called for new general elections to be held in April 2019, which resulted in repeal and reform initiatives being postponed.

The focus on the constriction and supervision of public space is no surprise. As David Graeber wrote in 2016:

> Mainstream pundits and Marxist theorists alike never tire of declaring the failure of the movements of 2011, but if Turkey, Brazil, Bosnia, Hong Kong—and now, France—are anything to go by, they have permanently changed the very language of popular democracy. In every case, popular uprisings no longer take the form either of armed revolution, or attempts to transform the system from within; the first move is always to create a territory outside the system entirely, if possible, outside the legal order of the state: a prefigurative space in which new forms of direct democracy could be imagined.[43]

As governments are making it more difficult and more dangerous to do that, occupations like Nuit Debout have responded by modifying their approach to space and time.

THE LIBRARY

In this national and international context of constriction of public space, by the time Nuit Debout began in 2016, French activists had already been considering how to circumvent spatial prohibitions. One of the tactics they adopted was to co-opt their spaces primarily at night and vacate them during the daytime. The activists took over Place de la République, which in its most immediate history had been where large crowds gathered to pay tribute to the *Charlie Hebdo* victims. On a typical day, it is a busy city plaza like Puerta del Sol, though smaller and more closely surrounded by retail shops, restaurants, and high-end hotels. After the day of action, the first day of protests against the Loi Travail, when protesters decided they just wouldn't go home, they hoped the novelty of a nighttime protest might gain media attention and prevent the police from cracking down, since the general public was not using the space as much as they would in the daytime. So they stayed in the plaza. Police evicted them around 5:00 a.m., but they returned the next day around 4:00 in the afternoon, with activity steadily picking up until the next morning. Each day they would haul in their "infrastructure," and each morning they would pack it up. They fell into this routine quickly, as the nighttime became their primary meeting time. This inverse approach to time meant that the whole encampment, and specifically the library embedded within it, existed in a nomadic state almost from the beginning.

On April 5, 2016, a blog post appeared calling for people to come to the Place de la République and help build the occupation's new library.[44] Silvère Mercier and Lionel Maurel, the founders of SavoirsCom1 and both professional librarians, were clearly knowledgeable about protest libraries in previous encampments. Their very first blog post asking for participation began by referencing BiblioSol, the People's Library, and the Gezi Park library. Just as the Nuit Debout activists were thinking through and documenting these conscious decisions regarding their movement's development, the protest library itself was also explicitly self-aware: of its space and its collection, of its history as a protest library, and of the value it contained.

Claire Richard was one of the people who answered the call to build a library. She and around a dozen others showed up on that first Saturday, her motivation stemming from seeing BiblioDebout as a chance to become a "biblioguerrilla." For her it represented an opportunity "to enter this movement by what is most dear to me, namely the books."[45] A few days later on April 12, she published a description of the library. It was comprised, she writes, of two rickety tables and several shelves made out of pallets, with five or six people volunteering their time as librarians. The day was busy, with people bringing a wide range of donations, from Delphine de Vigan novels to "a pile" of works by Michel Foucault. Maurel estimates that they could have had several hundred books on display at a time, but bringing more than a small number of volumes every day might cause trouble with the police, who were likely to disallow anything that looked like a "convoy." BilioDebout librarians estimate their collection grew to around five hundred books after the first month, although the total number of donated books was likely much higher. It is impossible to know, since so many books were subsequently "checked out" and not returned.

On an average day during the summer, BiblioDebout's long folding tables held several boxes of books protected by a tarp overhead and a large sign with the library's name to help claim the space. Some days a small area on the ground would be marked out by carpets and pillows, and people would sit together in conversation, surrounded by books. When I visited in June, there were around one hundred books on display. More were in storage at a friend's apartment down the street, the librarians told me, but lacking the resources to bring all the books every day, they rotated the collection and brought a different set of boxes each time. As with so many other systems that emerged within protest library sites, the rotation was a "system" only very loosely defined. In this case, the process of deciding which books to bring was left up to the discretion of the person who had volunteered to haul the boxes to and from the park that day. Librarians did try to bring different boxes each time so that "regulars" would find a nice variety of selections. Eventually a public Googledoc was created so people could sign up to bring supplies and books, but it simply listed a person's name and "whatever books."[46]

I had brought with me a box of books from the People's Library with "OWSPL" marked in black on the spines. These books were put out on the table right away, and the librarians tweeted a picture. They became instant "celebrity" books. On her blog, Claire Richard confessed her worries that people would take all the "good" books, the expensive, rare, or exceptionally beautiful ones, leaving only "flea-market finds," and I wondered how long the OWSPL texts would last. How many passers-by would recognize that mark and understand the history of that book? Earlier I discussed the decision-making process that Biblio-Sol and some other libraries used as their collection developed. They questioned what kinds of books their collections should include. Richard noticed that the same people would come by more than once over the weekend and handpick several "valuable" volumes, but she feared sounding too authoritarian if she said anything, and so she bit her lip. Another volunteer told her that despite the risk of losing it all, "maybe the important thing is that [the book] circulates." She spoke, too, with Lionel Maurel, who agreed with her that "this will perhaps be a tragedy of the commons, we will see," but advised that they should give the library a chance to work on its own. She decided to trust in the vision of the other librarians, the vision of the common good, and wait to see what would happen.

Eventually, Richard wrote on her blog, "throughout the weekend, people converge, stop, come back around the tables of BiblioDebout. As if the books continued to constitute a focal point, a point of warmth, presence and duration. On a sunny Sunday, people linger, glean, sit on the cushions . . . which are on the floor next to them. A space of slowness, of attention is created around the books." It turned out not to be a tragedy at all, she concluded. Additionally, through the emphasis on circulation, gleaning, slowness, and physical books, important undercurrents from other protest library narratives were echoed, again resulting in the triumph of creating the world the organizers wanted to see here and now. But this time they had several existing models to draw from. In the next chapter I address the patterns visible at BiblioDebut and other protest libraries in an effort to draw out the common phases that they pass through.

CHAPTER 12

PHASES OF THE PROTEST LIBRARY
BiblioDebout, Paris and Lyon

The strategy of circumventing some of the legal issues involved in occupying the plaza during the day was successful, but the nighttime nature of Nuit Debout might have been expected to lead to fatigue. Robert Shaw writes, "The move to the night might be seen as an attempt to find a timespace in which a more open and creative politics is possible, strategically responding to the reduction in the freedom to protest in the more heavily surveyed day." In interviews with activists, he found that, instead of increasing fatigue, "Nuit Debout's disruption of urban rhythms was cited as a key strength of the movement: the main aim wasn't only to occupy the place, it was," as one protester told him, "to disrupt 'the rhythm, the rhythm that we all follow. You know the protesting, you protest in the day and the beginning of the afternoon, and then you go home. We didn't want to do this, we wanted to disrupt the rhythm of the protest.'" Shaw continues, "Protesters use the night to stretch and frustrate attempts to constrain protest by pushing at rhythms of governance, an important technique in the context of France's state of emergency laws that were operating at the time of Nuit Debout." In disrupting the "rhythms of protest itself," the activists had found a method to overcome "protest fatigue."[1]

Even if the nighttime model combats protest fatigue, Shaw finds that it exerts its own toll on people, generating a very different kind of fatigue from that of daytime activity. Shaw compares it to the effects of shift work. He says that 'problems of fatigue, strains on family life and other emotional challenges are recurring issues" in all occupations, but these are exacerbated when the activism takes place at night. Though other protests had set up a permanent occupation that continued overnight, the rhythm of "living" in the park was different from the itinerant coming and going, and the need to balance a normal daytime life with nighttime activism. This tension resulted in degrees of weariness, despite initially high levels of hope and optimism, at the Occupy Wall Street People's Library as well.

These stresses that come with nighttime occupation are exacerbated by the presence of police and private security. Many of the raids I have discussed happened at night: the OWS People's Library, Gezi Park library, and Maidan library were all destroyed after the sun went down. Sometimes the nighttime weariness resulted not from a single, intense confrontation but from a slow, ongoing burn. For example, at Occupy Tampa in Florida, blogger and occupier Bill Livsey noted: "the nighttime harassment by the police is non stop and an effort to cause sleep deprivation. They mock us—laugh at us–and shine bright lights in our faces. Their behavior is much like a schoolyard bully!"[2] The books at Occupy Tampa were confiscated by police on November 27, 2011. Livsey writes: "The crates were forcefully snatched and thrown in the back of a truck for sanitation disposal. When one Occupy Tampa member attempted to retrieve a crate of books—he was thrown to the ground—arrested—and taken to jail."[3] And of the People's Library in New York, Jaime Taylor and Zachary Loeb, librarians from the Occupy Wall Street People's Library, wrote that as of April 2013, "we no longer have the capacity to rebuild the People's Library as it was, besides which we'd probably find our collection in the garbage again and ourselves in jail in short order if we tried."[4]

One other issue that Shaw points out is that the nighttime occupations limited the visibility of the encampment. While this was a positive aspect in terms of avoiding legal confrontations, it limited the overall number of participants who could be physically present. Social media participation, however, was booming. By David Graeber's count, "hundreds of thousands followed, and contributed, on social media."[5] But in terms of the occupation of Place de la République itself, the numbers were much smaller. France 24 reported on April 3, 2016, that "while the Indignados protests drew about 20,000 people in May 2011, and the Occupy movement gathered between 2,000 and 15,000 protesters in 2011 and 2012, Nuit Debout has so far reached at most 1000 to 2000, according to organisers."⁶

Because the entire movement of Nuit Debout itself ebbed and flowed with the daytime/nighttime rhythm, the attendance in the plaza did as well. As Raphaëlle Bats and Marilou Pain write: "The more the occupied square is empty, the less the library is frequented. The reports [on the BiblioDebout email list] often deplore the low level of participation at Nuit Debout and consequently the low involvement in the BD," the BiblioDebout library.⁷ From this perspective, BiblioDebout is more like Bloombergville than the People's Library. The restrictions on the use of space and the demand that these libraries essentially be in motion all the time prevented both of them from reaching critical mass. By July 2016, the BiblioDebout activists were meeting largely on the weekends and only occasionally during the week. And while the nighttime gatherings were thus innovative and necessary, they also entailed unique drawbacks.

Even with all these changes, however, the books continued to work their magic, attracting attention, pulling people in to stop and talk with the librarians at the table, and generating conversation about different texts and about the occupation itself. Bats and Pain write that despite the small number of visitors, "the interactions were strong. The visitors came rarely only to consume books. They have the will to discuss with the organizers. The speaking and the exchange are truly at the heart of the project."⁸

CONSTRUCTION PHASE

The rhythms identified by Shaw at BiblioDebout Paris point to other rhythms or patterns, specifically the identification of common stages or lifecycle events among the entire set of examples that I call protest libraries. Bats and Pain describe the typical states of being of a protest library, or what they call a "participative" library, and break them down into three phases. The first is "a construction and installation phase with many exchanges on the creation of the collection, the interactions, etc."⁹ In general, the physical emergence and rapid growth of the book collection marks the first phase of any protest library, bringing with it an extreme public visibility that can be at times a painful and violent one. The physical, visible act of taking over a space, reclaiming it, renaming it, and reusing it is radically provocative, especially in the case of a library, because it creates a heavy sense of permanence. This is the most obvious phase, the one that begins the narrative of most protest libraries.

Bats and Pain describe this first phase in regard to the BiblioDebout library sites in both Paris and Lyon, which sound very much like the initial libraries that emerged back in 2011: "During this phase, the BD establishes itself in the square and tries to build its nest: tarpaulins, cartons, bags, duvets, carpets, pallets." The types of book donations are similar to those that other protest libraries received: "The donors are either passers-by who deposited one or more document/s, or institutions (publishers, association, public institution, especially libraries)." In addition, "an academic institution will give a stock [of books] following the liquidation of a student association . . . , a TV [sic] will give digital files of one of its programs," and "a school publisher will give several boxes of textbooks." The questions of identity are also familiar. Bats and Pain write, "We can wonder whether these gifts are a reflection of a commitment of the institution in question, or rather, through these institutions, the manifestation of individual approaches, people who recognize themselves in the BD and in the movement." They say that "this phase lasted from the end of March to the end of April in Paris, and to the end of May in Lyon."[10]

While both the Paris and Lyon BiblioDebout sites were clearly identifiable as libraries because of the books and signage, the sites did not have the same sense of permanence experienced by other protest library sites. Without any permanent seating or "inside" area, and without a thriving, consistent presence of an enveloping larger occupation, the library was not as conducive to lounging, reading, or gaming as had been the libraries that inspired BiblioDebout, specifically BiblioSol and the People's Library. This was a big departure from the embedded library model I have discussed so far. Part of their effect on passers-by had to do with the magnetic pull the situation generated. Without the surrounding protest to insulate it, without the barricades to help define the perimeter, a library necessarily evolves differently.

Nevertheless, for Lionel Maurel, BiblioDebout was always an experiment that centered on the notion of the commons. About a month after BiblioDebout began, Lionel wrote a blog post titled "In What Way Is BiblioDebout a Common?" He reflects on the experience and explains how his previous research about the commons had driven his desire to create the library. A common, by his definition, requires three things: "1) a shared resource, 2) a community that gathers together to manage it, 3) rules designed to organize governance." He concludes that by this definition, BiblioDebout fits the bill. The books are the shared resource; the volunteer librarians are the community, "now distinct from the collective SavoirsCom1" as well as from the larger community of Nuit Debout; and they have all agreed to a set of rules that are evolving over time. But, he says, this is really too broad a definition to be useful, for it could "apply to very different phenomena." Maurel is interested in the specific connection of the concept to the library. "Is there only a metaphorical link between the Commons and this book-sharing mechanism," he asks, "or can we really apply the elements of Common theory to this experiment?" It is clear, he concludes, "that the concepts of the theory of the Commons, unlike the way in which a researcher approaches them, for example, have not only remained for us a framework for the analysis of reality but also played the role of guiding principles of action, with a direct influence on our behavior."[11]

STRUGGLE PHASE

The second phase of the library's lifespan is a post-eviction, nomadic, insubstantial phase. Bats and Pain call this the "struggle phase," one in which "the reports are focused on the interactions with forces of law and order . . . The BD is not anymore installed and occupying, it is nomadic and moving." This took place "especially in Paris, from the end of April to the end of June." In general, they say, "it is a nomadic phase, clearly affirmed in Lyon, where the BD follows an itinerant

Nuit Debout which does not occupy only one square anymore."[12] It is marked specifically by transition, and this phase is inevitable because the types of spaces selected during phase one affect the ways in which the library grows.

The People's Library and Gezi Park focused on visibility and transparency. The BiblioDebout organizers continued to be mindful of these factors, but their emphasis shifted to mobility, movement, and rapid circulation. When the OWS People's librarians had encounters with security in Zuccotti Park who enforced varying rules regarding the books, the conflict sometimes had to do with the visibility of the collection. Initially, they were not allowed to store the books in boxes because the police could not see what was inside, which was considered a security threat. But because of the outdoor nature of the library, being able to cover the boxes was an important aspect of protecting the books from the weather. Eventually the librarians were allowed to store the books in transparent plastic bins with lids.

What we notice with BiblioDebout is that the pace at which libraries shift out of phase one and into phase two seems to be accelerating. In Lyon, an anecdote reveals how the question of permanence and mobility was perhaps more intense there than at any other protest library. Like the Paris library, Lyon was nomadic from the beginning. One night in June, around ten thousand people participated in a Nuit Debout protest, and according to testimony published on the bibliodebout.org site, it was peaceful, without conflict or even the use of tear gas. The library was shut down by the police, however, who called it "occupation of the public domain without authorization." BiblioDebout librarians in Lyon had been using "quasi-mobile devices," which meant lightweight portable tables, but on this night, the police said that they were limiting access to public space. When the librarians asked if they could spread their books out on the brick walls and benches built into the park landscape, they were told no. "We are very surprised," wrote a blogger, "and will therefore equip our tables with wheels to be fully mobile. I fear, however, that next time we'll be told that the wheels are not mobile enough!"[13]

LIBRARIANS AS CATALYSTS

BiblioDebout sites are almost instantaneously nomadic, and this phase highlights the equally rapid pace at which the librarian identity is formed. The heavy emphasis on mobility helps underscore the tremendous energy the librarians must put into tending to and fostering the growth of the library. As we have seen in several cases, the librarians have persisted despite the fact that their collections were confiscated, in storage and inaccessible, or deliberately distributed to other libraries and groups. But even in these cases, the books preceded the library. Unlike with a public library, for a protest library the wave of giving precedes the library itself. The books arrive first, and a library forms around them. They serve as the catalyst for the library's very formation. The collection emerges before there are even any librarians around to consider rejecting the donation, and then a wider community of donors steps up to continue the process. As volunteers begin to take on their new identity as librarians, the identity of the library itself develops concurrently through the continued donations of the external community. The three identities enter into a feedback loop.

If we look at the collection through this lens of inversion, we see that these identities are all working well outside the typical subject-object relationship and begin to add up to a new whole. In this situation, human beings are not bestowing power upon the books. Rather they experience a reciprocity together with the books.

In all these examples, even in the protest libraries that immediately dissolved, talking with the librarians invokes a sense of currency and ongoing dedication. These people are still librarians, despite the lack of a physical book collection, a physical library space, or formal library training.

DIGITAL LIBRARIES

While their self-awareness served as a strong, conscious foundation for the new library and helped them draw from what had worked in previous protest libraries, BiblioDebout placed a heavier emphasis on digital texts than previous libraries had. The librarians had never drawn a sharp either/or line between the physical and digital options. A BiblioSol blogger on CounterCartographies.org writes: "Of course, we're in the plaza, and we're also in facebook, and the plaza is on facebook and we're in the facebook plaza. Our power lies in that we can go from facebook to the plaza and back again whenever we want." This worked to the advantage of the activists.[14] The other protest libraries made positive arguments to support the focus on physical books, and except for the argument from OWS against the proprietary orientation of publishers, none of their arguments were explicitly opposed to electronic texts. The protest libraries did not practice a rejection of digital texts but rather expressed a strong preference for physical books.

BiblioDebout chose to use PirateBox as a complement to the physical library. PirateBox functions as a server with its own local wireless connectivity. Its website describes it as "a self-contained and mobile digital collaboration and file sharing system. Inspired by pirate radio and the free culture movement, PirateBox utilizes Free and Open Source software to create mobile wireless communication and file sharing networks where users can communicate and anonymously exchange images, video, audio, documents, and other digital content." PirateBox was created in 2011 by David Darts, who is identified on the website as "artist, maker, and educator." In response to the question "Does PirateBox promote stealing," the team's answer is no. They describe the box as "designed to facilitate communication and sharing between friends and local community members."[15]

PirateBox is based on open-source coding and runs on the Linux operating system, making it an easy system to use. That is, it is easy to use in terms of not needing permission or access to proprietary computer code. For about $35, users can buy all the supplies they will need to build their own box. They can follow a tutorial to connect their own equipment to the BiblioDebout PirateBox, thus forming a "mesh network."[16] Because of the open, unrestricted nature of the PirateBox setup, other developers and artists have created their own "forks." The coding and technology are thus very much aligned with the spirit of the protest libraries.[17]

The equipment was portable, which allowed librarians to bring it on marches and larger demonstrations, giving anyone in proximity an opportunity to view texts that are considered public access or

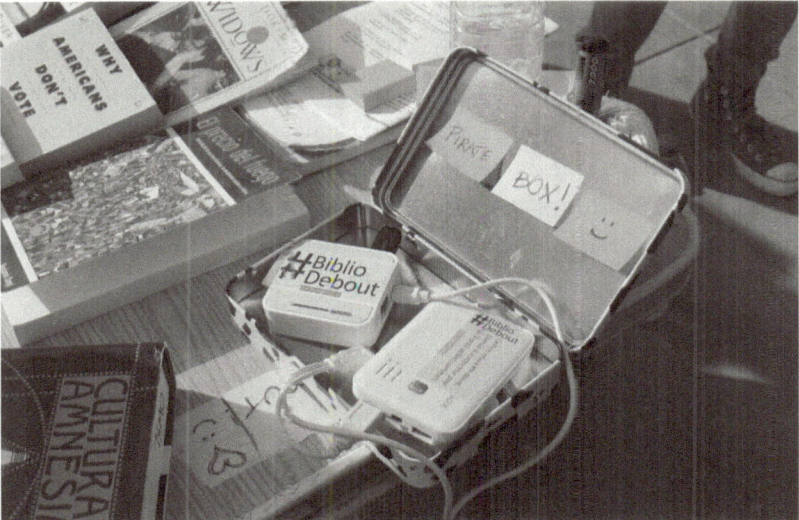

Figure 5. The BiblioDebout, Paris, PirateBox. Look closely to see "OWSL" on the edge of *Cultural Amnesia* at the bottom left. This was one of the books donated to BiblioDebout by the OWS People's librarians. Paris, July 2016. Courtesy of the author.

have free use licenses. Much like Stephen Boyer, the OWS librarian hauling around "People's Library 3.0" after its eviction from Zuccotti Park, BiblioDebout librarians could much more easily bring their library with them on marches and mobile excursions. Their PirateBox, however, had very limited broadcast range: according to one site, "the signal barely spans one meter."[18] On marches through the streets, this meant that in a crowd as large as ten thousand, not everyone would be able to access the files. The specific location of the librarian carrying the equipment made a big difference. While highlighting and actively developing their PirateBox was an innovation at BiblioDebout, it has not had a lasting impact, certainly not an impact any greater than the physical books have had.

FUTURES PHASE

Bats and Pain end their outline of protest library phases with a third stage "in which the exchanges are mostly concentrated on the future of BiblioDebout: what could we do with BiblioDebout after Nuit Debout?

During this last phase, the BD thought itself in other places than those of the original protest. In result of the protest itinerance observed in the previous phase, this phase is the one of the relation with other protests, other mobilisations."[19] With hindsight, we have now seen what has happened to some of these libraries.

BiblioDebout shows us that protest libraries can persist despite the removal of time, or rather, despite the passage of laws that prohibit occupation or protesting in public places. And even more precisely, they can change their relationship with time and still provide a disruption through a shift in rhythm. We also see that some of these evolutions—the self-awareness, the digital library, and the rapid shift into nomadism—are more accurately an increase in intensity than a significant shift within the protest library assemblage itself.

We saw in chapter 1 that a librarian community coheres around the physical library and that an identity begins to form. We also focused on the voice that social media provide, and in chapter 2 we looked at how that voice can be amplified to yield rhetorical power to great effect. Protest libraries and their secondary nomadic instantiations are innately temporary and ephemeral, and the traces they leave are most visible through social media and digital content. Ironically, the tweets, Facebook updates, and blog posts have lasted longer than the physical spaces and book collections, although they are slowly eroding as posts are deleted and accounts deactivated.

After the political encampment ends, both the librarians and the book collections persist in various nomadic incarnations. The librarian community often boxes up the collection and enters a mobile phase that lasts for weeks or, in some cases, years. For example, BiblioSol in Madrid moved its collection of several thousand books from squat to squat for two years until a permanent space was located. During that time the books were kept in storage, at one point becoming split into two sets of boxes in two different locations and would ultimately never be reunited. The fact that the collection existed, despite its inaccessibility, anchored the librarians to their work and their identities as BiblioSol librarians.

The Bats and Pain "futures" phase encompasses the point in time just before the end of the library, the moment at which the assemblage is at its most volatile and opportunity at its most available. But what do these "futures" become? Can a protest library exist perpetually in this phase, or must it necessarily transition into something else? And if "futures" is an in-between phase, how long can a protest library slow down its trajectory and remain here? When it speeds up again, in which directions can the library move? Often the end of the protest library is protracted and complex, so I would also add to the Bats and Pain life-cycle rhythms a fourth standard event, that of conclusion or transition, the phase in which the library either reinvents itself as a permanent space, becomes an archive, and/or is dismantled and redistributed. In the next chapter I will consider this "transitions" phase as I introduce Chicago's Freedom Square library, the last documented protest library of its kind.

We have already seen some of the answers to this question via the persistence of the librarians and the longevity of the social media accounts. But I want to broaden the question a bit as well. What do we do, not with the individual protest library called BiblioDebout, but with the genre of protest library? Is it possible that the short era of protest libraries is already over?

CHAPTER 13

REINVENTION AS COLLECTIVE
Freedom Square Library, Chicago

During the summer of 2016, at about the same time that BiblioDebout was developing in France, the occupation of "Freedom Square" began in Chicago. Freedom Square is the name that activists bestowed on an encampment in an empty lot across the street from Homan Square, the site of a huge warehouse that served as an unofficial detention center, where police were accused of using "Guantanamo-esque interrogation techniques" on suspects, a disproportionately large number of whom were people of color.[1] Freedom Square sprang from the work in which a collective of activists was engaged, work that already emphasized the material power of books in the streets.

The library in Freedom Square was the last of its kind to emerge. Nevertheless, it lies on a fuzzy border between the protest library I have been working to define and what we might consider to be the next phase of the protest library genre, just beyond the "futures" phase in the structure outlined by Raphaëlle Bats and Marilou Pain. When the Freedom Square occupation ended, the collective maintained its momentum and found a permanent (legal) space out of which it could operate. It is an old two-story house full of character, where a dedicated room has been set aside for a proper library. The room has shelves lining the walls, books protected behind glass doors, and a system of organization shaping up. Here the collective was able to reabsorb the library, now a library with a history of its own, into a less volatile space maintained by a self-defined community with an orientation sympathetic to that of prefigurative politics.

CONTEXT

As with so many of the other political movements that led to the occupations and libraries detailed in this book, the #LetUsBreathe Collective was both a singular event and part of a wider pattern. The collective's history was only peripherally inspired by Occupy and its prefigurative, austerity-focused encampments. Rather, it was much more intimately tied to direct action regarding the multitude of unarmed people of color who had died in the United States at the hands of the police. In 2014 the American general public would have recognized the highly publicized names of Trayvon Martin, Tamir Rice, Michael Brown, and Eric Garner, but the full list is much longer.[2] The #LetUsBreathe Collective itself derives its name from the tragic death of Eric Garner on July 17, 2014, who died in New York City from being held by a police officer in a chokehold. He told the officers restraining him as he died, "I can't breathe."

The Chicago activists who founded the collective originally came together in order to help and support the community in Ferguson, Missouri, in the wake of Michael Brown's death on August 9, 2014. Brown, an eighteen-year-old African American, was shot and killed by police in an event that sparked widespread protests not just in Ferguson but around the country. As Cassandra Chaney and Dannielle Joy Davis write in their introduction to a special issue of *Western Journal of Black Studies* dedicated to Brown, "the fatal shooting of Michael Brown serves as a painful reminder to African-Americans and other marginalized communities of their own mortality as well as the blatant disregard that police have for Black life."[3] The event catalyzed the #LetUsBreathe Collective, which formed "as a fundraising initiative to bring tear gas protection and remedies, medical and hygiene supplies, and water bottles" to people in Ferguson protesting the lack of justice in the Brown case and gross judicial inequities in the city of Ferguson.[4]

Through volunteer efforts in Ferguson, the collective worked with and was inspired by other groups such as the Black Youth Project 100 (BYP100), Lost Voices, and of course the more widely publicized Black Lives Matter, all of which have formed national networks and local coalitions throughout the United States. Additionally, the #LetUsBreathe Collective also drew support from other relevant existing groups such as Chicago's Emmaus House, "an intentional Christian community in North Lawndale, Chicago with a commitment to racial justice and affiliated with the Catholic Worker Movement."[5] This extended network supported local goals while reaching out as well to communities like Ferguson that needed immediate targeted support.

Between 2014 and 2016, the collective continued its outreach in Chicago neighborhoods and began to think strategically about long-term goals. "As we were analyzing our method of protest," says Damon Williams, co-founder of the collective, "we started trying to figure out how to be more communally facing and not just be downtown and on the north side. How do we move with our people?" In some ways these questions echo the "protest fatigue" that the Nuit Debout activists needed to counter, as we saw in the last chapter: How could the #LetUsBreathe Collective continue to spark attention and gather support from a community that had been exhausted by constant external pressures? In this case the pressures revolved around economic disparities explicitly based on a history of racism, segregation, and slavery.[6]

#LetUsBreathe tapped into the creative energy of its activists to come up with a solution. The collective's website says that as "a grassroots alliance of artists, journalists, and activists, we use our talents to amplify marginalized voices, disrupt the status quo, offer opportunities for healing and education, and provoke critical thought and dialog about the intersections of oppression through film, music, theater, poetry, and civil disobedience."[7] Thus, Williams says, "instead of protesting and chanting about death, we would organize in the same way but make it more like a parade. So we played music. We would carry books." They provided food, performed neighborhood cleanups, and hauled around free used books in a little wagon "as a way to start different political conversations . . . Books would be kind of our entry point: here, take a free book, and then we would have the conversation, instead of just walking up with a clipboard." Member and Freedom Square librarian Frank Bergh echoes Williams's narrative, noting that often just seeing someone pushing a car battery and amp down the street for an outdoor open-mic event was enough to "bring people out of their houses. Then come the books. Then comes the peanut butter and jelly." Lydia Wong, another member who helps organize many of the collective's book-related initiatives, adds that this kind of effort "also fights this misconception that divested neighborhoods don't read or don't want books. Very frequently we'd give out most of the books in the wagon."[8]

FREEDOM SQUARE

The collective had been engaged with this work for about a year when, in 2015, *Guardian* journalists Spencer Ackerman and Zach Stafford revealed the "overwhelming racial disparity at Homan Square, where detainees are still held for minor crimes with little access to the outside world." In a series of articles, Ackerman describes the facility as "an off-the-books interrogation warehouse in Chicago," a place "unique in not generating public records of someone's detention there, permitting police to effectively hide detainees from their attorneys."[9] In this way "police 'disappeared' more than 7,000 people."[10] His reporting generated public awareness and helped lead to several resignations and lawsuits.[11] By the summer of 2016, the public was loudly demanding that the facility be shut down. In collaboration with BYP100, the #LetUsBreathe Collective planned a local direct-action initiative that included a march, a human blockade of Homan Square, and the occupation of an empty lot across the street. According to Kristiana Rae Colón, one of the collective's co-founders: "Freedom Square first emerged on Wednesday, July 20, in collaboration with the Black Youth Project 100's civil disobedience blockade of Homan Square. The action was organized in conjunction with the July 21 #FreedomNow National Day of Action—a day of collective actions for justice simultaneously held across the US in response to a national call put out by the Movement for Black Lives."[12] The protesters pledged to occupy the lot until "city officials meet their demands—including shutting down Homan Square, revoking a proposed 'Blue Lives Matter' ordinance, and releasing reports about the death of 16-year-old Pierre Loury, who was fatally shot by police in April."[13]

The collective's distinct arts and humanities orientation influenced the type of action it took in opposition to the abuses at Homan Square. While supporting "traditional" protest and civil disobedience methods like the march and blockade, the activists also drew on their history of seeking different ways to start political conversations. They decided to set up seven tents on the abandoned property across the street from Homan Square. "The tents were originally meant to create a visual spectacle," Colón, told the press that summer.[14] "They were artistic pieces," explains Williams, "that represented the resources we wanted investment into in opposition to police and violence."[15] These resources included "restorative justice, education, employment, housing, mental health & physical wellness, addiction treatment, access to nutritional food, and art."[16]

THE LIBRARY

In addition to the seven primary, symbolic tents, the Freedom Square occupation also included a "Free Store." This was a space where members of the collective could redistribute clothing, books, and many of the items they already had on hand as part of their regular work in the community. While the Free Store offered a wide variety of items, according to Williams, "pretty quickly we started getting so many clothes and book donations that they were separated, and they all had their own canopy." Once the books were broken apart from the other Free Store items, several activists became heavily involved with the development of the new library space. They set up a number of milk crates to function as bookshelves and tried to keep up with the flood of donations. Their most urgent goals included unpacking the books from the boxes as fast as possible, placing them on the shelves, and trying to protect them from all the rain Chicago was experiencing that summer.

As with the other protest libraries, the book donations came from

Figure 6. Freedom Square's library tent. Chicago, July 2016. Photo by Sarah-Ji (Love + Struggle Photos). Courtesy of the photographer.

a variety of sources. One of the librarians told me: "People would pop up any time of the day with either a box or food or books, throughout the day, all day. I remember some people coming from out[side] of Chicago [who] had heard about Freedom Square from social media or a radio station, and they wanted to come drop off the books." She said that although no one had any formal library training, "people would come in probably every two to three days and try to organize it and try to either have some type of theme or keep it neat." The activists lamented the lack of organization, but they were just too busy to give the library their full attention. "Sorting [the books] was a challenge, and it got to a point where we weren't able to keep up with the cycle of people taking, people giving, and then it just getting rifled through." Additionally, with all the children on site, whatever organization existed often quickly disappeared.

In contrast to some of the other collections we have seen that indiscriminately accepted everything and made space for a wide variety of political opinions and worldviews, Freedom Square was much more closely aligned with the process at Maidan. Williams said the foundation of the collection was formed by "old classics" and a wide array of popular fiction and literature, but the volunteers actively curated what was on their shelves. And, said Lydia Wong, "if [building this collection of books] is also a form of propaganda, this is contributing to the education that is needed, if we're saying this is what true education is, there's no reason to put out certain books." In Williams's words, the Freedom Square library "started to build an aesthetic," and soon enough, publishers like Haymarket, "a radical, independent, nonprofit book publisher based in Chicago,"[17] were making donations. "You would look up and now there's ten copies of Assata Shakur's biography," he says, along with books by writers like the BreakBeat Poets and Ta-Nehisi Coates. Colón adds, "One of the things that I'm really proud of is how many children's books we have." The focus on children is a constant throughout the different book and library projects led by the collective.[18]

LEGITIMACY OF BOOKS

In conversation, the activists did refer to the space as a library, as do several newspaper articles, but they did not refer to themselves as librarians. "A 'librarian' might cringe at our library," said Williams. He points out that it was pretty different from what one might expect of a "library." "We never really got to full 'library' status," he admits, "and also, it was all for free so it's not a library in the sense that we're expecting it to be returned. It's more of a free bookstore." Wong says: "I think maybe library isn't necessarily the best word to describe it, unless you're just meaning it as a collection of books . . . Maybe people are taking some out and also returning them, but in Freedom Square it was more like book distribution." Nevertheless, like other protest libraries that did not have a return policy, the library at Freedom Square always had books on the shelves. The concerns expressed by Claire Richard at BiblioDebout in chapter 11, and the advice of Lionel Maurel to trust in the circulation of books within the space even at the risk of a "tragedy of the commons," apply here too.

Even if Freedom Square did not function like a library in terms of "borrowing" versus "taking," the librarians did agree that it certainly felt like a library.[19] Colón said: "I remember it being one of the cleaner, quieter places where you could sit and catch your breath when there was chaos all around. And so even if you weren't in there to read . . . here is a folding chair where I can sit, and here is a milk crate where I can sit, and here is clear space where I can sit, and just be surrounded by books." Another librarian echoed Colón's sentiment, saying, "I definitely caught a few quiet hours in the library." Colón continued, "One of the most beautiful things was seeing a young mother from the community that was camping with us reading the autobiography of Assata Shakur for the first time and carrying that around the space." Shakur's work, part autobiography and part poetry, "is really kind of aligned with our vision of using the arts as sort of an entry point for political education and access to social justice work." So "to see another young woman in the North Lawndale community have the mental space with four kids to sit down and read that book was pretty powerful." In the first part of this book I posed the question, what is a library? Whether or not the space was a "library" in some ways and not in others, on the basis of everything I have discussed so far, the answer here seems to be unequivocally yes, Freedom Square was a library, if for no other reason than that the librarians and patrons in that space of books practiced a slowing down, a curbing of circulation key to defining a heterotopic space as distinct from the surrounding social space. The echoes of the Beeb resonate here too, despite being separated by two thousand miles and having emerged four years apart.

In addition to defining the space, the books lent a certain legitimacy to the community being built inside the encampment. Regarding the magnetic quality of the books, Wong said, "There's such an emphasis in this culture on [the] written word that there's also something about a library that makes people—especially people of a dominant culture—feel like it's legitimate." Books, she says, seem to say to people: "You have this message that isn't just somebody speaking on a mic; you have a message that somebody has written something about. And for better or worse, probably worse, that's viewed as legitimacy. So I think there's something about books that makes people feel reassured." Coupling this sense of legitimacy with an emphasis on books is powerful. It is a form of nation-building akin to the work of the Maidan librarians, but with a different type of political border and a different type of barricade setting the space apart from established nationality. Colón says, "I will say, we did a pretty good job of sorting and grouping black political thought at Freedom Square," and in this way the librarians were able to harness some of the unwieldy power of a material book collection and turn it in a particular direction. The Freedom Square library was especially effective because these legitimacy-lending books revolving around black political thought came as gifts from the community itself.

THE RAID THAT NEVER CAME

The #LetUsBreathe activists had not originally intended on living or camping as part of this protest action. As at Nuit Debout, they were going to be there in person only some of the time, splitting their efforts between the protest and their regular daily lives. The rest of the time they would let the tents claim the space. "We had flirted with the idea of occupying the space and it being much more like contested, protest-style space," says Williams, but because they were explicitly opposing police presence, they figured their occupation "would be swept away within thirty-six to seventy-two hours." But as it turned out, some of the neighborhood kids "really wanted to sleep in the tents," and thus organization of the occupation began not with the activists themselves but with the wider neighborhood community, who were inspired by the sight of it all.

During this time, the #LetUsBreathe Facebook account issued a steady stream of invitations to events and pictures of the square full of people having a good time and engaging with one another. On their blog, members of the collective explained:

> We had no meetings, no budget, no dedicated staff, just a handful of people who were willing to camp out. We didn't know if we'd hold it through the night, but hoped the goal of opposing "Blue Lives Matter" legislation, calling out the illegal detention and torture happening across the street, and building consciousness for abolitionist politics would garner support. We figured however long we could hold the space, we'd use it as a tool to give out free clothes, free books, free food, and cold water to the community.

A "Final Reflection" on the blog states, "Freedom Square accomplished more beautiful things in each of its 41 days (and counting) than we can name: we built relationships with survivors of Homan Square torture, we fed 200–300 people a day, we taught kids pottery and about Assata Shakur, we chanted, we marched, we roasted marshmallows, and in every moment, we stood for love, no matter how violent or chaotic things became."[20]

Since the activists expected police to shut them down quickly, they were ready for a raid or eviction or confrontation of some sort. "We had all these contingency plans," says Bergh. "We didn't think we were going to be able to last the night. We had people wait up all night, not just the first night but every night. We had people awake all night in case we got raided, and so everything was kind of fluid." But night after night, they were not raided. The lack of city or police action against the encampment came as a surprise to the activists. It was the one thing they had *not* planned for. So Freedom Square continued developing and building its encampment for over a month, long enough for the books to cross a critical threshold into a library collection. What had begun with approximately two hundred books grew to around two thousand.

After forty-one days, the encampment ended voluntarily. Although the "Final Reflection" post on the blog conveys the weariness and fatigue the activists felt, they emphasize that "the occupation did not end because we ran out of energy or we were overwhelmed by the logistics of the site. It ended because it illustrated the tension between the world as it is and the world as we imagine it to be." They discuss several aspects of the encampment that might have been addressed differently had they expected to be living on site for an extended period of time. The organizers were striving to "maintain collective vision about the values and operation of the space. We wanted to empower everyone to take ownership of and claim leadership in the space, so folks with all levels of organizing backgrounds (or not) and intersectional analyses (or not) positioned themselves as leaders." Although the collective did not publicly elaborate on the details, its story is reminiscent of that of the Beeb. And like the Beeb, the #LetUsBreathe Collective is protective of its community, even—and especially—when it comes to the most vulnerable and volatile among them. As Williams says, "the real impact of this structural violence and oppressive power gets internalized by the people that are harmed. And so dealing with and trying to transform and heal those injuries is a non-linear and messy process." What the ending boiled down to was "limited capacity, drain, fatigue, and the honest realization that we are not ready yet." He compares the process to making the body stronger by working out regularly. One of the first things to do when you begin a new workout routine is to max out, to push as hard as possible and lift as much weight as you can just to see what your body's current limits are; but maxing out is not a daily workout activity. It becomes the benchmark toward which you can then work, using smaller goals and measuring daily, incremental progress. In Freedom Square, "we went past our max to see how strong we really are," he says, "and now we are building up and doing smaller sets to get stronger."

Toward the end of the Freedom Square lifespan, Bergh said, people unrelated to the original organizers and activists began "spending their nights in the space, and those people kind of inherited what was left of the tents—the first-aid tent and the library tent and everything else—and there was a night, several nights, where there were some threats of violence and then some escalated threats of violence." When the organizers returned after leaving the space, they found "the library tent, and all of the tents, pretty much knocked over." It had been raining, "so some of the books were wet and a lot of the books were just kind of lying there." They could see that "stuff was pretty badly damaged," and they "realized that probably within the next twenty-four hours everything would be either removed or destroyed because of the attitudes of the people who were still in that space." So he, Wong, and several other activists set their minds to saving the books, ignoring the food and tents and all the other supplies, and they simply "jumped into whatever was left of that tent. It's almost like that image of books in a puddle, it's like, I've got to save these books." The group made multiple car trips, "seven or eight runs, the cars were full to the brim," hauling the books out of the park. Bergh and Wong took most of them back to the basement at Emmaus House, the collective space where they lived.

Wong estimates that they probably ended up with twelve to fifteen crates of books, to which Bergh added in a personal communication, "Our ability to store the books for over a year is because our house is part of a radical movement which is all about these types of projects." As previous protest library stories have underscored, the strong networking of like-minded, sympathetic communities—and the librarians and book lovers living there—consistently help these book collections find new spaces and homes.

During our conversation, Bergh acknowledged that his narrow, dedicated focus on saving the books—when so many other materials and supplies also needed rescuing—was perhaps a somewhat irrational response. But he is not alone in his response, and in the context of the power of protest libraries and material book collections, it feels quite reasonable. The BiblioSo. librarians also had to move their massive collection several times; at one point they were evicted from an illegal squat and the police prohibited them from reentering the building to claim their books. They wrote about this on their blog, and the trauma of their experience is clear: "They have taken away our books. About ten thousand. They are behind a wall, locked . . We feel powerless and defenseless against this system that criminalizes some squatters."[21] These anecdotes about the need people feel to save books is yet again demonstrative of the power of book collections. These books, the books at all the protest libraries, function as catalysts, and what Bergh and Wong rescued from Freedom Square would provide the seeds for the next phase. The more they could collect, the stronger the magnetic pull would be, and the faster the new assemblage might reach critical mass the next time. Bergh and Wong ended up storing the books for about a year before the next phase of the library could begin. From the perspective of the books, the story of Freedom Square is not a pessimistic narrative of "the end" of anything but rather a cyclical story that began in the streets with a book wagon, reinvented itself in Freedom Square as a library under a tent, and then would begin again in a new place they named the "Breathing Room."

As we have already seen, the hope of permanence when it comes to a protest library is rarely realized. If one considers the permanence of the *idea* of the library, though, it becomes easier to find threads of continuity. And to return to one of the original points about the importance of the physical books, we can even consider that wherever the books have gone, the library still exists.

THE BREATHING ROOM

The Breathing Room, the #LetUsBreathe Collective's new permanent, legal home, hosts monthly community events and meetings. Its website describes it as "a Black-led liberatory space that produces cultural events, builds coalition with the Chicago resistance community, and incubates programs that aim to force prisons and policing into obsolescence."[22] The library, which is on the second floor of the group's headquarters, began with about one thousand books that had been salvaged from the occupation.

The books are a bit more organized now, although the project of categorizing and shelving the books is ongoing. Kristiana Colón told me, "We've had waves of volunteers come through and say, 'I want to help with the library,' and it often would get started and then it would be incomplete, and then another wave of volunteers would start to come through and they would have a slightly different vision." At one point, volunteers from HERstory, a young women's mentorship program, "were very inspired by the space." They "came for a few weeks in a row to shelve and sort the books," says Colón.

> I think it was really serendipitous and important that ultimately it was young black women that saw the library project through to completion, and so their vision for how books should be sorted and categorized. So we had one wave of volunteers that came through and collapsed queer authors and authors of color, and those were previously separate categories. We were like, "Why would you do that?" Those are separate for a reason. Those are not the same thing. It's not just like "minority authors" because we are not viewing those categories as minor in this space. We are centering those writings and that knowledge in this space. Epistemology is so political. Who gets to decide what knowledge is valuable?

Williams adds: "There have been many valiant efforts. This is probably the fifth attempt."

When I asked the Freedom Square activists if they would include a library again at their next occupation now that they knew how much work it had been, Colón was fast to reply, "Oh, absolutely." She sees "the library as a structure of the occupation. It's a symbol of the things we think we should invest in instead of the police. What are the things that are actually beneficial to communities?" For Colón, the library falls under the umbrella of education, but often, she says, "when we talk about education, schools, what we mean is structure. Folks just having access to literature and to books, I think, sometimes is more useful than paying someone money for a piece of paper." That is, sometimes just giving a community access to information without the institutional structure, pedagogy, and ideology is not only *enough* but *better*. Free books as part of community engagement and direct action will always be important to the #LetUsBreathe Collective, and to the other collectives I have addressed here.

CHAPTER 14

CIRCLING BACK
BiblioSol Reinvented as Tres Peces Tres, Madrid

Chapter 1 began the story of BiblioSol in Madrid, the first protest library of its kind, as it emerged from the Indignados/15-M encampment in Acampada Sol. BiblioSol served as the primary inspiration for the Occupy Wall Street People's Library as well as many others around the world. While BiblioSol was chronologically the first library, its conclusion also foreshadows the last documented protest library. Through flexibility and reinvention, BiblioSol has persisted now for the better part of a decade since leaving its original physical space. By the time of its transition, BiblioSol had more in common with Chicago's 2016 Freedom Square library than with the People's Library, pointing again to the notion that collectives may provide solid homes for libraries transitioning out of temporary phases.

After vacating the Plaza del Sol with the rest of the Indignados in June 2011, BiblioSol along with several other working groups moved to CSO Casablanca, a "squatted social centre," with its four thousand books safely in tow. In Spain, the names of squats often include the phrase "Centro Social Okupado y Autogestionado."[1] As "Y" explains in an interview with *Mutiny Zine* discussing how some squatters view these spaces: "Most of the squatted social centres here have social projects. That's why they're called 'social centres' . . . 'Centro Social Okupado Autogestionado' represents key ideas for us. Firstly, 'okupado'—squatted, and everyone who comes here must know we squatted it, with all the political implications that involves. Also, 'autogestionado'—self-managed, meaning we don't do things hierarchically, we do things horizontally. And 'social' because we want to share it." Says an activist named Mario in the same article: "I recognise that in Spain we have an anarchist movement that is more or less solid. It is like a rock with cracks in it. We have serious internal problems. But we have a strong movement of squatting—above all in Barcelona, but also in Madrid. We also have a strong culture—of music, zines, books, information to share and relationships between areas that connect lots of different people. We have a web. It is weak, but it exists."[2] That BiblioSol was able to bounce around for as long as it did is therefore, not a surprise. It was able to tap into an existing network of relevant, like-minded existing communities.

The BiblioSol team worked for about five months, putting in countless hours of prepping the new library space and setting up the books. They muddled through building shelves for thousands of books. They issued calls for help with cataloging via their blog and through announcements on other sites: "To those of us who work at Bibliosol, thousands of uncataloged books cry out to us every day to recover their voices. The task of cataloging books is slow, arduous, and requires the help of a multitude of friendly hands. Therefore, we invite you to collaborate with us in the task of putting books in circulation. No doubt books will find, on their own, the way to return the favor."[3]

Their collection absorbed the books already in place at the squat, and on November 25, 2011, they announced their grand opening at Casablanca. Librarian Bárbara spoke on their opening night about the work they had put into building a permanent space for their collection. "I do not know about the rest of the members of the commission," she said, "but my back, every time I enter the library . . . screams at me in a loud voice . . . 'run while you can and do not stop until you are well hidden' because as soon as someone from the library sees me, they will plant a box of books in my arms and make me carry it from one place to another." The overall tone of her message was jovial, despite her professed aches and pains, and her words convey the deep affection she feels for the space, the books, and the people with whom she had worked so hard for so long. "I would really love to say that what has happened to us in these one hundred and eighty days surrounded by books, is that culture has entered through the pores of our skin and today because of this, we know more, we have more vocabulary, we are even better people."[4] The evening of festivities included presentations from a few of Acampada's other working groups and an overview of the library activities, as well as readings, music, and a performance by Proyecto Fahrenheit 451 (Las Personas Libro), a group inspired by characters in Ray Bradbury's novel *Fahrenheit 451* who preserve books through memorization.[5]

For the next several months, the blog was full of posts documenting the active library schedule. The organizers announced the days they would be open and asked for help with cataloging and staffing. They posted reviews of publishers and conferences, and they marketed their catalog in clever ways. For example, in December they promoted "El Libro E-léctrico" (The E-lectric Book) to highlight some of the "jewels" of their collection—while, in their typical irreverent style, adding that the books themselves are not "e-books," but they are "electric" because you can read them only as long as the power company has not turned off the electricity.[6] For about a year, BiblioSol was able to settle in, and the librarians began to feel as if they were working in a permanent space. For librarians like Zeke Ochoa, the identity of BiblioSol is embedded as much or more in their Casablanca iteration as in the Acampada Sol emergence. In fact, whenever we talk about the story of BiblioSol, he is careful to end on a Casablanca reference and not on the eviction from the square.

But *Libraries amid Protest* is not about long periods of tranquillity, so I will fast-forward this story to September 2012. On September 19, almost a year after BiblioSol left the Plaza del Sol, the Casablanca squat was raided by police and everyone was evicted from the building. The police raid caught the librarians off guard. While they did have an emergency plan, they did not have enough time to put it completely into motion. They were able to save only a limited number of books before they were removed from and locked out of the building. They had created a system of prioritization which privileged saving the signed and original works held in the collection. The librarians acknowledged that they hated having "to put an order of priority to literature, but we had to start somewhere . . . and the books dedicated by the authors were chosen." Author Eduardo Galeano had visited BiblioSol while it was in the plaza and had donated some autographed copies of his novels. These were among the two hundred texts that they were able to save before leaving the building. They wrote to Galeano publicly via social media to ask for help and wryly joked with him: "You have been lucky. This is not the case for Faulkner or James or Cortázar."[7] It took months, but eventually they were granted access to the Casablanca space, where they retrieved their property.

BiblioSol then moved, with many others from the Casablanca CSO, to CSO Raíces. In April 2013, CSO Raíces was evicted in another surprise raid. This time the librarians were able to remove their entire collection from the squat, but the question was where to go from there. Because of storage constraints, the boxes of books were split up, with half of the books going to CSOA La Quimera and the other half to CSO EKO, while the librarians again decided what to do. Another year passed. All this time the collection was stored in different locations and inaccessible to the BiblioSol librarians as they tried to envision, yet again, a future for the library.

Finally, three years after it began, in May 2014, BiblioSol successfully merged with several other activist organizations to form "Centro Social Tres Peces Tres." This was BiblioSol's fourth phase, one marked by a conclusion of sorts. The librarians experienced the initial, rapid physical emergence in Acampada Sol. They spent the second phase, the period of nomadism, prepping for and moving into Casablanca and then bouncing among different squats for years. During that time, they engaged in the third phase—discussing their future. Would they reinvent their library as a permanent space, or would the book collection be dismantled and redistributed? Finally, after considering various futures and seeking spaces and networks, they became part of a collective.

Tres Peces Tres legally operates out of donated storefront space and hosts community events and "any other activity that has no place in traditional venues." It features performers and artists, movies, political activity and discussion, and passionate talk about future plans. Several of the original librarians continued to volunteer their time here,

Figure 7. The Tres Peces Tres space, set up to screen Vera Chytilová's film *Daisies*. The library is on the wall to the right, and signage from the occupation is on the top shelf. Madrid, June 2015. Courtesy of Robert Wall.

alongside volunteers who began Archivo 15-M, the group that collected and preserved signage, posters, and other realia related to the Acampada Sol protests. The new collective also includes a small independent press and another library, La Biblio, which emerged over twenty years ago from the vibrant squat community in Madrid and contributed its collection of approximately five thousand books.

When I visited Tres Peces Tres, the mood felt optimistic and determined. The Biblioteca librarians were striving to maintain the "counter space" that their history was founded on. As a formal storefront, however, the new space had swapped barricades for floor plans, and the library had to share the finite space with other groups. The librarians now found themselves in a position of needing to make choices about the library's collection. In order to have room to show movies and host dance performances, the library was able to put up only a certain number of shelves, so they rotated the books in and out in an approach similar to that of BiblioDebout. When I visited, they told me there was no formal schedule. Sometimes when events were planned, they tried to make relevant books available. If a librarian had the inclination, he or she might decide to put out new books. Generally, they tried to keep things "fresh" for readers. Ochoa was happy to have a space where some of the books were finally back on shelves and available for people to read, and the rest of the collection had a safe place to wait for its turn in the rotation.

While I was there, Ochoa took me over to CSOA La Quimera to visit the diaspora of BiblioSol books. It turns out that when La Quimera received the boxes, rather than putting them into storage while BiblioSol figured out another plan, the librarians there unpacked them. Ochoa and I toured the two rooms that they had set aside inside their large building to house the books. One is dedicated primarily to children's books, and the other holds everything else. Both rooms are lined with shelves, and the different categories are clearly marked. The BiblioSol books were stamped with the name of the protest library and still carried the BiblioSol category markings on their spines. But in La Quimera, they had become intermingled with additional books that were already shelved there. When La Quimera put the BiblioSol books on the shelves, Ochoa realized that part of their collection was gone for good. The BiblioSol librarians lamented the loss, but he says they never tried to reclaim the books. Taking them back from a squat that was actively putting them to good use was not really in the spirit of the protest library.

When piles of books appear from within a political occupation or encampment, an event with a prefigurative orientation, this orientation tends to foster an openness toward the books, and this openness allows them to aggregate and reach a critical mass, crossing a threshold from a pile to a collection. This identity shift gives the collection greater value than the books had individually, though having been part of such a collection gives a permanent identity and increased value to an individual book even after it is separated from the collection.

The activists-turned-librarians, those people who are drawn to the books and who take on the persona of "librarian" regardless of any formal librarian experience, support the development of this unique identity for the library via social media voices. The librarians help to define and name the library, create systems of organization and lending rules, create stamps to mark the books, and collect equipment to store, display, and protect the volumes. The libraries rely on the librarians to help them become dedicated spaces within the camps for conversation and activities like poetry readings, music, and chess.

This emergence and identity-building takes place within a type of space distinct from the everyday social space in which we all live. Our social space is full of actions and interactions that are embedded in the economy and institutional power. Protest libraries exist in a space that is "other than" social space, what I have referred to in previous chapters as heterotopic, an "other place." It lets us move freely in an area grounded in community, in relationships of choice, and in a radical redistribution of power. It lets us slow down, it requires that we slow down, much to the annoyance of everyone moving at a fast pace in a non-heterotopic mode.

As we have seen across five years of their history, the internal lifecycle of protest libraries generally unfolds in three phases: their initial material emergence, a nomadic phase, and the "futures" phase. These phases do not always last for the same amount of time, and often the nomadic and futures phases last longer than the emergence of the physical library within the heterotopic space. Once the aggregation crosses the critical threshold into a library, it no longer necessarily needs its physical space or collection, although it usually continues to draw strength from these variables as long as they persist. Eventually, the library transitions into something else more permanent, such as a collection housed within a collective or a squat space, and at this point the nature of the protest library crosses a new threshold into something different. The protest library proper no longer exists. What we perceive as the end of this pattern, though, may be only an interruption. When we look for places where books are reclaiming space of their own, we may better see the evolution rather than the repetition of the pattern.

Despite so many similarities from one protest library to the next, the most definitive things we can say about them are that they are necessarily temporary and that they resist permanence through deterritorialization. Said another way, they embody resistance to becoming static, expected, or institutionalized. This is part of why protest libraries are so difficult to define. When I started researching protest libraries, I was tempted to see the OWS People's Library as a natural outcome—and possibly the natural conclusion—of the evolution of the US public library. But now I see that protest libraries are just one more temporary stop on the chaotic, nonlinear trajectory of the long-lasting concept of "library." Every time we try to pin the concept down with a definition based on even the most basic of assumptions, that libraries have books, we are immediately confronted with myriad exceptions, iterations, and evolutions. I have also come to realize that these libraries resist definition because they are meant to be used and inhabited rather than written about. Protest libraries are experiential.

BABEL CONVERGENCE

On a fall day in 2015, I found myself in Toronto hauling a box of books down Bloor Street toward the Centre for Medieval Studies. Bloor Street is a typical big-city street. Four lanes of traffic cross smaller one-way streets at hectic intersections. Pedestrians crowd the sidewalks going to and from hotels, museums, and restaurants at a rapid pace. This place is not designed for people moving slowly, and my box and I were annoying everyone who was forced to veer around me in order to keep up their own speed. As part of a book-themed conference, I had enthusiastically proposed building a pop-up library, an activity that requires being very fast with objects that are inherently slow. The gist of a pop-up library, which is more of an art installation than a "real" library, is to collect books, spread them out in some kind of accessible order for people to browse and take away, and then pack everything up, all in a short period of time. In many ways, it is created very much in the spirit of a protest library. This pop-up library complemented a formal conference panel about protest libraries. The installation would last from Friday night through Sunday morning, not even two full days. In addition to hundreds of random books, it would also include an exhibit of posters, photography, and signage from several recent occupations.

This particular box that I was hauling down the street was special: Zachary Loeb had donated some of the last remaining boxes of

Figure 8. Zachary Loeb, Martin Zeke Ochoa, and Jaime Taylor building the pop-up library at the Fourth Biennial Meeting of the Babel Working Group. Toronto, October 2015. Courtesy of the author.

books from the Occupy Wall Street protest library. For our conference pop-up library, we brought in around five hundred books, which I estimate probably weighed around 375 pounds, give or take a few pulled muscles. But the protest libraries discussed in *Libraries amid Protest* routinely aggregate several thousand books, sometimes up to five or six thousand at a time. I thought about what it must have been like to tend to such a large collection in a public park, engaged in what Jaime Taylor had described as "happy non-work work."[8] I imagined the physical labor involved in the hurried packing and hauling of the books each time, not because conference organizers needed to lock up and return the building key, but because security or police were forcibly evicting people from the park. These evictions happened more than once, usually without notice. And then to haul them all back the next day and reconstruct the boundaries of the library space, to try to put things back where they had been and to provide some consistency for the people who were actually using this library on a regular basis—I could feel after just a few boxes how tiring this would become.

Librarians from several protest libraries had agreed to participate on the panel and help build the pop-up library. Zeke Ochoa had flown in from Madrid to be with us and represent BiblioSol. Jaime Taylor and Zachary Loeb had flown from New York to represent the OWS People's Library. And on the opposite coast, Jamie Omar Yassin had caught a flight from Oakland to represent the Beeb. While they were familiar with one another, and one another's libraries, this Toronto conference was the first time they had met in person. Once they were together in the same room, they formed what looked to me like a protest library dream team. We all had a lot to talk about regarding politics, public space, and occupation. Our conversations throughout the weekend formed the basis for many of the common themes and patterns detailed in this book and underscored what I had noticed during my research into each individual library.

PUBLIC LIBRARIES

What are we to make of American public libraries after having spent so much time thinking about protest libraries? What of the critical voices we heard in chapter 2, claiming that the People's Library was not a "real" library? To these people, I would say that protest libraries are realer than real: they are the ideal toward which we should be striving. Public libraries exist within and because of social space and are complicit with a capitalist economy. Public libraries need even more inertia than protest libraries to embody change because they are heavily institutionalized. Public libraries also encourage a slowing down, but they demand a certain kind of productivity that belies the relaxed, reflective pace. Not so with protest libraries.

As public libraries are working harder and harder to demonstrate their value and to entice the public with more digital resources, maker spaces, social services, and corporate partnerships, they are losing hold of the physical book collections. Without the books to anchor and ground the space as one of reading and the circulation of ideas and creative energy, the public library is at risk of crossing a threshold into something else, something more like a community center. The risk is too great, as the collection becomes invisible, that slowly the space will slip into something else in such a quiet, invisible way that the public does not even notice.

Protest libraries have more freedom to reconfigure themselves and cross different thresholds into new phases than public libraries, institutionalized and territorialized, have. While the identity of a protest library can persist without the collection, public libraries do not have the same luxury. While digital resources are assets—and I do not mean to argue that we should not acquire them, particularly for the scholars and researchers among us—I believe that public libraries need to make sure they are always able to surround their patrons with physical books, even if the books are just placeholders for the "real" information to be found online.

Underneath all the talk about identity and community, under the heady vocabulary of prefiguration and heterotopic space, under the symbolic value of the books and the different political and cultural content that makes up "knowledge," underneath all of this is a base, gross, brute materiality that physical books can never leave behind. The gift of a physical book is in some ways an albatross, bringing with it the heaviness of financial and material responsibility. Unsolicited, uncurated book donations can sometimes cause problems for regular public libraries, where they are just as often rejected as accepted. Public libraries are constrained by space and have limited funding—not just funding to acquire new texts, but the funding needed for ongoing care and maintenance. As libraries across the United States are actively swapping out their physical book collections for digital texts, the depth of their resources is becoming invisible to the everyday library user. Not only do we lose sight of what is coming and going from the collection, but also we risk losing sight of all the other values that make physical books not more trouble than they are worth but *worth* more than their *trouble*.

THE END AND THE BEGINNING

These are the things I was thinking about as I balanced the box of People's Library books on my knee and waited for the light to change. The work of the conference pop-up library demanded the team's immediate attention. Donations had come from a variety of sources, and we wanted to assess what kinds of books we had in our collection. We also needed to find some makeshift shelving, give ourselves a name and create some signage so people would know we existed, figure out how best to display the photography exhibit of political protest libraries that the team represented, and get the book stamp set up. My body was still surprised at the demands made by the materiality of the project, reminding me that part of the protest libraries' power comes from being in the world with them. Visiting a protest library is about more than sitting down and plugging in. It necessitates a creative, sustained energy from everyone involved.

It is easy to situate protest libraries as just a blip within the much longer US-specific public library history or the much wider international library history. But the undercurrents reveal narratives embedded in intercultural and international commonality, the power of the book, and the emergence and perseverance of a new, hopeful community. For Americans struggling to understand some of the conflicts playing out nationally and confounded by our shifting role internationally, this may provide a welcome connection to the rest of the world.

We need both the institutionalized public library *and* the protest-turned-collective library, because they serve different communities. Or, rather, they serve one community from different perspectives. Wherever you see an occupation or encampment or the claiming of public space by a group of people speaking from outside the mainstream, look to see if a library is emerging. Spaces that let this potential develop are valuable, and something special is happening there.

NOTES

PREFACE AND ACKNOWLEDGMENTS

1. Dramatic may be an overstatement, but the index card did revolutionize cataloging capabilities. For an easy introduction, see Jonathan Schifman, "How the Humble Index Card Foresaw the Internet," *Popular Mechanics,* February 11, 2016, https://www.popularmechanics.com/culture/a19379/a-short-history-of-the-index-card/.

INTRODUCTION

1. The librarians documented well over nine thousand individual books as part of their catalog, which is preserved at http://www.librarything.com/catalog/OWS Library. Books were coming and going at a rapid pace, and librarians estimate that the library only ever contained around seven thousand at its peak.
2. See "Wrapping Up," *Occupy Wall Street Library,* blog, February 12, 2014, https://peopleslibrary.wordpress.com/2014/02/12/wrapping-up/.
3. The NYPL main branch library is located at Forty-second Street and Fifth Avenue. This is the flagship library building with an entrance flanked by two iconic stone lions, Patience and Fortitude. The main branch was renamed the Stephen A. Schwarzman Building after the benefactor's $100 million gift in 2008. The library is also sometimes called the Forty-second Street branch or the Fifth Avenue branch.

CHAPTER 1: ORIGINS

1. "¿Quiénes Somos?," *Sin Bibliotecas No Hay Paraíso,* blog, https://bibliosol.wordpress.com/quienes-somos/.
2. When talking about people volunteering in the library sites, I refer to them as "librarians" whether or not they have any formal library experience. When I mention someone regarding his or her work in the occupation or political movement, I refer to that person as an "activist" or "protester." For the most

part, I do not provide additional biographical information about the librarians and activists for two reasons. One, most of them resist being defined by their "jobs." Two, some of them are still actively resisting and living in precarious political situations. Although they have all granted permission for me to quote them and use their real names, it seems imprudent to provide any more identifying information than that.

3. Most activists decided together that the camp should be dismantled on June 12. A small group of dissenters chose to remain in Puerta del Sol, however, and the camp also left an information booth in the square that was occupied during the day. For a detailed account of these decisions, see activist Oscar ten Houton's blog entry, https://spanishrevolution11.wordpress.com/2011/06/08/the-end-of-the-beginning/.

4. Outsider libraries are those libraries that are not funded by tax dollars or private donations. They appear in unusual places and are not managed by professional librarians. An example of a different kind of outsider library is the Free Underpass Library, which I visited in 2015. It was managed by two amateur librarians with no fixed address who lived with the library under a highway in Toronto.

5. Franco was in power from 1939 to 1975. The Casa served a couple of different purposes during this time.

6. Almudena Escobar López, "Invisible Participation: The Hologram Protest in Spain," *Afterimage* 43, no. 4 (January 2016): 8–11, doi:10.1525/aft.2016.43.4.8.10.

7. Jeremy, "Conversations with Anarchists in Madrid," *Mutiny Zine,* January–February 2013, https://www.scribd.com/document/137032941/Mutiny-Zine-A-Paper-of-Anarchist-Ideas-and-Actions.

8. The term 15-M references the first day of the protests, May 15, 2011. The movement is also referred to as "Los Indignados," which means "the indignant," and refers to the people rather than the date. The terms can be used interchangeably.

9. "Spain's Unemployment Total Passes Five Million," BBC News, January 27, 2012, https://www.bbc.com/news/world-16754600.

10. The name Tres Peces Tres comes from their address, 3 Tres Peces Street. Their full name is Centro Social Autogestionado Tres Peces Tres, sometimes shortened to CSA 3P3.

11. The name is a play on the title of a 2006 Columbian telenovela *Sin Tetas No Hay Paraíso* (Without Boobs There Is No Paradise). An American version was produced by Telemundo in 2008.

12. See BiblioMedia: El Archivo Grafico de Imagen y Video de Bibliosol, https://bibliofotos.wordpress.com/.

13. "¿Quiénes Somos?"

14. "Acampada Sol: Literatura y Cultura," June 5, 2011, *El Planeta de los Libros,*

produced by Círculo de Bellas Artes de Madrid, podcast, MP3 audio, 54:59, http://www.elplanetadeloslibros.com/html/audio-205-acampada-sol.htm.
15. Oscar ten Houten, "Portrait of an Acampada," *Revolução*, blog, May 25, 2011, https://spanishrevolution11.wordpress.com/2011/05/25/portrait-of-an-acampadaada/.
16. Jon L. Peacock, "Beginnings," https://www.jonlpeacock.com/beginnings.html.
17. Zeynep Tufekci, *Twitter and Tear Gas: The Power and Fragility of Networked Protest* (New Haven: Yale University Press, 2018), 87, 90.
18. Jaime Taylor and Zachary Loeb, "Librarian Is My Occupation: A History of the People's Library of Occupy Wall Street," in *Informed Agitation: Library and Information Skills in Social Justice Movements and Beyond*, ed. Melissa Morrone (Sacramento: Library Juice Press, 2014), 273.
19. Bárbara, "Welcome to BiblioSol," *Sin Bibliotecas No Hay Paraíso*, blog, November 29, 2011, https://bibliosol.wordpress.com/2011/11/29/bienvenida-a-bibliosol/#more-501.
20. David Graeber, "La Nuit Debout against le Panama Partout," *Le Monde*, April 14, 2016, https://www.lemonde.fr/idees/article/2016/04/12/la-nuit-debout-against-le-panama-partout_4900825_3232.html.
21. For an extended discussion, see Marina Sitrin, ed., *Horizontalism: Voices of Popular Power in Argentina* (Oakland: AK Press, 2006)..
22. Jeremy, "Conversations with Anarchists in Madrid."
23. Taylor and Loeb, "Librarian Is My Occupation," 277.
24. Raphaëlle Bats and Marlou Pain, "Bibliodebout: A Collaborative Library in a Social Movement," Bobcatsss symposium, January 2017, Tampere, Finland, <hal-01496139>.
25. Kristiana Rae Colón (co-founder of the #LetUsBreathe Collective), in discussion with the author, September 7, 2018.

CHAPTER 2: MATERIALITY AND VIRTUALITY

1. When a man named Mohamed Bouazizi set himself on fire in a public square after ongoing harassment and humiliation from local officials, the wider Tunisian public responded passionately, ultimately forcing President Zine el-Abidine Ben Ali to resign. The umbrella movement known as the Arab Spring is generally understood to include not only these actions in Tunisia but also protests in several other countries, including Syria, Libya, Egypt, and Bahrain.
2. Manuel Castells. *Networks of Outrage and Hope: Social Movements in the Internet Age* (Malden, MA: Polity Press, 2015), 23, 60.
3. Mohamed Fadel Fahmy, "In Tahrir Square, a Tent City Blooms," CNN, July 14, 2011, https://www.cnn.com/2011/WORLD/meast/07/13/egypt.tahrir.color/index.html.
4. Anastasiia Makarenko, in discussion with the author, June 27, 2016.

5. Mandy Henk, "A People's Digital Library and Prefigurative Politics," *Occupy Wall Street Library*, blog, December 9, 2011, https://peopleslibrary.wordpress.com/2011/12/08/a-peoples-digital-library-and-prefigurative-politics-2/.
6. Cory Doctorow, "Microsoft Is About to Shut Off Its Ebook DRM Servers: 'The Books Will Stop Working,'" Boing Boing, June 28, 2019, https://boingboing.net/2019/06/28/jun-17-2004.html.
7. Writers of the 99%, *Occupying Wall Street: The inside Story of an Action That Changed America* (Chicago: Haymarket Books, 2012), 72.
8. See http://occupyarchive.org/ for more information about the archive group. Librarians and archivists frequently collaborate. For example, the collective that BiblioSol eventually joined included archivists from the Acampada Sol. But in the case of OWS, the archives were developed and managed by a separate working group. This book limits its scope to the library.
9. Jaime Taylor and Zachary Loeb, "Librarian Is My Occupation: A History of the People's Library of Occupy Wall Street," in *Informed Agitation: Library and Information Skills in Social Justice Movements and Beyond*, ed. Melissa Morrone (Sacramento: Library Juice Press, 2014), 271–88.
10. Lionel Maurel, "En Quoi la BiblioDebout Constitue-t-elle un Commun?" [In What Way Does BiblioDebout Constitute a Commons?], *S.I.Lex*, blog, May 14, 2016, https://scinfolex.com/2016/05/11/en-quoi-la-bibliodebout-constitue-t-elle-un-commun/.
11. Martin Ezequiel Ochoa, "Protest Libraries as Attractor Fields during a State of Exception," presentation at the Fourth Biennial Meeting of the BABEL Working Group, Toronto, October 11, 2015. See also my article "OWS People's Library and Jorge Luis Borges: Radical Politics, Heterotopic Spaces, and the Practice of Hope," *CTheory*, July 10, 2014, http://ctheory.net/ctheory_wp/ows-peoples-library-and-jorge-luis-borges-radical-politics-heterotopic-spaces-and-the-practice-of-hope/, for a similar discussion.
12. Jane Bennett, *Vibrant Matter: A Political Ecology of Things* (Durham: Duke University Press, 2010).
13. Mercedes del Valle, in conversation with the author, July 2015.
14. Del Valle, conversation with the author.
15. "Acampada Sol: Literatura y Cultura," June 5, 2011, *El Planeta de los Libros*, podcast, produced by Círculo de Bellas Artes de Madrid, MP3 audio, 54:59, http://www.elplanetadeloslibros.com/html/audio-205-acampada-sol.htm.
16. Martin Ezequiel Ochoa, in conversation with the author, July 2015.
17. Ochoa, discussion with the author.
18. Ochoa, discussion with the author.
19. Maurel, "En Quoi la BiblioDebout Constitue-t-elle un Commun?"
20. Makarenko, discussion with the author.
21. Maurel, "En Quoi la BiblioDebout Constitue-t-elle un Commun?"

22. Zachary Loeb, "Where Are They Now? The People's Library Today," *Librarian Shipwreck*, blog, March 19, 2015, https://librarianshipwreck.wordpress.com/2015/03/19/where-are-they-now-the-peoples-library-today/.
23. "¿Quiénes Somos?," *Sin Bibliotecas No Hay Paraíso*, blog, https://biblioso.wordpress.com/quienes-somos/.

CHAPTER 3: BEHAVIOR IN SPACE

1. Micah White, "Case Study: #OccupyWallStreet," original poster and email, https://www.micahmwhite.com/occupywallstreet/.
2. "'Occupy Wall Street' Library Shows Spine," *The Rachel Maddow Show*, MSNBC, November 15, 2011, http://www.msnbc.com/rachel-maddow-show/watch/occupy-wall-street-library-shows-spine-44136515904?v=railb&.
3. See Karen McVeigh, "Wall Street Protesters Divided over Occupy Movement's Demands," *The Guardian*, October 18, 2011, https://www.theguardian.com/world/2011/oct/19/occupy-wall-street-protesters-divided, for example.
4. David Graeber, *Direct Action: An Ethnography* (Oakland: AK Press, 2009), 210.
5. Zeynep Tufekci, *Twitter and Tear Gas: The Power and Fragility of Networked Protest* (New Haven: Yale University Press, 2018), 95–97. See also "Congressman John Lewis Denied Opportunity to Address 'Occupy Atlanta,'" *AFRO: The Black Media Authority*, October 14, 2011, https://www.afro.com/congressman-john-lewis-denied-opportunity-to-address-occupy-atlanta/; and John Walsh, "The Man Who Blocked John Lewis Speaks," October 13, 2011, *Salon*, https://www.salon.com/test/2011/10/13/the_man_who_blocked_john_lewis_speaks/.
6. "Updated Solidarity Letter from Acampada Sol Library," *Occupy Wall Street Library*, blog, October 19, 2011, https://peopleslibrary.wordpress.com/2011/10/19/updated-solidarity-letter-from-acampada-sol-library/.
7. Ishaan Tharoor, "From Chomsky to the Onion: What's on the Shelves at Occupy Wall Street's Library," *Time*, October 25, 2011, http://newsfeed.time.com/2011/10/25/from-chomsky-to-the-onion-whats-on-the-on-the-shelves-at-occupy-on-the-shelves-at-occupy-wall-streets-library/.
8. Betsy Fagin, Mandy Henk, Zachary Loeb, Daniel Norton, and Jaime Taylor, "People's Library Presentation at ALA Midwinter," *Occupy Wall Street Library*, blog, January 24, 2012, https://peopleslibrary.wordpress.com/2012/01/24/peoples-library-presentation-at-ala-midwinter/.
9. OWS Library catalog, LibraryThing, http://www.librarything.com/catalog/OWSLibrary.
10. Michael, "No Due Date Books of the People's Library," *Occupy Wall Street Library*, blog, March 11, 2015, https://peopleslibrary.wordpress.com/2015/03/11/no-due-date/.
11. Fagin et al., "People's Library Presentation."

12. Doug Singsen and Sarita Flores, "What Bloombergville Achieved," *Socialist Worker,* July 25, 2011, https://socialistworker.org/2011/07/25/what-bloombergville-achieved.
13. Matt Sledge, "Reawakening the Radical Imagination: The Origins of Occupy Wall Street," *Huffington Post,* January 23, 2014, https://www.huffpost.com/entry/occupy-wall-street-origins_n_1083977.
14. "NYCLU v. Giuliani: First Amendment Cases," New York Civil Liberties Union, October 1, 1999, https://www.nyclu.org/en/press-releases/nyclu-v-giuliani-first-amendment-cases.
15. John Sullivan, "Judge Strikes Down Rule Limiting City Hall Protests," *New York Times,* April 7, 2000, https://www.nytimes.com/2000/04/07/nyregion/judge-strikes-down-rule-limiting-city-hall-protests.html.
16. Jerold S. Kayden with the New York City Department of City Planning and the Municipal Art Society of New York, *Privately Owned Public Space: The New York City Experience* (New York: John Wiley & Sons, 2000), 11, 73.
17. Kayden, *Privately Owned Public Space,* 21.
18. S. J. Makielski Jr., *The Politics of Zoning: The New York Experience* (New York: Columbia University Press, 1966), 14, quoted in Kayden, *Privately Owned Public Space,* 7.
19. Kayden, *Privately Owned Public Space,* 11.
20. Kayden, *Privately Owned Public Space,* 11.
21. Kayden, *Privately Owned Public Space,* 16, 51–53.
22. Sam Roberts, "A Public Servant Whose Name Is Now on Protesters' Lips," *City Room,* blog, October 5, 2011, https://cityroom.blogs.nytimes.com/2011/10/05/zuccotti-by-roberts/.
23. Fagin et al., "People's Library Presentation."
24. "'Occupy Wall Street' Library Shows Spine."
25. Zachary Loeb, personal communication, August 12, 2018.
26. Jaime Taylor and Zachary Loeb, "Librarian Is My Occupation: A History of the People's Library of Occupy Wall Street," in *Informed Agitation: Library and Information Skills in Social Justice Movements and Beyond,* ed. Melissa Morrone (Sacramento: Library Juice Press, 2014), 278.
27. David Graeber, "La Nuit Debout against le Panama Partout," *Le Monde,* April 14, 2016, https://www.lemonde.fr/idees/article/2016/04/12/la-nuit-debout-against-le-panama-partout_4900825_3232.html.

CHAPTER 4: VISUAL SPECTACLE

1. Betsy Fagin, Mandy Henk, Zachary Loeb, Daniel Norton, and Jaime Taylor, "People's Library Presentation at ALA Midwinter," *Occupy Wall Street Library,* blog, January 24, 2012, https://peopleslibrary.wordpress.com/2012/01/24/peoples-library-presentation-at-ala-midwinter/.
2. William Scott, "The People's Library of Occupy Wall Street Lives On," *The*

Nation, November 22, 2011, https://www.thenation.com/article/peoples-library-occupy-wall-street-lives/.

3. "Statement of Mayor Bloomberg on Clearing and Re-Opening of Zuccotti Park," November 15, 2011, https://www1.nyc.gov/office-of-the-mayor/news/410-11/statement-mayor-michael-bloomberg-clearing-re-opening-zuccotti-park.
4. Christian Zabriskie, "A Library Occupies the Heart of the Occupy Movement," *American Libraries Magazine,* October 18, 2011, https://americanlibrariesmagazines.org/2011/10/18/a-library-occupies-the-heart-of-the-occupy-movement/.
5. "Opening Message from a BiblioSol Participant," *Sin Bibliotecas No Hay Paraíso,* blog, November 29, 2011, https://bibliosol.wordpress.com/page/15/.
6. New York City mayor's office, November 15, 2011, 12:43, https://twitter.com/NYCMayorsOffice/status/136544900815663106.
7. Fagin et al., "People's Library Presentation." Loeb later told me that at first the librarians thought "that they simply gave us back every book they had confiscated. But because of how we had cataloged and marked things we could tell that many of the books they gave to us weren't actually ours." Personal communication, August 12, 2018.
8. Michael, "UPDATE: State of Seized Library," *Occupy Wall Street Library,* blog, November 16, 2011, https://peopleslibrary.wordpress.com/2011/11/16/update-state-of-seized-library-items/.
9. The People's Library, November 16, 2011, 8:06, https://twitter.com/OWSLibrary/status/136837595459100672.
10. Tommy Ben Bergman (@TBApple), November 15, 2011, https://twitter.com/TBApple/status/136461042296438784; Glenn Rosado, November 17, 2011, https://twitter.com/GlennRosado/status/137223705049829376; Bill Buster (@wtb6chiny), November 16, 2011 https://twitter.com/wtb6chiny/status/136916773982310400.
11. Paul M. Davis, "Authors, Publishers, and Supporters React to the Seizure of the People's Library," *Shareable,* November 16, 2011, https://www.shareable.net/blog/authors-publisher-and-supporters-react-to-the-seizure-of-the-peoples-library.
12. OccupyElders, November 16, 2011, https://twitter.com/OccupyElders/status/136837430824280064.
13. "ALA Alarmed at Seizure of Occupy Wall Street Library, Loss of Irreplaceable Material," American Library Association, November 17, 2011, http://www http://www.ala.org/news/press-releases/2011/11/ala-alarmed-seizure-occupy-wall-street-library-loss-irreplaceable-material.
14. Karen McVeigh, "Destruction of Occupy Wall Street 'People's Library' Draws Ire," *The Guardian,* November 23, 2011, https://www.theguardian.com/world/blog/2011/nov/23/occupy-wall-street-peoples-library.
15. Tricia McKinney, "Update: The People's Library Not So 'Safely Stored,'" *The MaddowBlog,* MSNBC, November 16, 2011, http://www.msnbc.com/rachel-maddow-show/update-the-peoples-library-not-so-saf.
16. Keith Olbermann, "Occupy Wall Street Needs Michael Bloomberg," *Reader*

Supported News, November 17, 2011, https://readersupportednews.org/opinion2/275-42/8451-occupy-wall-street-needs-michael-bloomberg.

17. Feliz L. Molina, "Interview with OWS Poetry Anthology Editor Stephen Boyer," *Huffington Post*, April 4, 2012, https://www.huffpost.com/entry/interview-with-ows-poetry_b_1395555.
18. Scott, "The People's Library of Occupy Wall Street Lives On."
19. Molina, "Interview with OWS Poetry Anthology Editor."
20. Jaime Taylor and Zachary Loeb, "Librarian Is My Occupation: A History of the People's Library of Occupy Wall Street," in *Informed Agitation: Library and Information Skills in Social Justice Movements and Beyond*, ed. Melissa Morrone (Sacramento: Library Juice Press, 2014), 281.
21. Stephen Boyer, "People's Library in Action: Free Books!," *Occupy Wall Street Library*, blog, November 25, 2011, https://peopleslibrary.wordpress.com/2011/11/25/peoples-library-in-action-free-books/.
22. Hristovoynov, "Macy's at Midnight," *Occupy Wall Street Library*, blog, November 25, 2011, https://peopleslibrary.wordpress.com/2011/11/25/macys-at-midnight/.
23. Stephen Boyer, "Happy 2012: You Are Not Alone!!!," *Occupy Wall Street Library*, blog, January 2, 2012, https://peopleslibrary.wordpress.com/2012/01/02/happy-2012-you-are-not-alone/.
24. Taylor and Loeb, "Librarian Is My Occupation," 286, 287.
25. Alison Flood, "Occupy Movement Attracts Support of Top Authors," *The Guardian*, October 20, 2011, https://www.theguardian.com/books/2011/oct/20/occupy-movement-authors-atwood-rushdie.
26. Fagin et al., "People's Library Presentation."
27. Laurie Gries, *Still Life with Rhetoric: A New Materialist Approach for Visual Rhetorics* (Boulder: University Press of Colorado, 2015), 3, 16.
28. Steve Matthews, "Librarian or Radical Social Activist?," *21st Century Library Blog*, January 23, 2012, https://21stcenturylibrary.com/2012/01/23/librarian-or-radical-social-activist/.
29. Lionel Maurel, "En Quoi la BiblioDebout Constitue-t-elle un Commun?" [In What Way Does BiblioDebout Constitute a Commons?], *S.I.Lex*, blog, May 14, 2016, https://scinfolex.com/2016/05/11/en-quoi-la-bibliodebout-constitue-t-elle-un-commun/.
30. Matthews, "Librarian or Radical Social Activist?"
31. Dan Kleinman, "Occupied ALA Ignored Cuban Librarians; OWSLibrary Is Not a Real Library and People Knew It Would Be Removed," *SafeLibraries*, blog, November 17, 2011, http://safelibraries.blogspot.com/2011/11/occupied-ala-ignored-cuban-librarians.html.
32. "Library Lions Gala," New York Public Library, November 1, 2010, https://www.nypl.org/events/programs/2010/11/01/library-lions-gala.

CHAPTER 5: LIBRARY AS A DEMOCRATIC INSTITUTION

1. Sara @Likelydisaster, November 17, 2011, https://twitter.com/likelydisaster/status/137379680025190400.
2. Annoyed Librarian, "What Is an American Library?," *Library Journal*, blog, November 21, 2011, https://lj.libraryjournal.com/blogs/annoyedlibrarian/2011/11/21/what-is-an-american-library/ (no longer available).
3. Wayne A. Wiegand, *Part of Our Lives: A People's History of the American Public Library* (New York: Oxford University Press, 2015), 104.
4. "How Americans Value Public Libraries in Their Communities," Pew Research Center, December 11, 2013, http://libraries.pewinternet.org/2013/12/11/libraries-in-communities/.
5. See Wiegand, *Part of Our Lives*; Abigail Van Slyck, *Free to All: Carnegie Libraries and American Culture, 1890–1920* (Chicago: University of Chicago Press, 1995); Robert Dawson's *The Public Library* (2014), Frederick Lerner's *The Story of Libraries* (2009), and even, to some degree, Matthew Battles's *Library: An Unquiet History* (2015).
6. Note that this does not mean an increase in funding but rather a decrease in other sources of revenue.
7. Betsy Fagin, Mandy Henk, Zachary Loeb, Daniel Norton, and Jaime Taylor, "People's Library Presentation at ALA Midwinter," *Occupy Wall Street Library*, blog, January 24, 2012, https://peopleslibrary.wordpress.com/2012/01/24/peoples-library-presentation-at-ala-midwinter/.
8. John Chrastka and Erica Findley, "Breaking Records at the Polls: Budgets and Funding," *Library Journal*, February 20, 2018, https://www.libraryjournal.com/?detailStory=breaking-records-polls-budgets-funding.
9. Scott Sherman, "Upheaval at the New York Public Library," *The Nation*, November 30, 2011, https://www.thenation.com/article/upheaval-new-york-public-library/.
10. Annoyed Librarian, "The People's Library... Again," *Library Journal*, blog, March 28, 2012, https://lj.libraryjournal.com/blogs/annoyedlibrarian/2012/03/28/the-peoples-library-again (no longer available).
11. Scott Sherman, *Patience and Fortitude: Power, Real Estate, and the Fight to Save a Public Library* (Brooklyn: Melville House, 2017), 70.
12. The two properties proposed for sale in the CLP were the Mid-Manhattan Library and the Science, Industry, and Business Library. See Sherman, *Patience and Fortitude*.
13. Paul Goldberger, "The Surprising Controversy around the New York Public Library's $300 Million Remodeling Project," *Vanity Fair*, December 2012, https://www.vanityfair.com/culture/2012/12/new-york-public-library-re-model-controversy.
14. Sherman, *Patience and Fortitude*, 107; "Anthony W. Marx: Reconsider the $350 Million Plan to Remake NYC's Landmark Central Library," Change.org, March

2014, https://www.change.org/p/anthony-w-marx-reconsider-the-350-million-plan-to-remake-nyc-s-landmark-central-library.

15. "Occupy Wall Street Becomes Highly Collectible," Fox News, December 24, 2011, http://www.foxnews.com/us/2011/12/24/occupy-wall-street-becomes-highly-collectible.html. Additionally, the Tamiment Library and Robert F. Wagner Labor Archives at New York University also acquired a large portion of Occupy materials. To search Tamiment holdings, see https://specialcollections.library.nyu.edu.
16. Edmund Morris, "Sacking a Palace of Culture," *New York Times*, April 21, 2012, https://www.nytimes.com/2012/04/22/opinion/sunday/sacking-a-palace-of-culture.html.
17. "State of America's Libraries Report 2018," American Library Association, March 30, 2018, http://www.ala.org/news/state-americas-libraries-report-2018.
18. Nathan Schneider, "Occupy Wall Street Icons: Where Are They Now?," Al Jazeera America, September 17, 2013, http://america.aljazeera.com/multimedia/2013/9/ows-icons-where-aretheynow.html.
19. Sherman, "Upheaval at the New York Public Library."
20. Michael, "Irony of What Bloomberg's Done, Threw Out Fahrenheit 451," *Occupy Wall Street Library*, blog, November 18, 2011, https://peopleslibrary.wordpress.com/2011/11/18/irony-of-what-bloombergs-done-threw-out-fahrenheit-451/.
21. William Scott, "The People's Library of Occupy Wall Street Lives On," *The Nation*, November 22, 2011, https://www.thenation.com/article/peoples-library-occupy-wall-street-lives/.
22. Zachary Loeb, "OWS People's Library: Unseen Labor and Low-Tech Environments," presentation at the Fourth Biennial Meeting of the BABEL Working Group, Toronto, October 11, 2015). Loeb also mentioned the kitchens and medics as aspects remembered fondly.
23. For "punctum," see Roland Barthes and Richard Howard, *Camera Lucida: Reflections on Photography* (New York: Hill and Wang, 1981).

CHAPTER 6: CARNEGIE'S INFLUENCE

1. In March 2015 I visited 1449 Miller and the Biblioteca Popular. The city allowed me access to the interior of the building, and I spent several days in the outdoor Biblioteca space. Unless otherwise noted, descriptions and details about these spaces are my own based on that visit.
2. Charles Berkowitz, Sam Rolens, and Angela Hart, "A Look Back on Occupy Oakland a Year after the First Raid on the Camp," *Oakland North*, October 25, 2012, https://oaklandnorth.net/2012/10/25/a-look-back-on-occupy-oakland-a-year-after-the-first-raid-on-the-camp/.
3. Zachary Loeb, personal communication, August 11, 2018.
4. Berkowitz, Rolens, and Hart, "A Look Back."

5. "Man Fatally Shot Near Occupy Oakland Camp," CBS News, November 10, 2011, https://www.cbsnews.com/news/man-fatally-shot-near-occupy-oakland-camp/.
6. Jess Bidgood, Dan Frosch, and Malia Wollan, "Other Sites Hope N.Y. Raid Will Energize Cause," *New York Times*, November 16, 2011, https://www.nytimes.com/2011/11/15/us/other-occupy-sites-hope-ny-raid-energizes-movement.html.
7. Andre Damon, "Mayors Conspired to Close Occupy Wall Street Encampments," International Committee of the Fourth International, World Socialist Website, November 17, 2011, https://www.wsws.org/en/articles/2011/11/occu-n17.html.
8. Jaime Omar Yassin, "#Occupy Meets Community Organizing: Biblioteca Popular Victor Martinez," *North Star*, September 6, 2012, http://www.thenorthstar.info/?p=2255 (no longer available).
9. Daniel Brownstein, "More Better Mapping of Oakland's Population," *Musings on Maps*, blog, October 24, 2013, https://dabrownstein.wordpress.com/2013/10/24/more-better-mapping-of-oaklands-populations/.
10. Garrett Caples, "Turf's Up," *Bay Guardian* (San Francisco), September 12, 2006, https://48hills.org/sfbgarchive/2006/09/12/turfs/. Most references to "Murder Dubs" attribute the name to the generally high levels of violence in the area. Writer Garrett Caples claims in the *Bay Guardian* article that the area got this name "in the early '90s, when a neighborhood hustler named P-Dub began a lethal reign of terror in an effort to control the local drug trade. Naturally, this didn't endear him to the community, which locked its collective doors to him the night his number came up, leaving him to be gunned down in the street by pursuers circa 1994."
11. Yassin, "#Occupy Meets Community Organizing."
12. Jaime Omar Yassin, "Biblioteca Popular Victor Martinez Update: Occupy Tactics Meet Community Organizing," San Francisco Bay Area Independent Media Center, August 23, 2012, https://www.indybay.org/newsitems/2012/08/28/18720431.php.
13. Cheryl Knott, *Not Free, Not for All: Public Libraries in the Age of Jim Crow* (Amherst: University of Massachusetts Press, 2015), 40–56.
14. Knott, *Not Free, Not for All*, 50.
15. Abigail A. Van Slyck, *Free to All: Carnegie Libraries and American Culture, 1890–1920* (Chicago: University of Chicago Press, 1995), 124.124, 65, 101–2.
16. Van Slyck, *Free to All*, 42–43.
17. Andrew Carnegie, *The Gospel of Wealth, and Other Timely Essays* (Cambridge: Belknap Press of Harvard University Press, 1962), 27.
18. Van Slyck, *Free to All*, 109.
19. Van Slyck, *Free to All*, 21, 77.
20. Tim Kelley, "Landmark Nomination: Carnegie Branch Libraries of San Fran-

cisco," San Francisco Public Library, January 2001, https://sfpl.org/pdf/librar ies/main/about/carnegie_branch_libraries.pdf.
21. Charles A. Julian, "History of the OCPL," Ohio Country Public Library Lunch with Books Series, April 16, 2013, http://ww.ohiocountylibrary.org/uploads/wy _OCPLHistory-LWB-2013-04-16-PDFLibraryFile.pdf.
22. Nelson Lichtenstein, *The Most Dangerous Man in Detroit: Walter Reuther and the Fate of American Labor* (New York: Basic Books, 1995), 2.
23. Andrew Carnegie, *The Gospel of Wealth*, 15–19.
24. Knott, *Not Free, Not for All*, 47.
25. National Park Service, "California Carnegie Libraries," National Register of Historic Places Multiple Property Documentation Form, US Department of the Interior, 1990, https://npgallery.nps.gov/NRHP/GetAsset/a0edf010-9916 -4cb9-a4ff-59d0c7ab4fc1?branding=NRHP.
26. "History of the Oakland Public Library," Oakland Public Library, http://www .oaklandlibrary.org/about/history-oakland-public-library.
27. Abigail Ayres Van Slyck, "Free to All: Carnegie Libraries and the Transformation of American Culture, 1886–1917" (PhD diss., University of California, Berkeley, 1989), 204. Van Slyck's dissertation includes a much more detailed history of the Oakland library than is included in her book by the same title.
28. "Oakland Free Library 23rd Avenue Branch," National Register of Historic Places Registration Form, National Park Service, US Department of the Interior, 1996, https://npgallery.nps.gov/GetAsset/052c4920-a66a-4597-8b99 -23b4220b0dc1.
29. "Oakland Free Library 23rd Avenue Branch."
30. Van Slyck, *Free to All*, 207.
31. Henry Root, *Personal History and Reminiscences with Personal Opinions on Contemporary Events, 1845–1921* (San Francisco: Antique Reprints, 2016), 83–84, Kindle.
32. City of Oakland Public Works Call Center records from November 2007 through July 2013. Nine calls are logged. These are only building-related complaints. They do not include calls made to the police related to violent crime.

CHAPTER 7: LIBRARY AS SOCIAL SPACE

1. John Palfrey, *BiblioTech: Why Libraries Matter More Than Ever in the Age of Google* (New York: Basic Books, 2015), 2.
2. Agibail A. Van Slyck, *Free to All: Carnegie Libraries & American Culture, 1890–1920* (Chicago: University of Chicago Press, 1995), 77.
3. "Biblioteca Popular Victor Martinez," Facebook, https://www.facebook.com /Biblioteca-Popular-Victor-Martinez-406510572731289/.
4. Jaime Omar Yassin, in discussion with the author, February 2015.
5. Jaime Omar Yassin, "Biblioteca Popular and the Question of Simultaneous

Politicized Environment and Horizontal Leadership," presentation at the BABEL Working Group Biennial Meeting, Toronto, October 9–11, 2015.

6. "California Carnegie Libraries," National Register of Historic Places Multiple Property Documentation Form, National Park Service, US Department of the Interior, 1990, https://npgallery.nps.gov/NRHP/GetAsset/a0edf010-9916-4cb9-a4ff-59d0c7ab4fc1?branding=NRHP.

7. Kyung-Jin Lee, "The People's Library Continues Despite City Crackdown," KALW, September 5, 2012, http://cpa.ds.npr.org/kalw/audio/2013/07/WEB.PeoplesLibrary.mp3.

8. Sarah LeTrent, "Restaurants' Table Turnover Tricks Boost Business," CNN, April 30, 2010, http://www.cnn.com/2010/LIVING/04/30/noisy.restaurant.business/index.html.

9. "Library Rules and Policies," Houston Public Library, http://houstonlibrary.org/library-rules-policies.

10. "Houston Bans Offensive Odor in Libraries," Fox News, April 28, 2005, http://www.foxnews.com/story/2005/04/28/houston-bans-offensive-odor-in-libraries.html; Joe Stinebaker, "Library Looks to Ban Those Who Smell Bad," *Houston Chronicle*, April 26, 2005, http://www.chron.com/news/houston-texas/article/Library-looks-to-ban-those-who-smell-bad-1513431.php.

11. Jaime Taylor and Zachary Loeb, "Librarian Is My Occupation: A History of the People's Library of Occupy Wall Street," in *Informed Agitation: Library and Information Skills in Social Justice Movements and Beyond*, ed. Melissa Morrone (Sacramento: Library Juice Press, 2014).

12. David Graeber, "La Nuit Debout against le Panama Partout," *Le Monde*, April 14, 2016, https://www.lemonde.fr/idees/article/2016/04/12/la-nuit-debout-against-le-panama-partout_4910825_3232.html.

13. Guylaine Beaudry, "Academic Libraries, Digital Culture, Spaces, and Public Life," Around the World Library Conference, virtual conference, May 4, 2016, https://aroundtheworld.ualberta.ca/2016/05/around-the-world-2016-guylaine-beaudry/.

14. Tea Lobo, Facebook photo comment, August 3, 2011, https://www.facebook.com/photo.php?fbid=116876385068585&set=a.111337398955867.20696.100002388223395&type=3&theater.

15. Jaime Omar Yassin, "Engagement Not Displacement: A Story about Public Places," *Hyphenated-Republic*, blog, January 30, 2016, https://hyphenatedrepublic.wordpress.com/2016/01/30/engagement-not-displacement-a-story-about-public-places/.

16. Mark Jenkins, "D.C. Adds a Social Worker to Library System to Work with Homeless Patrons," *Washington Post*, August 27, 2014, https://www.washingtonpost.com/local/dc-adds-a-social-worker-to-library-system-to-work-with-homeless-patrons/2014/08/26/2d80200c-2c96-11e4-be9e-60cc44c01e7f_story.html.

17. "Library Outreach," Brooklyn Public Library, htttps://www.bklynlibrary.org/outreach.
18. "Extending Our Reach: Reducing Homelessness through Library Engagement," American Library Association, http://www.ala.org/aboutala/offices/extending-our-reach-reducing-homelessness-through-library-engagement.
19. Kristiana Rae Colón in discussion with the author, September 7, 2018.
20. Yassin, "Engagement Not Displacement."
21. Yassin, "Engagement Not Displacement."
22. "The Beeb is back, but it never left," Facebook post, February 12, 2017, https://www.facebook.com/permalink.php?story_fbid=1246270638755274&id=406510572731289; "The Beeb had a rough year in 2016." Facebook post, March 18, 2017, https://www.facebook.com/permalink.php?story_fbid=1277990108916660&id=406510572731289.
23. Kimberly Veklerov, "Oakland Fire Officials Upset over Blazes in City-Owned Building," *San Francisco Chronicle*, May 17, 2017, http://www.sfchronicle.com/bayarea/article/Oakland-fire-officials-fret-over-blazes-in-11154413.php.
24. Biblioteca Popular Victor Martinez, "Update on Biblioteca Popular," Facebook post, May 4, 2017, https://www.facebook.com/permalink.php?story_fbid=1332982356750768&id=406510572731289.
25. Kimberly Veklerov, Sophie Haigney, and Erin Allday, "Historic Oakland Building with History of Problems Destroyed by Fire," *SFGATE*, February 24, 2018, https://www.sfgate.com/bayarea/article/Large-fire-breaks-out-at-vacant-Oakland-library-12704478.php.
26. Aaron Davis and Angela Ruggiero, "Former Historic East Oakland Library Branch Burns Second Time in a Year," *San Jose Mercury News*, February 23, 2018, https://www.mercurynews.com/2018/02/23/fire-erupts-at-former-east-oakland-library-damaged-by-blaze-last-year/.

CHAPTER 8: BORDERS AND BARRICADES

1. Senem Sadri, "Oeuvre vs. Abstract Space: Appropriation of Gezi Park in Istanbul," *Contemporary Urban Affairs* 1 (2017): 5, https://doi.org/10.25034/1762.ijcua.3643.
2. Activists argued that that this underpass would not make any difference, and in fact would make the square more dangerous than it already was.
3. Leyla Önal, "Gezi Park and EuroMaidan: Social Movements at the Borders," *Innovation: The European Journal of Social Science Research* 29, no. 1 (2016): 21, https://doi.org/10.1080/13511610.2015.1089473.
4. "Erdoğan Vows to 'Rebuild' Ottoman Military Barracks in Istanbul's Gezi Park—Turkey News," *Hürriyet Daily News* (Istanbul), June 18, 2016, http://www.hurriyetdailynews.com/erdogan-vows-to-rebuild-ottoman-military-barracks-in-istanbul-gezi-park-100645.
5. Thomas de Monchaux, "The Mixed-Up Files of Taksim Square Architecture,"

The New Republic, June 10, 2013, https://newrepublic.com/article/113410/taksim-square-protests-over-new-building.
6. Sadri, "Oeuvre vs. Abstract Space," 3.
7. *Taksim Commune: Gezi Park and the Uprising in Turkey*, prod. and dir. Brandon Jourdan and Marianne Maeckelbergh August 5, 2013), video, 32:33, http://www.globaluprisings org/taksim.commune-gezi-park-and-the-uprising-in-turkey/.
8. Nick Ashdown, "Five Years after the Gezi Protests, the Legacy Lives On," *Los Angeles Review of Books*, blog, June 8, 2018, http://blog.lareviewofbooks.org/essays/five-years-gezi-protests-legacy-lives/.
9. Reuben Fischer-Baum, "Stop Calling Gezi Park a 'Small Green Space,'" *Gawker*, blog, June 6, 2013, http://gawker com/stop-calling-gezi-park-a-small-green-space-511660654.
10. Beiran Konte, "Court Decision Cancels Taksim Artillery Barracks Project That Triggered Gezi Protests," *Turkish Greek News*, March 7, 2013, https://www.turkishgreeknews.org/en/court-decision-cancels-taksim-artillery-barracks-project-triggered-gezi-protests/10273.html.
11. *Cennetin Düşüşü (The Fall of Heaven)*, dir. Ersin Kana (Pancard Film, 2014), video (in Turkish with English subtitles).
12. *Cennetin Düşüşü (The Fall of Heaven)*.
13. *Taksim Commune*.
14. *Taksim Commune*.
15. Mark Bergfeld, "Turkey's Ultras at the Forefront of Resistance," *GCC News*, Al Jazeera, December 16, 2014, https://www.aljazeera.com/indepth/opinion/2014/09/turkey-ultras-at-forefront-resi-201492310517225921.html. The entire team would eventually go on trial for plotting to overthrow the government.
16. Oscar ten Houten, "Historical Atlas of Gezi Park," *Revolução*, blog, June 27, 2013, https://postvirtual.wordpress.com/2013/06/27/historical-atlas-of-gezi-park/.
17. Zeynep Tufekci, *Twitter and Tear Gas: The Power and Fragility of Networked Protest* (New Haven: Yale University Press, 2018), 52.
18. "Publishing Houses to Unite in Gezi Park to Distribute Major Resistance Material: Books," *Hürriyet Daily News* (Istanbul), June 4, 2013, http://www.hurriyetdailynews.com/publishing-houses-to-unite-in-gezi-park-to-distribute-major-resistance-material-books-48234.
19. *Kütüphaneci—Bir Gezi Parkı Belgeseli* [Librarian: A Gezi Park Documentary], trans. Katherine Belliel (YouTube video, June 1, 2014), https://www.youtube.com/watch?v=oRdH8mxVQEw.
20. Jaime Taylor and Zachary Loeb, "Librarian Is My Occupation: A History of the People's Library of Occupy Wall Street," in *Informed Agitation: Library and Information Skills in Social Justice Movements and Beyond*, ed. Melissa Morrone (Sacramento: Library Juice Press, 2014), 20.
21. Jeffrey Wasserstrom, "Hong Kong Visions," *Los Angeles Review of Books*, November 21, 2014, https://lareviewofbooks.org/article/hong-kong-visions/.

22. Jaime Omar Yassin, "Engagement Not Displacement: A Story about Public Places," *Hyphenated-Republic*, blog, January 30, 2016, https://hyphenatedrepublicwordpress.com/2016/01/30/engagement-not-displacement-a-story-about-public-places/.
23. Yassin, "Engagement Not Displacement."
24. Rachel Swan, "Oakland Letting Activists Tend Land They Seized—For Now," *San Francisco Chronicle*, August 14, 2015, http://www.sfchronicle.com/bayarea/article/Oakland-letting-activists-tend-land-they-seized-6445558.php.
25. Oscar ten Houten, "No Pasaran," *Revolução*, blog, June 10, 2013, https://postvirtual.wordpress.com/2013/06/10/no-pasaran/.
26. Oscar ten Houten, "Community Occupation," *Revolução*, blog, June 22, 2013, https://postvirtual.wordpress.com/2013/06/22/community-occupation/.
27. Oscar ten Houten, *#OccupyGezi*, (Morrisville: Lulu Press, 2013), 59–60.
28. Hakim Bey, *TAZ: The Temporary Autonomous Zone: Ontological Anarchy, Poetic Terrorism* (Brooklyn: Autonomedia, 2003), 61.
29. "Kütüphaneci—Bir Gezi Parkı Belgeseli."

CHAPTER 9: ENGAGING IN NATION-BUILDING

1. Maria Haigh, "Escaping Lenin's Library: Library and Information Science Education in Independent Ukraine," *International Information and Library Review* 39, no. 2 (2007): 77, 73, https://doi.org/10.1016/j.iilr.2007.02.002.
2. Serhy Yekelchyk, "The Making of a 'Proletarian Capital': Patterns of Stalinist Social Policy in Kiev in the Mid-1930s," *Europe-Asia Studies* 50, no. 7 (1998): 1229, 1242.
3. Tetyana Ogarkova, "The Truth behind Ukraine's Language Policy," Kharkiv Human Rights Protection Group, March 13, 2018, http://khpg.org/en/index.php?id=1520890100.
4. See Karina V. Korostelina, "Ukraine Twenty Years after Independence: Concept Models of the Society," *Communist and Post-Communist Studies* 46, no. 1 (2013): 53–64, https://0-doi-org.library.svsu.edu/10.1016/j.postcomstud.2012.12.008.
5. Volodymyr Ishchenko, "The Ukrainian Left during and after the Maidan Protests," ResearchGate (2016): 12, 6, https://doi.org/10.13140/RG.2.2.23614.69447.
6. Leonid Peisakhin, "Answering Remaining Questions about Ukraine's Maidan Protests, One Year Later," *Washington Post*, February 25, 2015, https://www.washingtonpost.com/news/monkey-cage/wp/2015/02/25/answering-remaining-questions-about-ukraines-maidan-protests-one-year-later/.
7. "Khreshchatyk Included into List of Most Expensive Streets in the World," *MIG News* (Ukraine), June 15, 2010, http://mignews.com.ua/en_events/2785320.html.
8. "Khreshchatyk Rated among Europe's Top 20 Most Expensive Streets," *Kiev*

Weekly, July 1, 2011, http://kyivweekly.com.ua/accent/news/2011/07/01/163211.html.

9. Bohdan Kordan, "Maidan and the Politics of Change: Meaning, Significance, and Other Questions," *East/West: Journal of Ukrainian Studies* 3, no. 137 (2016): 139, https://doi.org/10.21226/T2001Q.
10. Others called for protests as well, but it is Nayyem who is consistently credited by name as the originator.
11. For example, as pointed out in the documentary *Winter on Fire*, although the opposition leader Vitali Klitschko, more famous at that point for his boxing career, was there and eventually tried to broker an agreement, he was far from "in charge." See *Winter on Fire: Ukraine's Fight for Freedom*, dir. Evgeny Afineevsky (Afineevsky-Tolmor Production, 2015), DVD.
12. Ishchenko, "The Ukrainian Left," 27, 7.
13. Ishchenko, "The Ukrainian Left," 6, 8.
14. *Winter on Fire*
15. Leonid Peisakhin, "Answering Remaining Questions about Ukraine's Maidan Protests, One Year Later," *Washington Post*, February 25, 2015, https://www.washingtonpost.com/news/monkey-cage/wp/2015/02/25/answering-remaining-questions-about-ukraines-maidan-protests-one-year-later/.
16. While the documentary was met with favorable reviews and is fascinating to watch, Netflix has been criticized for "whitewashing" the fascist leanings of some of the protesters out of the story. See Lev Golinkin, "The Heartbreaking Irony of 'Winter on Fire,'" *The Nation*, February 18, 2016, https://www.thenation.com/article/the-heartbreaking-irony-of-winter-on-fire/.
17. Roman Goncharenko, "Titushki—The Ukrainian President's Hired Strongmen," *Deutsche Welle*, February 19, 2014, https://www.dw.com/en/titushki-the-ukrainian-presidents-hired-strongmen/a-17443078.
18. Owen Hatherley, "Architects of Revolt: The Kiev Square That Sparked Ukraine's Insurrection," *The Guardian*, April 8, 2014, https://www.theguardian.com/cities/2014/apr/08/architects-revolt-kiev-maidan-square-ukraine-insurrection.
19. Paul Waldie, "The Globe in Kiev: Ukrainian Opposition Movement Has Its Own Library," *The Globe and Mail*, January 29, 2014, https://www.theglobeandmail.com/news//world/the-globe-in-kiev-ukranian-opposition-movement-has-its-own-library/article16599200/.
20. Nataliya Trach, "EuroMaidan Library Is Relief for Protesters," *Kyiv Post*, January 30, 2014, https://www.kyivpost.com/article/guide/about-kyiv/euromaidan-library-is-relief-for-protesters-335913.html.
21. Waldie, "The Globe in Kiev."
22. "Maidan Library," Facebook, www.facebook.com/MaidanLibrary/.
23. "Tension and Unrest in Ukraine: Statement by the Ukrainian Library

Association," International Federation of Library Associations, March 4, 2014, https://www.ifla.org/node/8422.
24. "Maidan Library."
25. Anastasiia Makarenko and Viktoriia Kolesnikova, in discussion with the author, June 27, 2016. Subsequent quotations from Makarenko and Kolesnikova in this chapter and the next are identified in the text.
26. Trach, "EuroMaidan Library Is Relief."
27. "Ukrainian House Occupied by Opposition in Kyiv," Interfax, January 26, 2014, http://www.interfax.com/newsinf.asp?id=475812.
28. "Tension and Unrest in Ukraine."
29. A small militia remained, but most protesters disbanded.
30. Eight if we include December, when police were occupying the space.
31. *Ukrainian House—Center of National Idea, the International Convention Center*, 2014, www.icc-kiev.gov.ua/en.

CHAPTER 10: A LIBRARY WITHOUT BOOKS

1. Alex Kleimenov, "Battle Rap Kiev," *Roads and Kingdoms,* August 31, 2015, https://roadsandkingdoms.com/2016/rap-battle-kiev/ ("reactor"); Keith Gessen, "The Orange and the Blue," *The New Yorker,* March, 2010, 30 ("Guggenheim"): Owen Hatherley, "Architects of Revolt: The Kiev Square That Sparked Ukraine's Insurrection," *The Guardian,* April 8, 2014, https://www.theguardian.com/cities/2014/apr/08/architects-revolt-kiev-maidan-square-ukraine-insurrection ("classical building").
2. Kleimenov, "Battle Rap Kiev."
3. Trevor J. Smith, "The Collapse of the Lenin Personality Cult in Soviet Russia, 1985–1995," *Historian* 60, no. 2 (Winter 1998): 325.
4. Smith, "The Collapse of the Lenin Personality Cult," 333.
5. *Lenin, Krupskaia and Libraries,* ed. Sylva Simsova, trans. G. Peacock and Lucy Prescott (London: Clive Bingley, 1968), 10.
6. *Lenin, Krupskaia and Libraries,* 20.
7. Maria Haigh, "Escaping Lenin's Library: Library and Information Science Education in Independent Ukraine," *International Information and Library Review* 39, no. 2 (2007): 73, 77, https://doi.org/10.1016/j.iilr.2007.02.002.
8. Susan Benz, "Ukrainian Libraries through the Eyes of an American Librarian," *International Leads: A Publication of the International Round Table of the American Library Association* 22, no. 2 (June 2008): 1, 7.
9. "Библиотеки вынуждены избавляться от книг. Как и почему это происходит" [Libraries Are Forced to Get Rid of Books. How and Why Does This Happen?], ОВД-Инфо [OVD-Info], May 31, 2017, https://ovdinfo.org

/articles/2017/05/31/biblioteki-vynuzhdeny-izbavlyatsya-ot-knig-kak-i-pochemu-eto-proishodit.

10. Damien Sharkov, "Head of Moscow's Ukrainian Library Arrested, Could Face Four Years in Prison," *Newsweek*, October 29, 2015, https://www.newsweek.com/head-moscows-ukrainian-library-arrested-could-face-four-years-prison-388507.
11. Alec Luhn, "Moscow Library of Ukrainian Literature Raided by 'Anti-Extremist' Police," *The Guardian*, November 3, 2015, https://www.theguardian.com/books/2015/nov/03/ukrainian-literature-library-moscow-raided-anti-extremist-police.
12. Howard Amos, "'We Are Worried about the Books': Kremlin Targets Moscow's Ukrainian Library," *International Business Times*, February 10, 2016, https://www.ibtimes.com/we-are-worried-about-books-kremlin-targets-moscows-ukrainian-library-2301219.
13. "The Power of the Russian State vs. a Librarian," *New York Times*, June 11, 2017, https://www.nytimes.com/2017/06/10/opinion/sunday/the-power-of-the-russian-state-vs-a-librarian.html.
14. Amos, "We Are Worried."
15. Ihor Vynokurov, "Academia Again Serves State Ideology as Russia Convicts Ukrainian Library Head," *Euromaidan Press: News and Views from Ukraine*, June 14, 2017, http://euromaidanpress.com/2017/06/14/academia-again-serves-state-ideology-as-russia-convicts-ukrainian-library-head-sharina/.
16. Sharkov, "Head of Moscow's Ukrainian Library Arrested."
17. "The Power of the Russian State vs. a Librarian."
18. Amos, "We Are Worried."
19. "Library of Ukrainian Literature Destroyed in Moscow," *Euromaidan Press: News and Views from Ukraine*, April 23, 2018, http://euromaidanpress.com/2018/04/23/library-of-ukrainian-literature-destroyed-in-moscow/.
20. "Украинцы России просят защитить Библиотеку украинской литературы" [Ukrainians of Russia Ask to Protect the Library of Ukrainian Literature], *Levyy Bereg* (Kiev), February 23, 2018, https://lb.ua/world/2018/02/23/391036_ukraintsi_rossii_prosyat_zashchitit.html.
21. "Library of Ukrainian Literature Destroyed."
22. Andrew Osborn, "Head of Moscow's Ukrainian Library Convicted of Incitement against Russians," *U.S. News and World Report*, June 5, 2017, https://www.usnews.com/news/world/articles/2017-06-05/head-of-russias-only-ukrainian-library-gets-suspended-jail-term.
23. Vynokurov, "Academia Again Serves State Ideology."
24. Haigh, "Escaping Lenin's Library," 75, 77.
25. Paul Waldie, "The Globe in Kiev: Ukrainian Opposition Movement Has Its Own Library," *The Globe and Mail*, January 29, 2014, https://www.theglobeandmail

.com/news/world/the-globe-in-kiev-ukrainian-opposition-movement-has-its-own-library/article16599200/.

CHAPTER 11: THE NEW SHAPE OF SPACE

1. The translation of Nuit Debout varies, including "We Stand through the Night," "Rise Up at Night," and "Standing Up All Night."
2. The "1" in French is pronounced *une*, forming a play on the French word *commune* (the commons).
3. Silvère Mercier and Lionel Maurel, "BiblioDebout: SavoirsCom1 Appelle à Créer une Bibliothèque Éphémère sur la Place de la République!" [BiblioDebout: SavoirsCom1 Calls for Creating an Ephemeral Library on the Place de la République!], SavoirsCom1, April 5, 2016, http://www.saviorscom1.info/2016/04/savoirscom1-appelle-a-creer-une-bibliotheque-ephemere-sur-la-place-de-la-republique-bibliodebout/.
4. "Nuit Debout," Facebook event, March 31, 2016, https://www.facebook.com/events/573412422835483/.
5. Alix Mugnier, "Labour Law Reform in France," Mondaq.com (UK), October 27, 2016, https://o-infoweb-newsbank-com.library.svsu.edu/apps/news/document-view?p=AWNB&docref=news/16049BCEE2613178.
6. Guy Jackson, "French Minister Defends Contested Labour Reform," Agence France-Presse, May 3, 2016, https://www.yahoo.com/news/french-minister-defends-contested-labour-reform-163236227.html.
7. Sophie Béroud, "French Trade Unions and the Mobilisation against the El Khomri Law in 2016: A Reconfiguration of Strategies and Alliances," *Transfer: European Review of Labour and Research* 24, no. 2 (May 2018): 182.
8. David Graeber, "La Nuit Debout against le Panama Partout," *Le Monde*, April 14, 2016, https://www.lemonde.fr/idees/article/2016/04/12/la-nuit-debout-against-le-panama-partout_4900825_3232.html.
9. Ari Davis, "Could the #NuitDebout Movement Become France's Indignados?," France 24, April 3, 2016, https://www.france24.com/en/20160403-can-nuitdebout-movement-become-france-indignados.
10. Louise Nordstrom, "In Numbers: Behind France's Two-Year State of Emergency," France 24, October 31, 2017, https://www.france24.com/en/20171031-france-anti-terror-law-numbers-record-long-state-emergency-macron-civil-liberties.
11. "Paris Attacks: Bataclan and Other Assaults Leave Many Dead," BBC News, November 14, 2015, https://www.bbc.com/news/world-europe-34814203.
12. "Hollande Says Paris Attacks an 'Act of War' by Islamic State Group," France 24, November 14, 2015, http://www.france24.com/en/20151114-paris-attacks-president-hollande-act-war-islamic-state-group-terrorism-france.

13. "What Does a 'State of Emergency' Mean in France?," France 24, November 15, 2015, http://www.france24.com/en/20151115-what-does-france-state-emergency-mean.
14. Nicholas Vinocur, "Emmanuel Macron's Long War," Politico, October 3, 2017, https://www.politico.eu/article/macron-terrorism-borders-long-war/.
15. "French Parliament Votes to Extend State of Emergency until after 2017 Elections," Agence France-Presse, The Guardian, December 13, 2016, https://www.theguardian.com/world/2016/dec/14/french-parliament-votes-to-extend-state-of-emergency-until-after-2017-elections; Nordstrom, "In Numbers."
16. Samuel Osborne, "France Declares End to State of Emergency Almost Two Years after Paris Terror Attacks," Independent, October 31, 2017, https://www.independent.co.uk/news/world/europe/france-state-of-emergency-end-of-terror-attacks-end-terror-attacks-paris-isis-terrorism-alerts-warning-risk-reduced-a8029311.html.
17. "Projet de Loi," Assemblée Nationale, October 11, 2017, http://www2.assemblee-nationale.fr/documents/notice/15/ta/ta0025/(index)/ta.
18. Vinocur, "Emmanuel Macron's Long War."
19. "France: Don't 'Normalize' Emergency Powers," Human Rights Watch, June 27, 2017, https://www.hrw.org/news/2017/06/27/france-dont-normalize-emergency-pofrance-dont-normalize-emergency-powers.
20. William Scott, "The People's Library of Occupy Wall Street Lives On," The Nation, November 22, 2011, https://www.thenation.com/article/peoples-library-occupy-wall-street-lives/.
21. "*People v. Nunez* (Challenging Trespassing Arrests of Occupy Wall Street Protesters at Zuccotti Park)," trial judge's order, ACLU of New York (2012), para. 22, https://www.nyclu.org/sites/default/files/Order.pdf.
22. Jerold S. Kayden with New York City Department of City Planning, and the Municipal Art Society of New York, *Privately Owned Public Space: The New York City Experience* (New York: John Wiley & Sons, 2000), 21.
23. "*People v. Nunez*," para. 9.
24. Cao Hao, "A Noneventful Social Movement: The Occupy Wall Street Movement's Struggle over Privately Owned Public Space," *International Journal of Communication* 11 (January 2017): 3176.
25. "Anti-Protest Bills around the Country," ACLU, June 23, 2017, https://www.aclu.org/issues/free-speech/rights-protesters/anti-protest-bills-around-country.
26. "House Bill 176," South Dakota legislature, February 3, 2017, http://sdlegislature.gov/docs/legsession/2017/Bills/SB176ENR.pdf.
27. Tim Goodwin, "SD District 30 Rep. Tim Goodwin against SB176—The Creation of Public Safety Zones," *Custer (SD) Free Press*, March 6, 2017, https://custerfreepress.com/2017/03/05/sd-district-30-rep-tim-goodwin-against-sb176-the-creation-of-public-safety-zones/.

28. Lacey Louwagie, "SD Passes Law to Crack Down on Pipeline Protests," Courthouse News Service, March 14, 2017, https://www.courthousenews.com/s-d-passes-law-crack-protests/.
29. Goodwin, "SD District 30 Rep. Tim Goodwin against SB176."
30. Mitra Ebadolahi, "The Border Patrol Was Monstrous under Obama. Imagine How Bad It Is under Trump," ACLU, May 23, 2018, https://www.aclu.org/blog/immigrants-rights/ice-and-border-patrol-abuses/border-patrol-was-monstrous-under-obama-imagine.
31. Franklin Foer, "How Trump Radicalized ICE," *The Atlantic*, September 2018, https://www.theatlantic.com/magazine/archive/2018/09/trump-ice/565772/.
32. Jonathan Blitzer, "The Government Has No Plan for Reuniting the Immigrant Families It Is Tearing Apart," *The New Yorker*, June 18, 2018, https://www.newyorker.com/news/news-desk/the-government-has-no-plan-for-reuniting-the-immigrant-families-it-is-tearing-apart.
33. Occupy ICE, https://occupyice.org/ (no longer available).
34. Jason Wilson, "'Occupy Ice': Activists Blockade Portland Building over Family Separations," *The Guardian*, June 20, 2018, https://www.theguardian.com/us-news/2018/jun/20/occupy-ice-portland-protest-immigration-family-separations.
35. Lukas Mikelionis, "Portland, Ore., to Clean Up 'Disgusting' Occupy ICE Camp, Calling It Biohazard," Fox News, July 26, 2018, http://www.foxnews.com/politics/2018/07/26/portland-to-clean-up-disgusting-up-disgusting-occupy-ice-camp-calling-it-biohazard.html.
36. "OccupyICE Portland," Facebook, https://www.facebook.com/AbolishICEPortland/.
37. "Democrasy [sic] on Trial in Turkey," Türkiye Devrimci İşçi Sendikaları Konfederasyonu [The Confederation of Progressive Trade Unions of Turkey], February 19, 2015, http://disk.org.tr/2015/02/democrasy-on-trial-in-turkey/.
38. Wendy Zeldin, "Turkey: Recent Developments in National and Public Security Law," Global Legal Research Center, Law Library of Congress, November, 2015, https://www.loc.gov/law/help/national-security-law/turkey-recent-developments-2015.pdf.
39. Ayla Jean Yackley, "Turks Mark May Day Far from Traditional Rallying Site," *Al-Monitor*, May 1, 2018, http://www.al-monitor.com/pulse/originals/2018/05/turkish-workers-rally-may-day-arrests.html#ixzz5OBlsonHn.
40. Carlotta Gall, "In Istanbul, Erdogan Remakes Taksim Square, a Symbol of Secular Turkey," *New York Times*, March 22, 2019, https://www.nytimes.com/2019/03/22/world/europe/in-istanbul-erdogan-remakes-taksim-square-a-symbol-of-secular-turkey.html.
41. Almudena Escobar López, "Invisible Participation: The Hologram Protest in Spain," *Afterimage* 43, no. 4 (January 2016): 8, 9, https://doi.org/10.1525/aft.2016.43.4.8.10.
42. Óscar López-Fonseca, "Government Plans to Repeal Core of Spain's 'Gag

Law' Before Year's End," *El País*, June 25, 2018, https://elpais.com/elpais/2018/06/25/inenglish/1529918352_148656.html.
43. Graeber, "La Nuit Debout against le Panama Partout."
44. Mercier and Maurel, "BiblioDebout."
45. For remarks from Claire Richard's blog, see "BiblioDebout: Ce Qu'on Apprend en Tenant une Bibliothèque Éphémère" [What One Learns by Building an Ephemeral Library], *L'Obs*, Groupe Nouvel Observateur, April 12, 2016, https://www.nouvelobs.com/rue89/rue89-rue89-culture/20160412.RUE2659/bibliodebout-ce-qu-on-apprend-en-tenant-une-bibliotheque-ephemere.html.
46. The Googledoc spreadsheet was still accessible as of November 2019 at https//:docs.google.com/spreadsheets/d/19FIpILy2Ge_mvzek-NhtmOtait3ki5LGwYHgq6qqNQ/edit. A Dropbox folder with some of the BiblioDebout digital texts was also still accessible as of November 2019 at https://www.dropbox.com/sh/ige7s3fh2fq6czo/AAAXyF36UPwp6xE6XPmgoOx9a?dl=0.

CHAPTER 12: PHASES OF THE PROTEST LIBRARY

1. Robert Shaw, "Pushed to the Margins of the City: The Urban Night as a Timespace of Protest at Nuit Debout, Paris," *Political Geography* 59 (2017): 117, 120, 121.
2. Bill Livsey, "Occupy Tampa Continually Occupies!," *Occupy Wall Street Library*, blog, December 3, 2011, https://peopleslibrary.wordpress.com/2011/12/03/occupy-tampa-continually-occupies-by-bill-livsey/.
3. Bill Livsey, "Thanksgiving at Occupy Tampa," *Occupy Wall Street Library*, blog, November 27, 2011, https://peopleslibrary.wordpress.com/2011/11/27/thanksgiving-at-occupy-tampa-by-bill-livsey/.
4. Jaime Taylor and Zachary Loeb, "Librarian Is My Occupation: A History of the People's Library of Occupy Wall Street," in *Informed Agitation: Library and Information Skills in Social Justice Movements and Beyond*, ed. Melissa Morrone (Sacramento: Library Juice Press, 2014), 286.
5. David Graeber, "La Nuit Debout against le Panama Partout," *Le Monde*, April 14, 2016, https://www.lemonde.fr/idees/article/2016/04/12/la-nuit-debout-against-le-panama-partout_4910825_3232.html.
6. Ari Davis, "Could the #NuitDebout Movement Become France's Indignados?," France 24, April 3, 2016, https://www.france24.com/en/20160403-can-nuitdebout-movement-become-france-indignados.
7. Raphaëlle Bats and Marilou Pain, "Bibliodebout: A Collaborative Library in a Social Movement," *Bobcatsss* (January 2017), Tampere, Finland, <hal-01496139>.
8. Bats and Pain, "Bibliodebout."
9. Bats and Pain, "Bibliodebout."
10. Bats and Pain, "Bibliodebout."
11. Lionel Maurel, "En Quoi la BiblioDebout Constitue-t-elle un Commun?"

[In What Way Does BiblioDebout Constitute a Commons?], *S.I.Lex*, blog, May 14, 2016, https://scinfolex.com/2016/05/11/en-quoi-la-bibliodebout-constitue-t-elle-un-commun/.
12. Bats and Pain, "Bibliodebout."
13. "À Lyon, une BiblioDebout Interdite par la Police" [In Lyon, a BiblioDebout Prohibited by Police], *BiblioDebout,* blog, June 15, 2016, http://biblio-debout.org/index.php/2016/06/15/a-lyon-une-bibliodebout-interdite-par-la-police/.
14. "Part Two: What Is Acampada Sol?," Counter-Cartographies Collective, June 1, 2011, https://www.countercartographies.org/part-2-what-is-acampada-sol/.
15. "PirateBox FAQ," PirateBox, February 21, 2018, https://piratebox.cc/faq.
16. Elsa Ferreira, "Nuit Debout: Preparing for Maker Night," *Makery: Media for Labs,* April 19, 2016, http://www.makery.info/en/2016/04/19/nuit-debout-preparer-la-nuit-makeuse/.
17. LibraryBox is one such example. See http://librarybox.us/.
18. Ferreira, "Nuit Debout."
19. Bats and Pain, "Bibliodebout."

CHAPTER 13: REINVENTION AS COLLECTIVE

1. Tanya Basu, "Behind 'the Disappeared' of Chicago's Homan Square," *The Atlantic,* February 24, 2015, https://www.theatlantic.com/national/archive/2015/02/behind-the-disappeared-of-chicagos-homan-square/385964/.
2. Rich Juzwiak and Aleksander Chan, "Unarmed People of Color Killed by Police, 1999–2014," *Gawker,* blog, December 8, 2014, http://gawker.com/unarmed-people-of-color-killed-by-police-1999-2014-1666672349.
3. Cassandra Chaney and Dannielle Joy Davis, "Introduction: 'No Justice, No Peace': Social Unrest in Ferguson," *Western Journal of Black Studies* 39, no. 4 (Winter 2015): 267–71.
4. "Our Story," #LetUsBreathe Collective, https://www.letusbreathecollective.com/history.
5. "Community Interview: Emmaus House, Chicago USA," *Back Again Cait,* blog, April 9, 2018, https://backagaincait.com/emmaus-house-interview/.
6. One could argue that at its heart, all the inequities of Occupy can be traced back to America's foundation based on slavery. #LetUsBreathe is the first movement addressed in this book that brings these issues to the forefront in this way.
7. "Our Story."
8. Frank Bergh, in discussion with the author, September 7, 2018; Lydia Wong, in discussion with the author, September 7, 2018. All further quotations from Bergh and Wong are from these discussions.
9. Spencer Ackerman and Zach Stafford, "Chicago Police Detained Thousands

of Black Americans at Interrogation Facility," *The Guardian*, August 5, 2015, https://www.theguardian.com/us-news/2015/aug/05/homan-square-chicago-thousands-detained.

10. Spencer Ackerman, "Homan Square Revealed: How Chicago Police 'Disappeared' 7,000 People," *The Guardian*, October 19, 2015, https://www.theguardian.com/us-news/2015/oct/19/homan-square-chicago-police-disappeared-thousands.

11. Spencer Ackerman, "Chicago Police Commander Resigns in Wake of Homan Square Revelations," *The Guardian*, March 19, 2015, https://www.theguardian.com/us-news/2015/mar/15/senior-chicago-police-commander-resigns-homan-square.

12. Kristiana Rae Colón, "At Freedom Square, the Revolution Lives in Brave Relationships," *Truthout*, August 7, 2016, https://truthout.org/articles/at-freedom-square-the-revolution-lives-in-brave-relationships/.

13. Derrick Clifton, "How Protests in Ferguson Inspired the Occupation of 'Freedom Square,'" *Chicago Reader*, August 9, 2016, https://www.chicagoreader.com/chicago/freedom-square-homan-square-occupation-ferguson/Conent?oid=23089791.

14. Clifton, "How Protests in Ferguson."

15. Damon Williams, in discussion with the author, September 7, 2018. All further quotations from Williams are from this discussion.

16. "Imagining a World," #LetUsBreathe Collective, https://www.letusbreathecollective.com/freedomsquare.

17. "About Haymarket Books," Haymarket Books, https://www.haymarketbooks.org/pg/about.

18. Kristiana Rae Colón in discussion with the author, September 7, 2018. All further quotations from Colón are from this discussion.

19. I refer to the Freedom Square organizers and activists as librarians in order to remain consistent with the book's naming conventions and because in the context of this volume it is a compliment, an honorific. I do acknowledge, however, the problem with giving people a name that they do not necessarily take themselves.

20. "Imagining a World."

21. "#Carta a @EduardoGaleano de @SolBiblio: Nos Han Quitado los Libros" [#Letter to @EduardoGaleano from BiblioSol: They Have Taken the Books from Us], *Sin Bibliotecas No Hay Paraíso*, blog, September 25, 2012, https://bibliosol.wordpress.com/2012/09/25/carta-a-eduardogaleano-de-solbiblio-nos-han-quitado-los-libros/.

22. "The #BreathingRoom Space," #LetUsBreathe Collective, https://www.letusbreathecollective.com/what-is-breathing-room.

CHAPTER 14: CIRCLING BACK

1. "Centro Social Okupado y Autogestionado" is shortened to CSOA, and sometimes the "Autogestionado" is dropped and only CSO is used. Both CSOA and CSO generally signify the same type of squat space in Spain.
2. Jeremy, "Conversations with Anarchists in Madrid," *Mutiny Zine*, January–February 2013, https://www.scribd.com/document/137032941/Mutiny-Zine-A-Paper-of-Anarchist-Ideas-and-Actions.
3. "Opening Message from a Bibliosol Participant," *Sin Bibliotecas No Hay Paraíso*, blog, November 29, 2011, https://bibliosol.wordpress.com/2011/1/29/mensaje mensaje-de-inauguracion-de-un-participante-de-bibliosol/
4. "Welcome to BiblioSol," *Sin Bibliotecas No Hay Paraíso*, blog, November 29, 2011, https://bibliosol.wordpress.com/2011/11/29/bienvenida-a-bibliosol/#more-501.
5. See https://personaslibro.wordpress.com/ for more information about Proyecto Fahrenheit 451 (Las Personas Libro).
6. "El Libro E-léctrico II" [The E-lectric Book, II], *Sin Bibliotecas No Hay Paraíso*, blog, December 16, 2011, https://bibliosol.wordpress.com/2011/12/16/el-libro-e-lectrico-ii/.
7. "#Carta a @EduardoGaleano de @SolBiblio: Nos Han Quitado los Libros" [#Letter to @EduardoGaleano from BiblioSol: They Have Taken the Books from Us], *Sin Bibliotecas No Hay Paraíso*, blog, September 25, 2012, https://bibliosol.wordpress.com/2012/09/25/carta-a-eduardogaleano-de-solbiblio-nos-han-quitado-los-libros/.
8. Jaime Taylor, email message to author, March 11, 2014.

INDEX

Page references in *italics* refer to figures.

Acampada Sol: dismantling of, 16, 38–39, 200n3; Indignados and occupation inception, 15, 18–19, 22; as Occupy Wall Street inspiration, 42. *See also* BiblioSol
Ackerman, Spencer, 175
ACLU (American Civil Liberties Union), 153
Adams, Sam, 83
Adbusters, call for Occupy Wall Street, 41, 46
African Americans: Freedom Square library collection about, 177–79, 181; Occupy inequities and slavery, 222n6; prefigurative politics and, 25; unarmed victims of police, 172–76. *See also* Freedom Square library
AKP (Justice and Development Party, Turkey), 108
Al Jazeera America, on Occupy Wall Street, 72
American Library Association: "Extending Our Reach: Reducing Homelessness through Library Engagement," 99; on funding of libraries, 67–68; on People's Library destruction, 58, 62–64; "The State of American Libraries," 71
American Library Magazine, on spread of Occupy libraries, 55–56
Amos, Howard, 140
anarchism: horizontalism and, 24, 42, 100; prefigurative politics and, 24; squatting and, 186–89, 224n1; temporary autonomous zone (TAZ) and, 115–16; terminology of, 25
Annoyed Librarian (blogger), 65–66, 68
Arab Spring, 28–30, 124, 201n1
Archivo 15-M, 191
Argentina, prefigurative politics of, 24
Arias Navarro, Carlos ("Butcher of Málaga"), 17
Arkin, Ozelm, 107
Atalay, Cam, 107
Atwood, Margaret, 61

Babel Working Group pop-up library, 193–95, *194,* 197–98
Bald Eagle, Remi, 153–54
Bárbara (BiblioSol librarian), 23, 187
Bataclan concert hall, attack on, 150–51
Bats, Raphaëlle, 163–65, 169–72
BBC, on Paris terrorist attacks, 150–51
Beaudry, Guylaine, 97
Beeb. *See* Biblioteca Popular Victor Martinez
behavior in space, 40–53; government response to protests and new shape of space, 149–57; Occupy Wall Street inception and, 40–42; overview, 7; People's Library inception and, 43–46, *44;* public space vs. public property, 48. *See also* borders and barricades; library as social space; People's Library

225

Ben Ali, Zine el-Abidine, 201n1
Bennett, Jane, 33
Bergfeld, Mark, 108
Bergh, Frank, 175, 181, 182–83
Béroud, Sophie, 150
Bey, Hakim, 115–16
BiblioDebout (Nuit Debout, Paris), 147–60, 161–71; as "biblioguerrilla," 158; books donated to, 38; cataloging by, 158–60, 221n46; government policy change on protests and, 147, 152–57; libraries and social protest criticism, 63; library inception and self-awareness, 148–49, 157–60, 170; Lyons location of, 164–66; materiality of book collection, 33; Nuit Debout as nighttime protest, 10, 157, 161–63, 174; Nuit Debout inception, 147–52; prefigurative politics of, 25; as tragedy of the commons, 159, 165, 178
BiblioSol (Indignados movement, Spain), 15–26; Acampada Sol occupation, 16, 19, 22, 25; archivists of Acampada Sol and, 202n8; Babel Working Group pop-up library and, 195; BiblioDebout inspired by, 164; book donations to, 15–16, 34–37, 189; 15-M and Indignados background, 15, 17–19, 22; as first protest library, 2, 6, 11–12, 16–17, 29; library catalog of, 74, 187; materiality of book collection, 30–33; physical features and infrastructure of, 20–23, 21; prefigurative politics and, 23–26; productivity expectations for, 97; *Sin Bibliotecas No Hay Paraíso*, 20, 56, 200n11; social media use of, 29, 109, 168; society and community of, 22; as Tres Peces Tres, 19, 186–93, 190, 200n10
Biblioteca Popular Victor Martinez (Beeb, Occupy Oakland), 79–84, 81, 88–91, 209n10; Babel Working Group pop-up library and, 195; boundary of, 111–14; Carnegie's legacy and, 8–9; "Casita de Libros" and "Our Principles" of, 81, 93–94, 112–13; closure and reopening by, 92–93, 100; fires in, 101–3; gentrification via outreach by, 98–101; permission vs. law and, 92–95, 101–3; productivity expectations of, 95–98. *See also* Carnegie, Andrew
"Big Deal" packages, 31
Birkut (riot police, Ukraine), 124, 125
Bisovetskyi, Inna, 126, 143
Bisovetskyi, Viktor, 126, 143
Black Lives Matter, 174, 176
black political thought. *See* Freedom Square library
Black Youth Project 100 (BYP100), 174, 175
Bloomberg, Michael: as author, 45; "Bloombergville," 46–48; on New York Public Library, 64, 69; Occupy Wall Street raid and, 57–59, 73, 205n7
Book of Embraces, The (Galeano), 34–35
borders and barricades, 104–17; barricades and books as romantic, 114; boundary of Beeb, 111–14; boundary of Gezi encampment, 110–11; creation of boundaries, 103; Gezi Park library events and inception, 9–10, 35, 104–11, 213n15; lack of barricade and library evolution, 165; legitimacy of books and, 180; Maidan library and, 114, 125, 127–29
Bouazizi, Mohamed, 201n1
Boyer, Stephen, 59, 60, 169
Breathing Room, 183–85
Brookfield Properties, 48, 51, 153
Brooklyn Public Library, social services of, 98
Brown, Michael, 173

Carlos, Juan (Prince of Spain), 17
Carnegie, Andrew, 79–91; "The Gospel of Wealth," 86; library grants and legacy of, 8–9, 79–81, 84–91, 92, 100, 133; Oakland (California) public library history and, 80–84, 81, 88–91; race and class issues of branch libraries, 79, 84–88; values of, 86, 92, 134
Çarşı soccer team, 108, 213n15
Castells, Manuel, 28

cataloging and circulation: by BiblioDebout, 158–60, 221n46; by BiblioSol, 74, 187, 191–92; book stamps and souvenir status of books, 37–39, 128–29, 142–43, 159; by Maidan library, 126, 128–29; by People's Library, 45, 74–75, 199n1
Catholic Worker Movement, 174
censorship: People's Library destruction as, 58; Sel Publishing and, 109–10
Chaney, Cassandra, 173
Charlie Hebdo (Paris), attack on, 150–51, 157
Chicago. *See* Freedom Square library; #LetUsBreathe Collective
Citizen Security Law (2015, Spain), 155–56
class issues: of branch libraries, 79, 84–88; Carnegie libraries and, 79, 84–88; productivity expectations in library spaces, 95–98; social services provided by public libraries, 98
collection management. *See* cataloging and circulation; donations of books; materiality and virtuality; visual spectacle
Colón, Kristiana Rae, 25, 99, 175, 176, 179, 180, 184–85
common, BiblioDebout as a, 159, 165, 178
construction phase of protest libraries, 163–65
Countdown with Keith Olbermann (MSNBC), on Occupy Wall Street, 59
CounterCartographies.org, on digital libraries, 168
CSOA La Quimera, 189, 191–92
CSO Casablanca, 186–89, 224n1
CSO EKO, 189
CSO Raíces, 189

Davis, Dannielle Joy, 173
del Valle, Mercedes, 34
de Monchaux, Thomas, 105
Department of Homeland Security (United States), 154
Detroit Evening News, on Carnegie library grants, 87
digital book collections. *See* materiality and virtuality
digital rights management (DRM), 31–32
direct action, 42
Domestic, or Homeland, Security Package (2015, Turkey), 155
donations of books: archive initiatives by protest libraries, 32, 191, 202n8; to Beeb, 94; to BiblioDebout, 158–60, 164; to BiblioSol, 15–16, 20–23, 21, 34–37, 189; to Freedom Square, 176–81, 177; to Gezi Park library, 110; labeling of donated books, 37–39; to Maidan library, 127–29, 136; to People's Library, 38, 40, 52–53; subject matter and sources of, 34–37, 60–61

e-books and e-readers. *See* materiality and virtuality
economic issues: banking crisis (2008), 41, 67–69; labor movements and historic perspective, 86–88; Loi Travail, 149–50, 157; Ukraine and European Union Association Agreement, 120–24, 129. *See also* African Americans; class issues; *individual names of countries*
Egypt, Arab Spring in, 28–30, 124
El Khomri, Myriam, 149–50
Emmaus House, 174
Erdoğan, Recep Tayyip, 105, 108, 109, 155
Escobar López, Almudena, 17–18, 155–56
EuroMaidan occupation. *See* Maidan library
Euromaidan Press, on Maidan library, 140–41
European Union Association Agreement, with Ukraine, 120–24, 129
"Extending Our Reach: Reducing Homelessness through Library Engagement" (American Library Association), 99

Fagin, Betsy, 61–62
Ferguson (Missouri), #LetUsBreathe Collective on, 173–74
15-M. *See* Indignados (15-M) movement
first sale doctrine, 31
Fischer-Baum, Reuben, 106
France: *Charlie Hebdo* and Bataclan attacks in, 150–51, 157; labor reform (Loi Travail) in, 149–50, 157; Law to Strengthen Internal Security and the Fight against Terrorism, 151–52; Opération Sentinelle in, 151. *See also* BiblioDebout
France 24, on BiblioNuit, 162–63
Franco, Francisco, 17–18, 200n5
Freedom Square library (#LetUsBreathe Collective, Chicago), 172–85; Breathing Room as permanent space resulting from, 172–73, 183–85; destruction of books at, 74; events leading to #LetUsBreathe, 99, 173–75; #FreedomNow National Day of Action and emergence of, 175–76; Free Store and, 176; goals of, 174–75; legitimacy of books and, 178–80; library inception, 10, 176–77, *177*; prefigurative politics of, 25–26; raid anticipated by, 180–84; transition phase of, 171, 172–73
Free Underpass Library (Toronto, Canada), 200n4
Frick, Henry Clay, 86
futures phase of protest libraries, 169–71, 192–93

Gaiman, Neil, 61
Galeano, Eduardo, 23, 34–35, 189
Gallo, Noel, 101, 113
Garner, Eric, 173
Gezi Park library (Istanbul), 104–17; barricades and books as romantic, 114; books donated to, 35, 110; boundary of Beeb and, 111–14; boundary of encampment and, 110–11; government policy and new shape of space, 154–55; library inception, 9–10, 35, 104–11; "neighborhoods" model and, 108–9; raid events, 106–10, 162; struggle phase of, 166; Taksim Solidarity protest and police action, 106–8, 213n15; Taksim Square/Gezi Park urban renewal project plans, 104–10, 144, 212n2; temporary lifespan of political occupations, 114–17
Giuliani, Rudolph, 47
Globe and Mail (Toronto, Canada), on Maidan occupation, 126
Gonzalo (BiblioSol librarian), 22, 34
Goodwin, Tim, 153–54
"Gospel of Wealth, The" (Carnegie), 86
government and law enforcement, 147–60; African Americans and police action, 172–76, 222n6; Beeb and, 92–95, 101–3, 112–14; Casablanca squat raid, 188; Freedom Square anticipation of raid, 180–84; Gezi Park raid, 106–10, 162; government policy change, overview, 147; international response to protests as new shape of public spaces, 149–57; Maidan raid, 122–24, 129–31, 162; Occupy Oakland and police presence, 83, 209n10; Occupy Wall Street (People's Library) destruction and rebirth, 1–2, 40, 54, 59–61, 68, 152–53, 162, 169; Occupy Wall Street raid, 54–59, 61–64, 73, 111, 205n7; racial disparity at Homan Square, 172–73, 175–76; Spain on protest movements, 155–56; temporary lifespan of protest libraries and, 114–17; Turkey on protest movements, 155; unarmed victims of police, 173–75
Graeber, David: on behavior in space, 53; on creativity, 97; on direct action, 42; on French labor reform, 150; on prefigurative politics/spaces, 23–24, 147; on public space constriction/supervision, 156; on social media participation, 162
Grammaticas, Damian, 150–51
Grant, Oscar, 82–83
Gries, Laurie, 62

Guardian, The (United Kingdom): on Maidan library, 139; on Occupy ICE, 154; on People's Library rebirth, 61; on racial disparity at Homan Square, 175

Haigh, Maria, 119, 141
Hatherley, Owen, 125
Haymarket (publisher), 178
"Heavenly Hundred" (Revolution of Dignity, Ukraine), 130, 136, 142–43
Henk, Mandy, 31
here and now ideology. *See* prefigurative politics
"Heroes of the Heavenly Hundred" (Poshyvaylo), 142
HERstory, 184
"hit and kill" bills (United States), 153
Hollande, François, 149–50, 151
homelessness, and public libraries, 95–98
Hong Kong, Umbrella Revolution of, 111
horizontalism: of Beeb, 100; defined, 24; of Occupy Wall Street, 42
Houston, public library system of, 96
Huffington Post, on Bloombergville, 47
Human Rights Watch, 151–52
Hürriyet Daily News, on Gezi Park, 110

Immigration and Customs Enforcement (United States), 154
Ince, Sevgi, 107–8
Indignados (15-M) movement: Acampada Sol occupation inception by, 15, 18–19, 22; Archivo 15-M, 191; background and inception of, 2, 17–19, 22, 29; Indignados and 15-M, defined, 200n8; motivation of, 123, 124; name of, 22; prefigurative politics of, 23–26; size of movement, 163; Spanish politics and background of, 17–18, 24–25, 200n5. *See also* BiblioSol
International Business Times, on Maidan library, 140
International Conference Center (Ukraine). *See* Ukrainian House
International Federation of Library Associations and Institutions (IFLA), 126, 130
"In What Way Is BiblioDebout a Common?" (Maurel), 165
Ishchenko, Volodymyr, 120–22
Istanbul Chamber of Architecture, 106
Istanbul Chamber of Urban Planners, 106

Jones, Ellis, 58
Jourdan, Brandon, 107
Justice and Development Party (AKP, Turkey), 108

Kayden, Jerold S., 48, 49
KESK Public Worker's Union, 107–8
Keystone Pipeline, 153–54
Kiev International Institute of Society, 123
Kleimenov, Alex, 132, 216n1
Klitschko, Vitali, 215n11
Knott, Cheryl, 84, 88
Kolesnikova, Viktoriia, 127–31, 137–38, 142
Krikunenko, Vladimir, 140
Krupskaya, Nadia, 133–34

law enforcement. *See* government and law enforcement
Law to Strengthen Internal Security and the Fight against Terrorism (France), 151–52
Lenin, Vladimir, 132–35
#LetUsBreathe Collective (Chicago), 172–85; Breathing Room as permanent space resulting from, 172–73, 183–85; events leading to, 99, 173–75; Freedom Square library inception, 10, 175–77, 177; goals of, 174–75; legitimacy of books and, 178–80; prefigurative politics of, 25–26; raid anticipated by, 180–84; transition phase of, 171, 172–73. *See also* Freedom Square library
Levinson, Gabriel, 58
Ley Mordaza (Citizen Security Law, 2015, Spain), 155–56

librarians: BiblioDebout and self-awareness, 148–49, 157–60, 170; as catalysts, 167, 192; defined, 16, 199–200n2; librarian-as-activist-as-other, 27–28, 178–79, 192, 223n19

libraries: archive initiatives by protest libraries and, 32, 191, 202n8; government funding of, 67–69, 207n6; "library concept" and, 4–5, 63–66, 76, 179, 193; outsider libraries, defined, 6, 16, 200n4; private libraries (pre-Carnegie era), 85; public's perception of role of, 71; "thing-ness" of, 33. *See also* libraries as democratic institutions; library as social space; protest libraries; public libraries

libraries as democratic institutions, 65–76; budget considerations for public libraries, 66–69, 207n6; democratic ideals and, 72–73; destruction of physical books vs. deleting digital books/files, 73–76; libraries as cornerstone of democracy, 75–76; New York Public Library's Central Library Plan and, 63–64, 69–72; overview, 7–8; protest libraries vs. public libraries and "library" concept, 64, 65–66, 76

library as social space, 92–103; assemblage in outdoor vs. indoor space, 102; gentrification via outreach and, 98–101; identity-building and, 192–93; permission vs. law and, 92–95, 101–3; productivity expectations and, 95–98; rhetoric of libraries as "free to all," 9

Library Journal: blogger on "library" concept/funding, 65–66, 68; on funding of libraries, 67

Library of Ukrainian Literature (Moscow), 10, 132–35, 139–40. *See also* Ukrainian House

LibraryThing, 45, 74–75, 199n1

Lichtenstein, Nelson, 87

lifespan of protest libraries. *See* phases of protest libraries

Livsey, Bill, 162

Lobo, Tea, 97–98

Loeb, Zachary: Babel Working Group pop-up library and, *194*, 195; on boundaries, 111; on Occupy "spinoffs," 82; on Occupy stereotypes, 97; on Occupy Wall Street's legacy, 75; on People's Library destruction, 57, 162, 205n7; on People's Library identity, 38; on People's Library inception and organization, 23, 32–33, 45, 52; on People's Library rebirth, 60–61

Loi Travail (labor reform, France), 149–50, 157

Los Angeles County public library system, 68

Lost Voices, 174

Loury, Pierre, 176

Macron, Emmanuel, 151–52

Maddow, Rachel, 41, 59

Maeckelbergh, Marianne, 107

Maidan library (Kiev, Ukraine), 118–31, 132–43; barricades used by, 114, 125, 127–29; books donated to, 35, 37; book stamps and souvenir status of books, 37–39, 128–29, 142–43; goals of, 118; library inception and organization, 124–29, 177; lifespan of, 117; liquidated collection and subsequent work of, 135–43; Maidan occupation goals, 121–24, 129–30; Maidan occupation location, 118; materiality of book collection, 30–31; police action against, 122–24, 129–31, 162; Ukraine history and events leading to, 10, 118–22, 132–35, 139–40; Ukrainian House location of, 125–26, 128–31; Ukrainian Revolution (2014, Revolution of Dignity) and, 124, 130

Makarenko, Anastasiia, 30–31, 37, 127–31, 135–38, 142

"marginal" spaces, 49–50

Mario (Spanish activist), 187

Martin, Trayvon, 173

Martinez, Victor. *See* Biblioteca Popular Victor Martinez

Marx, Anthony, 69–70, 72
materiality and virtuality: BiblioDebout's use of digital files, 145; BiblioSol physical features and book donations, 15–16, 20–23, 21; destruction of physical vs. digital books, 73–76; digital libraries, 167–69, 169; donations accepted by occupation movements, 35–39; DRM, 31–32; identity of public libraries vs. protest libraries and, 6–7, 196–97; People's Library and, 31, 38, 40, 45, 48, 52–53, 72; physical books as assets, 32–33; physical vs. digital book collections, 27–28, 30–32, 68; prefigurative politics and physical occupation of space, 24–26; public libraries use of digital resources over print, 75; social media used by occupation movements, 27–30; subject matter and donors of books, 34–37, 60–61; symbolism of "collections," 73; visibility of community and books, 98, 102. *See also* library as social space; visual spectacle
Matthews, Stephen A., 63
Maurel, Lionel, 33, 36–37, 63, 157, 159, 165, 178
McAneny, George, 48
McCann, Colum, 70
McKinney, Tricia, 59
Mercier, Silvère, 157
Mercury News (San Jose, California), on Beeb fires, 101
Microsoft, 32
Miller Library (Oakland, California), 80–84, 81, 88–91
Morris, Edmund, 71
Movement for Black Lives, 175
MSNBC: *Countdown with Keith Olbermann,* 59; on Occupy Wall Street, 41; *The Rachel Maddow Show,* 41, 59
Mubarak, Hosni, 29–30
Museum of the Revolution of Dignity (Kiev, Ukraine), 142–43
Mutiny Zine (Spain): on Indignados, 18; on squatters, 186

Nation, The (magazine): on funding of libraries, 67, 69–70; on Occupy Wall Street raid, 55
nation-building, 118–31; legitimacy of books and, 180; Library of Ukrainian Literature and, 10, 132–35, 139–40; Maidan occupation goals and, 121–24, 129–30; protest libraries as free from indoctrination, 102; Ukraine history and events leading to Maidan occupation, 10, 118–22, 132–35, 139–40. *See also* Maidan library
Nayyem, Mustafa, 121, 122
Netflix, on Ukraine, 123, 215n11, 215n16
Networks of Outrage and Hope (Castells), 28
New Republic, The, de Monchaux article in, 105
Newsweek, on Maidan library, 139
New York City: police raid of Occupy Wall Street by, 1–2, 54–59, 61–64, 111, 162, 205n7; POPS policy of, 46–53, 152–53; public property closed at night by, 46–47; space usability issues in, 48–50; Zoning Resolution (1961), 47–49, 51. *See also* New York Public Library; Occupy Wall Street; People's Library
New York Civil Liberties Union, 58–59, 63
New Yorkers against Budget Cuts, 47
New York Public Library: Central Library Plan, 63–64, 69–72; endowment of, 68; funding after banking crisis (2008), 67; letter of opposition to, 70, 73–76; main branch of, 7, 199n3; reference collection of, 70
New York Times: on Maidan library, 135; on Occupy "spinoffs," 83; on Occupy Wall Street, 51; on public library access, 71
Not Free, Not for All (Knott), 84
Nuit Debout (#NuitDebout, Paris): Lyon location of, 164–66; name of, 218n1; as nighttime protest, 10, 157, 161–63, 174; Place de la République (Paris) location of, 157, 164; Saviors-

Nuit Debout (*continued*)
    Com1 and, 148, 157, 165; size of movement, 163. *See also* Biblio-Debout

Oakland (California): Beeb boundary and, 111–14; Beeb eviction by, 92–93; Beeb fires and, 101–3; Occupy Oakland and police presence, 83, 209n10; permission vs. law and Biblioteca Popular Victor Martinez, 92–95, 101–3; public library history of, 80–84, *81*, 88–91, 209n10. *See also* Biblioteca Popular Victor Martinez
"Obama Hope" image, 62
occupation movements. *See* Arab Spring; Biblioteca Popular Victor Martinez; Gezi Park library; Indignados (15-M) movement; #LetUsBreathe Collective; Nuit Debout; Occupy Wall Street; Ukraine
Occupy ICE, 154
Occupy Tampa, 162
Occupy Wall Street (New York City), 40–53, 54–64; archive initiative of, 32, 202n8; Biblioteca Popular Victor Martinez, 79–84, *81*, 88–91; boundary of, 111; inception of, 40–42; lack of demands by, 42; legacy of, 75; library concept critique resulting from raid, 63–64; motivation of, 123; network activation following New York raid, 61–62; prefigurative politics of, 23–25; in POPS, 46–53, 152–53; raid events, 1–2, 54–59, 61–64, 111, 162, 205n7; size of movement, 163; society and community of, 22; spread ("spinoffs") to multiple locations, 55–56, 79, 82–83; stereotypes of activists, 97. *See also* People's Library
OccupyWriters.com, 41, 61, 70
Ochoa, Martin Zeke, 19, *21*, 33, 35, 188, 191, *194*, 195
Ohio Valley Trades and Labor Assembly, 87
"On the Principles of the State Language Policy" (2012, Ukraine), 120
On the Role of the St. Petersburg Public Library (Lenin), 133–34
Opération Sentinelle (France), 151
outsider libraries, defined, 6, 16, 200n4
Öztürk, Çigdem, 105

Pain, Marilou, 163–65, 169–72
Peisakhin, Leonid, 121
People's Library (Occupy Wall Street), 40–53, 54–64; American Library Association endorsement of, 64; archive initiative of, 32, 202n8; Babel Working Group pop-up library and, 195; as behavior in space, overview, 7; BiblioDebout inspired by, 164; books donated to, 38, 40, 52–53; book stamps and souvenir status of books, 159; destruction and rebirth, 1–2, 40, 54, 59–61, 68, 152–53, 169; library catalog on LibraryThing, 45, 74–75, 199n1; library concept critique resulting from raid, 63–64; library inception, 43–46, *44*; materiality of book collection, 31, 38, 40, 45, 46, 52–53, 72; network activation following New York raid, 61–62; Occupy Wall Street raid events, 1–12, 54–59, 61–64, 111, 162, 205n7; physical location of, within Occupy Wall Street, 42; prefigurative politics of, 23–25; protectiveness over collection in, 70–71; social media use of, 109; struggle phase of, 166; as visual spectacle, overview, 7; workers of, 23. *See also* libraries as democratic institutions
Pew Research Center, 66
phases of protest libraries, 161–71; Breathing Room as permanent space, 172–73, 183–85; construction phase, 163–65; digital libraries and role in, 167–69, *169*; futures phase, 169–71, 192–93; librarians as catalysts of, 167, 192; lifespan of protest libraries, 11, 114–17; Nuit Debout as nighttime protest, 10, 157, 161–63,

174; permanent vs. temporary status of protest libraries, 95, 172–75, 183–85, 187–89, 192–93; protest rhythm disruption/protest fatigue and, 157, 161–63, 174; social media and, 162, 170; struggle (nomadic) phase, 165–66, 192–93; temporary autonomous zone (TAZ), 115–16; transition/reinvention phase, 171. *See also* reinvention as collective
Pinkerton (security agency), 85–88
PirateBox, 168–69, *169*
police action. *See* government and law enforcement
Politico, on France's counterterrorism law, 151
Portland (Oregon), Occupy ICE in, 154
Poshyvaylo, Igor, 142
prefigurative politics: anarchism and, 24; Argentina as example of, 24; defined, 23–24; Maidan occupation and, 126; materiality of protest libraries and, 27–28; Occupy Wall Street and, 42; physical occupation of space and, 24–26; protest libraries' evolution and, 147. *See also* reinvention as collective
private libraries (pre-Carnegie era), 85
privately owned public space policy (POPS, New York City): behavior and use of, 52–53; "Bloombergville" and, 46–47; "marginal" spaces of, 49–50; as new shape of public space, 152–53; Zoning Resolution (1961), 47–49, 51
productivity, in library spaces, 95–98
protest libraries: archive initiatives by, 32, 191, 202n8; BiblioDebout as self-aware, 148–49, 157–60, 170; BiblioSol as first protest library, 2, 6, 11–12, 16–17, 29; common features and patterns of, 2–4; defined, 4–6, 16–17; destruction of physical vs digital books, 73–76; identity of public libraries vs., 6–7, 196–97; international instances from 2011–2016, 1–3; outsider libraries, defined, 6, 16,

200n4; as participative libraries, 163; permanent vs. temporary status of, 95, 172–75, 183–85, 187–89, 192–93. *See also* librarians; *individual names of protest libraries*
Proyecto Fahrenheit 451, 188
public libraries: benefits of, 5–6; identity of protest libraries vs., 6–7, 195–97; Lenin and, 132–35. *See also* Carnegie, Andrew; library as social space; New York Public Library

Quan, Jean, 83

race issues. *See* African Americans; class issues
Rachel Maddow Show, The (MSNBC), on Occupy Wall Street, 41, 59
Raphael, Molly, 58
reinvention as collective, 172–85, 186–98; Babel Working Group pop-up library, 193–95, *194*, 197–98; BiblioSol phases leading to Tres Peces Tres, 186–93, *190*; Breathing Room as permanent space, 172–73, 183–85; Freedom Square library inception, 11, 175–77, *177*; identity of public libraries vs. protest libraries and, 196–97; legitimacy of books and, 178–80; #LetUsBreathe Collective background and events, 173–75, 180–84; as transition phase, 171, 172–73
Revolutionary Anarchist Action, 107
Revolution of Dignity (2014, Ukrainian Revolution), 124, 130, 136, 142–43
Rice, Tamir, 173
Richard, Claire, 158, 159, 178
Roberts, Sam, 51
Root, Henry, 90–91
Rushdie, Salman, 61, 70
Russia: Crimea seized by (2014), 136; on Maidan protests, 139. *See also* Maidan library

Sadri, Senem Zeybekoglu, 105
SafeLibraries (blog), on American Library Association, 64

Sanchez, Arturo, 94–95
Sánchez, Pedro, 156
San Francisco: Carnegie library grants to, 87; social services by public library of, 98
San Francisco Chronicle, on Beeb, 113
SavoirsCom1, 148, 157, 165
Scott, William, 55, 59–60, 74, 152
Seattle Public Library, 68
Sel Publishing, 109–10
Shakur, Assata, 178, 179, 181
Shareable (blog), on People's Library destruction, 58
Sharina, Natalia, 140–41
Sharlet, Jeff, 41, 61
Shaw, Robert, 161–62
Sherman, Scott, 67, 69
Siegel, Norman, 58–59
S.I.Lex (blog), on book donations, 36–37
Sin Bibliotecas No Hay Paraíso (Without Libraries, There Is No Paradise blog): on BiblioSol physical features, 20, 200n11; on People's Library, 56
Smith, Patti, 52
Smith, Trevor, 132
social media: #LetUsBreathe on, 180; Maidan library inception and, 126; occupation movements and use of, 27–30, 37; People's Library destruction and, 56–59; protest library phases and, 162, 170
Soviet Union, and Ukraine history. *See* Ukraine
Spain: Citizen Security Law of, 155–56; political history of, 17–18, 24–25; squats in, 186–89, 224n1. *See also* BiblioSol
spatial issues. *See* behavior in space; BiblioDebout; library as social space
squats, 186–89, 224n1
Stafford, Zach, 175
Stalin, Joseph, 119
"State of American Libraries, The" (American Library Association), 71
Still Life with Rhetoric (Gries), 62
struggle phase of protest libraries, 165–66, 192–93

Taksim Gezi Park. *See* Gezi Park library
Taksim Solidarity, 106–8
Talcott, J. R., 90–91
Taylor, Jaime: Babel Working Group pop-up library and, *194*, 195; on boundaries, 111; on Occupy stereotypes, 97; on People's Library destruction, 162; on People's Library inception and organization, 23, 32–33, 45; on People's Library rebirth, 60–61; Zuccotti Park raid and, 55
temporal (time) issues of protest libraries. *See* phases of protest libraries
ten Houten, Oscar, 22, 109, 114, 115
Time, on People's Library, 45
Titushki (mercenaries, Ukraine), 124
Tres Peces Tres, 19, 186–93, *190*, 200n10. *See also* BiblioSol
Trump, Donald, on immigration, 154
Tufekci, Zeynep, 22–23, 109
Tunisia, Arab Spring in, 28, 201n1
Turkey: AKP, 108; Taksim Square Pedestrianization plan of, 104–10, 144, 212n2; Turkish government on protest movements, 155. *See also* Gezi Park library
21st Century Library Blog, on libraries and social protest, 63
Twitter and Teargas (Tufekci), 22–23

Ukraine: Birkut of, 124, 125; independence claimed by, 135, 142; language of, 119, 135; literacy rate in, 134; Museum of the Revolution of Dignity, 142–43; Soviet history of, 118–22 (*see also* Maidan library); Titushki of, 124; Ukrainian Revolution (2014, Revolution of Dignity), 124, 130, 136, 142–43; United Left and Peasants party (ULP), 122; Yanukovych and, 120–24, 130
Ukrainian House (International Conference Center): Lenin's impact on libraries and, 132–35; as Library of Ukrainian Literature, 10, 132, 139–40; Maidan library housed in, 125–26, 128–31, *133*, 135–43; naming of, 132
Umbrella Revolution (Hong Kong), 111

United States: labor movements and historic perspective, 86–88; laws on protest movements, federal, 154; laws on protest movements, state, 153–54; Occupy inequities and slavery, 222n6. *See also* Biblioteca Popular Victor Martinez; #LetUsBreathe Collective; Occupy Wall Street

Van Slyck, Abigail, 85–87, 90, 92
Vargas Llosa, Mario, 70
Vinocur, Nicholas, 151
visual spectacle, 54–64; library concept critique resulting from, 63-64; network activation following New York raid, 61–62; of Occupy Wall Street raid, 54–59, 205n7; overview, 7; of People's Library destruction and rebirth, 54, 59–61

Walker, Alice, 61
Washington, DC, public library social services, 98
"We Are Worried about the Books" (Amos), 140
Western Journal of Black Studies, dedicated to Michael Brown, 173
"What Lenin Wrote and Said about Libraries" (Krupskaya), 133–34

Wheeling (West Virginia), Carnegie library grants to, 87
Wiegand, Wayne A., 66
Williams, Damon, 174, 176–78, 180, 182
Winter on Fire (Netflix), 123, 215n11, 215n16
Wong, Lydia, 175, 178, 179, 182–83
working group model: of BiblioSol, 22–23, 25, 28; of Occupy Wall Street and People's Library, 40, 42–43, 45–46
Writers for the 99%, 32

"Y" (Spanish student), 18, 24–25, 185
Yanukovych, Viktor, 120–24, 130
Yassin, Jaime Omar, 82, 83, 84, 98, 99, 112, 113, 195
Yekelchyk, Serhy, 119, 214n2

Zakharov, Dmitry, 140
Zoning Resolution (1961, New York City), 47–49, 51
Zuccotti, John, 51
Zuccotti Park (New York City): boundary of, 111; Occupy Wall Street location choice of, 32; POPS designation, 46–53, 152–53 (*see also* Occupy Wall Street); raid of, 54–59, 205n7. *See also* Occupy Wall Street

www.ingramcontent.com/pod-product-compliance
Lightning Source LLC
Chambersburg PA
CBHW032213230426
43672CB00011B/2539